"*Through the Heart of St. Joseph* is an invaluable source for discovering, or deepening knowledge and love of, St. Joseph, particularly during this 150th anniversary year of his proclamation as Patron of the Universal Church. Fr. Boniface Hicks' gracious accompaniment of the reader takes the form of an extended *lectio divina* of St. Joseph's portrayal in the Gospels, specifically his primary role in the lives of Jesus and Mary and thus in salvation history, that is both accessible and profound."

FR. JOSEPH F. CHORPENNING, OSFS, EDITORIAL DIRECTOR
St. Joseph's University Press

"*Through the Heart of St. Joseph* is packed with insights, wisdom, and application, and it highlights the important message that God is speaking to the Church today, namely, *Go to Joseph*! I very highly recommend this book. Now is the time of St. Joseph!"

FR. DONALD CALLOWAY, MIC
Author, *Consecration to St. Joseph*

"Fr. Boniface speaks of St. Joseph in a way that is perfectly contemporary—and yet always grounded in tradition, engaging the reflection of many saints. I know no book that so thoroughly plumbs the spiritual depths of St. Joseph's life. *Through the Heart* has become my favorite book about the holy patriarch."

MIKE AQUILINA
Author, *St. Joseph and His World*

"In the pages of this book, you will glimpse Father's devotion to St. Joseph and discover new aspects of the heart of this silent saint. You will encounter his tender fatherhood, his courageous masculinity, his fierce and chaste spousal love for Our Lady, and his fatherly heart for you. May you welcome St. Joseph into your heart!"

"St. Joseph, known in this book through Scripture, saints, homilies, and theological reflection, encourages us to embrace our authentic humanity. Most powerfully, he fathers us into loving the ordinary . . . that which we normally wish to escape. Joseph burrowed deep within the ordinary and found there life and life to the full. Let's join him."

"Contrary to certain hyper-pious theories, Fr. Boniface portrays St. Joseph in his red-blooded humanity as a passionate spouse and tender father who is the vigorous head and strong protector of the Holy Family."

"Reading this book helped me and will help you to love St. Joseph even more deeply! Beyond guiding us into the St. Joseph option, Fr. Boniface engages us in a real relationship with St. Joseph in such a way that we experience the love of the tender heart of this fatherly saint."

Through *the* Heart *of*
St. Joseph

Through *the* Heart *of*
St. Joseph

FR. BONIFACE HICKS, OSB

Steubenville, Ohio
www.emmausroad.org

Emmaus Road Publishing
1468 Parkview Circle
Steubenville, Ohio 43952

Library of Congress Control Number: 9781645850946
ISBN: 978-1-64585-094-6 (paperback) / 978-1-64585-095-3 (ebook)

Imprimi Potest:
The Right Reverend Martin R. Bartel, OSB
Archabbot of Saint Vincent Archabbey

Nihil Obstat:
The Most Reverend Larry J. Kulick, JCL
Bishop-elect of the Diocese of Greensburg

Imprimatur:
The Most Reverend Gregory J. Mansour, STL
Bishop of the Eparchy of St. Maron of Brooklyn
Date: January 15, 2021

The *nihil obstat, imprimatur* and *imprimi potest* are official declarations that a book or pam-
phlet is free of doctrinal or moral error. No implication is contained therein that those
who have granted the *nihil obstat, imprimatur* or *imprimi potest* agree with the contents,
opinions or statements expressed.

Cover design and layout by Emily Demary
Cover image: *The Nativity* by Melchers Gari (1860–1932)

For Pope Benedict XVI (Joseph Ratzinger) who has shared with his baptismal patron St. Joseph a tender and abiding love for the Incarnate Word of God and who has been a true father in faith for me through his teaching and inspirational witness.

FOREWORD

Catholicism in the United States is still relatively young, and in theology we're rushing to catch up with our elders. The French, the Italians, and the Spaniards have been at this a lot longer. They have more than a millennium's lead time.

Nevertheless, we Americans have made great strides in certain subfields. In Mariology, for example, Americans have established an international presence. We have journals, institutes, associations, publications, and conferences that command attention on the other side of the Atlantic. When American mariologists speak, the continent listens.

In Josephology, however, we've lagged. Yes, we've produced some extraordinary scholars. The achievement of Father Joseph F. Chorpenning, OSFS, is astonishing—prolific and prodigious in its excellence—and all by itself should put our country on the map. But one scholar does not constitute a field, and so too few researchers are engaging the work of Father Chorpenning. And it's been more than a half-century since Father Francis Filas produced such great works as *St. Joseph after Vatican II*. I've long lamented that the world needs a robust and distinctively American Josephology.

This present book is not a work of academic theology. It is unpretentious, simple, readable, and accessible to any motivated Catholic. Nevertheless, it is the product of great learning and greater prayer. And it gives me hope for my country's future with St. Joseph.

Father Boniface Hicks is a seminary professor and an author of respected works of spiritual theology—but he is also a professional communicator. He is a radio personality. He is a preacher of exceptional power. In this book he is marshaling all that power as he proposes a profound Christian spirituality of St. Joseph.

Through the Heart of St. Joseph is unique for its theological synthesis of the reflections of the saints. Father Boniface examines the major motifs associated with St. Joseph in Christian tradition, and he invokes the saints and doctors as his witnesses. He is also adept in the application of modern methods and disciplines, especially those of psychology and anthropology, though he never does this to excess.

Throughout the book, Father Boniface remains grounded in the biblical text and actual history. He scrupulously avoids the flights of fancy and lazy use of legend that are common flaws in devotional works on St. Joseph.

I have often encouraged my students to consider the saints as fellow members of their "Bible study group." They are our true and most reliable interpretive community. Their works are the monuments of Sacred Tradition and witnesses for the Church's magisterium. In the future I will invoke this book as an exemplar of that principle.

Through the Heart of St. Joseph is a hint of the distinctive Josephology I've been waiting for. I suspect it's what you, too, have been missing, even if you didn't know it. In these pages, perhaps, we Americans have finally begun to catch up.

Scott Hahn

ACKNOWLEDGMENTS

I am so grateful for those who introduced me to St. Joseph, beginning with the Passionist Nuns in Pittsburgh, PA, whose statue of St. Joseph inspired my initial prayer to ask him to help me know him. Shortly after that, Dr. Scott Hahn introduced me to the field of Josephology, which I had never even heard of. Then it was the enthusiasm of my Benedictine confrere Fr. Jerome Purta that lit a fire in me as he shared his discoveries from Andrew Doze's *Saint Joseph: Shadow of the Father*. My first chance to share my growing love for St. Joseph came thanks to Fr. Richard Karenbauer, who invited me to preach for the Solemnity of St. Joseph at St. Joseph Parish in New Kensington, where I had served as a deacon with Fr. (now Bishop) Larry Kulick. The insights that came to me from preparing that homily were fostered in many loving conversations with Br. (now Fr.) Elijah Joseph Cirigiliano. These reflections came to a fuller fruition when I was invited by Matthew Gorsich (in whom I also found a wonderful echo of St. Joseph) and Tom Marinchak to be a part of Saint Joseph Missions® and We Are One Body radio®. I will always be grateful for these occasions of God's providence that drew me into relationship with St. Joseph.

I also want to acknowledge the men in my life who have helped me personally experience the virtues of St.

Joseph, starting with my dad, William, and my brother, Michael. Following my entrance into the Catholic Church and monastic life, I was fathered by several St. Joseph figures in my spiritual directors and formators, most especially Fr. Thomas Acklin, O.S.B. These strong men with tender hearts helped me experience the loving, masculine care that I have come to associate with the heart of St. Joseph.

I am so thankful to several reviewers who responded so quickly to my request to read this book and who provided excellent feedback, especially Fr. Joseph Chorpenning, O.S.F.S., and Msgr. Brian Bransfield. Finally, I am deeply grateful for Scott Hahn, Chris Erickson, Melissa Girard, Madeleine Cook, and the whole staff at Emmaus Road for their sacrifices to bring this text into print so quickly after the beginning of the Year of St. Joseph. They are a joy to work with, and the excellence of their work makes the text shine more brightly for the glory of God and the veneration of St. Joseph!

Table of Contents

INTRODUCTION

"Unwilling to expose her . . ." (Matt 1:19, NABRE)

It took the Church nearly 1,500 years (in 1481) to establish a liturgical feast for St. Joseph and nearly 1,900 years (in 1889) to publish the first encyclical about him. This encyclical came just after he was officially raised up to a great status in devotion by Bl. Pius IX, who officially declared him the protector of the universal Church in 1870. Every subsequent pope has published a significant teaching on St. Joseph, and many of them have inscribed that teaching in the official liturgical practice of the Roman Rite.[1] In honor of the 150th anniversary of Bl. Pius IX's declaration in 1870, Pope Francis even declared a Year of St. Joseph for the year 2020–2021.[2] St. Joseph has surged in popularity among the faithful as well. For

---

[1] For example, the first concrete action of the Second Vatican Council was to add St. Joseph's name to the heart of every Mass by inserting him into the Roman Canon. Furthermore, his name was carefully placed in the Roman Canon just after the Blessed Virgin Mary, but before the other saints, including all the Apostles and martyrs. Pope Benedict XVI then initiated, and Pope Francis promulgated, the inclusion of the name of St. Joseph in all the new Eucharistic Prayers of the New Rite of the Mass.

[2] Pope Francis, Apostolic Letter on the 150th Anniversary of the Proclamation of Saint Joseph as Patron of the Universal Church *Patris Corde* (December 8, 2020).

example, an international movement of consecration began in 2020, set in motion by Fr. Don Calloway's comprehensive collection of teaching on St. Joseph packaged in his wonderfully accessible book.[3] Just prior to that, a forty-four-day consecration to St. Joseph was published to bridge the days between the Solemnity of St. Joseph on March 19 and the memorial of St. Joseph the Worker on May 1.[4] Another approach to St. Joseph was a recent exploration of his world as revealed in ancient documentary sources and archaeological records.[5]

In spite of all this, it seems there is still much mystery and even confusion that surrounds St. Joseph in the Christian imagination. Even for those who have come to know him through devotional and liturgical prayers, there is so much more that can be gained through deepening one's relationship with him. My hope, with this book, is that the reader will be moved to develop a deeper relationship with St. Joseph. On the one hand, I hope to provide enough trustworthy teaching to give starting points for prayer. On the other hand, I acknowledge that the only way to get to know St. Joseph, ultimately, is to spend time developing a relationship with him. This is necessarily a slow process, because the silent and hidden St. Joseph does not readily reveal his secrets.

The slow development of the Church's teaching on

---

[3] Donald H. Calloway, *Consecration to St. Joseph: The Wonders of Our Spiritual Father* (Marian Press, 2020).

[4] Dr. Gregory Bottaro and Jennifer Settle, *Consecration to Jesus through Saint Joseph: An Integrated Look at the Holy Family* (self-pub., 2019).

[5] Mike Aquilina, *St. Joseph and His World* (New York: Scepter Publishers, 2020).

St. Joseph is itself a teaching on St. Joseph. After all, the role he played in salvation history, as we read in Scripture, was not to reveal, but to hide. When men would have desecrated the mystery, he was "unwilling to expose her" (Matt 1:19, NABRE), and when deadly envy threatened, he disappeared: "[He] took the child and his mother by night, and departed to Egypt" (Matt 2:14). Amazingly, we see also that after decades in Nazareth, the neighbors had no idea that the Incarnate Word and the Immaculate Conception were living next door. Poor Joseph, who could only offer a pair of turtledoves in the Temple to fulfill the law toward his Son (see Luke 2:24), served as a living veil that disguised the Riches of Heaven, Whom he kept all those years in his home.

Growing in relationship with St. Joseph is a slow process because it is the development of a human relationship. In our humanity, it takes us time to open our hearts and trust, even when we are relating with a canonized saint. We must spend time together, gradually share more deeply from the heart, endure trials together, and eventually see the way our dear friend comes through for us. We also develop human relationships through mutual friends and family members. It stands to reason that no one can introduce us to St. Joseph better than his Divine Son and his immaculate wife. Of course, St. Joseph has much to teach us about them as well.

It is also important to approach St. Joseph with the right dispositions in order to come to know him better and be more united with him. These include dispositions that can receive love and help from him, such as vulnerability that trusts in his protection (Chapter 1) and littleness that opens to his fatherhood (Chapter 3). These also include dispositions that make us like him, such as silence (Chapter 2) and hiddenness (Chapter 4). There is also an unchosen path of suffering, fear, doubt, and anxiety on which we can choose to reach out to this strong and loving guardian and guide (Chapter 5). These are the pathways that lead us into his home. At the end of each of these chapters, we offer a traditional prayer to help us embrace that particular way to Jesus and Mary through the heart of St. Joseph. When we pass through his heart and arrive in his home, we discover that it is a kind of monastery where we can live out the wisdom of the Rule of St. Benedict. When we choose to live there, we could call it the Joseph Option, and we will discover some additional friends who have already moved in (Chapter 6).

A Journey through the Heart

St. Joseph is God's chosen protector, and the only way into his home is through his heart. The journey into the heart of St. Joseph requires us to disarm ourselves, take down our defenses, and become vulnerable, little, hidden, silent, and poor. When we are willing to come before him as a child, we will discover the heart of a father. When we enter into the hidden places of our hearts, we will find that he is there with us in the darkness. When we learn to silence our interior noise, we will become sensitive to his silent, loving presence. When we empty ourselves of the riches of worldly success and self-sufficiency and embrace our poverty, we will receive from him the greatest treas-

ure—all the Love of Heaven. The heart of St. Joseph is not
the destination, but only a door through which we must
pass in order to enter into the home in Nazareth, which is
truly heaven on earth. And although he has a great heart,
it has only a very little opening, because as Jesus clearly
taught us, only children are allowed in (see Matt 18:3).

We hope to set out now on a journey of prayerful discovery. This journey leads us to the center of the Christian
faith, namely, to Our Lord Jesus Christ, but it approaches
it from a different starting point. We focus our attention
in this book on St. Joseph, but not because he is more
important than his Son. To the contrary, he happily stands
back and disappears, like St. John the Baptist, knowing
that "He must increase, but I must decrease" (John 3:30).
Our recent popes have made the same observation. Pius
XII instructed us: "If you want to be close to Christ,
'Ite ad Joseph'—Go to Joseph."[6] Likewise, Pope Benedict XV wrote, "Increase of devotion to St. Joseph among
the faithful is bound to result in an increase of devotion
toward the Holy Family of Nazareth of which he was the
illustrious head, for these devotions spring spontaneously
from one another. St. Joseph leads us directly to Mary,
and Mary leads us directly to the source of holiness, Jesus
Christ, who sanctified the domestic virtues by His obedience to Joseph and Mary."[7]

This makes sense, because there is no competition in

[6] Pope Pius XII, Homily on the Feast of St. Joseph the Worker, May 1,
1955, quoted in Henri Rondet, *Saint Joseph*, trans. Donald Attwater
(New York: P. J. Kenedy & Sons, 1956), 222.
[7] Pope Benedict XV, Motu Proprio *Bonum Sane* (July 25, 1920), quoted
in Rondet, *Saint Joseph*, 206.

the communion of saints, let alone in the Holy Family. Each saint has the same hope, which is the fulfillment of the prayer of Jesus, that "they may all be one" (John 17:21). Each saint helps to bring that about in different ways as they form friendships with us. But St. Joseph is a special saint, intended for all of us. He is a father who will help all of us to be the children who can enter the kingdom of heaven. Jesus made St. Joseph who he is, and in a way, St. Joseph made Jesus who He is by being the human father who formed His humanity. Jesus is not envious if we allow St. Joseph to form us in a fatherly way, as he formed Jesus. There is a way that a human father can help us, and because he was called by the heavenly Father to be a human father to the Divine Son, we can all look to St. Joseph to be a father for us as well.

So, a first point to keep in mind throughout this book is that the orientation is always on Christ, but we approach by way of His Childhood, as His brothers and sisters, who are therefore also sons and daughters of St. Joseph. A second point is that we will refer to St. Joseph as the father of Jesus throughout this book, because we want to emphasize the special status and relationship that he had with Our Lord. We fully acknowledge that he is not the biological father of Jesus. He is the legal father of Jesus, however, and his role fulfills the role of fatherhood toward Jesus in His humanity. Furthermore, in calling him the father of Jesus, we are following the example of the Blessed Virgin Mary, who told Jesus, "Your father and I have been looking for you anxiously" (Luke 2:48). We are also following the example of the evangelist Luke, who wrote, "His father and his mother marveled at what was said about him" (Luke 2:33), and who, without qualification, calls Mary and Joseph the "parents" of Jesus (Luke 2:41, 43). We fully acknowledge the importance and great miracle of the virginal conception by the Holy Spirit in the Blessed Virgin Mary, but we want to emphasize the human reality that marked the childhood of Jesus, namely, that he was raised as "the carpenter's son" (Matt 13:55). In this way, we hope to reinforce the value for each of us to turn to St. Joseph as a father for us as well.

Now let us find some pathways by which we can draw close to our father St. Joseph in order to learn from him the way of Christ, who is our Brother and his Son.

Chapter One

St. Joseph's Protection

Protecting the Vulnerable

"You shall call his name Jesus . . ." (Matt 1:21)

St. Joseph faced a great trial when he discovered Mary was pregnant. Pope Francis described that trial beautifully:

> The Gospel tells us: "Joseph, being a just man and unwilling to put her to shame, resolved to send her away quietly" (1:19). This brief sentence reveals a true inner drama if we think about the love that Joseph had for Mary! But even in these circumstances, Joseph intends to do the will of God and decides, surely with great sorrow, to send Mary away quietly. We need to meditate on these words in order to understand the great trial that Joseph had to endure in the days preceding Jesus' birth. It was a trial similar to the sacrifice of Abraham, when God asked him for his son Isaac (cf. Gen

22): to give up what was most precious, the person most beloved.[1]

St. Joseph's internal struggle to understand this trial has been interpreted in several ways. The first is a natural explanation, namely, that he believed Mary was impregnated by a man, with or without her consent. This "suspicion theory" supposes that St. Joseph suspected Mary of consenting to sexual relations and therefore of being guilty of adultery. The second approach is a supernatural explanation, namely, that St. Joseph believed Mary was impregnated by the Holy Spirit and he knew the greatness of the mystery taking place in his midst. The third is simply bewilderment and perplexity, that St. Joseph believed something great had happened but did not understand what it meant. Although the modern translations seem to favor a theory of suspicion, this has not been promoted by any papal teaching, nor by doctors or saints in the last millennium. Pope St. John Paul II, Pope Benedict XVI, and Pope Francis all describe the events under the assumption that St. Joseph was perplexed by what was taking place. His presumption was not that *Mary* was unworthy or unfaithful, but rather that *he* was unworthy of being part of this amazing series of events. As Pope Francis described so beautifully, however, removing himself from these events was no small sacrifice. It was a sacrifice of Abrahamic proportions, both

---

[1] Pope Francis, Angelus Address, December 22, 2013, http://w2.vatican.va/content/francesco/en/angelus/2013/documents/papa-francesco_angelus_20131222.html.

emotionally for St. Joseph and in its significance for the entire human race.

Fortunately, God had other plans. Not only did He not want St. Joseph to separate himself from Mary and her Child, but God also wanted St. Joseph to be a father for Mary's Child. He indicates this by giving him a father's authority by empowering him to name this Child: "You shall call his name Jesus" (Matt 1:21). After this revelation in his dream, St. Joseph awoke to the startling mystery that the Divine Father was entrusting His eternal Son to St. Joseph's human fatherhood. St. Joseph was called to stand in the place of the heavenly Father as a human father for the Son of God. He needed to carry out a human fatherhood for Jesus, while at the same time, he had to represent the heavenly Father in raising His Son and preparing Him for His divine mission. St. Joseph carried out these roles already in giving the infant the name prepared for Him in heaven. With this significant action, St. Joseph placed Jesus in his own human, ancestral line and at the same time bestowed on Him the mission given Him by the heavenly Father. "In conferring the name, Joseph declares his own legal fatherhood over Jesus, and in speaking the name he proclaims the child's mission as Savior."[2] God did not force St. Joseph to accept this humanly impossible responsibility or the subsequent requests God made of him. This was the first in a series of ways that God became vulnerable and entrusted Himself

---

[2] Pope St. John Paul II, Apostolic Exhortation on the Person and Mission of Saint Joseph in the Life of Christ and of the Church *Redemptoris Custos* (August 15, 1989), §13. Hereafter cited in text as RC.

to St. Joseph's protection and paternal care.

From the vulnerability of the tiny baby in Mary's womb to the delivery of the baby in Bethlehem to the protection from Herod's wrath to the daily care and upbringing of the Divine Child, St. Joseph was God's choice for fatherly strength and tenderness. In our path to holiness, we are called to internalize God's wisdom. He has sowed the seeds of the divine logic (*Logos*) in our hearts through Baptism, and the more we let that logic guide our actions, the more divine we become by participation. Part of God's logic is to become vulnerable and entrust Himself to the loving fatherhood of St. Joseph. The infancy and childhood of Jesus is a model of vulnerability for us.

Jerónimo Gracián, the spiritual director of St. Teresa of Ávila, went so far as to say that St. Joseph was not only the adoptive father, but also the Guardian Angel of the Child Jesus:

> Learned authors say that Jesus had no Guardian Angel but many angels who served and ministered to Him, and that the office of Jesus' Guardian Angel was entrusted to St. Joseph. If this were not so, who protected Him from King Herod so that he would not kill Him? Why was St. Joseph so upset when Jesus was lost for three days, if he was not His Guardian Angel? Who protected and carried Him on the road when He went to Egypt, returned from Egypt, and went to the temple in Jerusalem from Nazareth? And neither the road from Nazareth to Jerusalem nor that to Egypt

was level ground; there was rough terrain, rocky ground, mud holes and streams.[3]

St. John Henry Newman went so far as to call St. Joseph "the Cherub, placed to guard the new terrestrial paradise from the intrusion of every foe."[4]

To reinforce this point, we can notice that when the Child was in mortal danger, God did not notify His Mother, but rather communicated the danger first to St. Joseph in a dream, warning him: "Herod is about to search for the child, to destroy him" (Matt 2:13). All this gives us courage to come to St. Joseph in our need. Although we are often tempted to rely only on ourselves, establish our own defenses, and cover up our vulnerabilities and sensitivities, God shows us a new way of dependence and trust by His own example.

This constitutes our first pathway to Jesus through the heart of St. Joseph.

The Weapons of Obedience

The manner of St. Joseph's protection is also noteworthy. St. Joseph does not utilize the methods of worldly power.

---

[3] Joseph F. Chorpenning, O.S.F.S., trans. and ed., *Just Man, Husband of Mary, Guardian of Christ: An Anthology of Readings from Jerónimo Gracián's Summary of the Excellencies of St. Joseph (1579)*, 2nd ed. (Philadelphia: Saint Joseph's University Press, 1995), 190–91.

[4] St. John Henry Newman, *Meditations and Devotions of the Late Cardinal Newman*, ed. Rev. W. P. Neville (New York: Longmans, Green & Co., 1907), 269.

He does not raise up armies or fashion more powerful weapons. He does not dominate through anger or defend by intimidation. These methods, in fact, have a dark side when it comes to protecting helpless, vulnerable children, because while they can scare away the enemy, they can also scare the child. At some level, the child knows that if his father can act that way toward someone else, he can act that way toward him as well. That can drive a wedge of fear into the child's heart and limit the intimacy and vulnerability of the child toward his father. God guides St. Joseph in taking a different approach: "Rise, take the child and his mother, and flee to Egypt, and remain there till I tell you" (Matt 2:13). St. Joseph protects Mary and Jesus from Herod, but more fundamentally he is protecting the Child and His Mother from Satan's wrath that is only working through Herod. Even if St. Joseph had defeated Herod, Satan would have found another way to attack the Child and His Mother.

The ultimate weapons for defeating Satan are humility and obedience. These are the weapons God gave to St. Joseph, and these are the weapons that St. Joseph eventually gave back to God in Jesus. Rather than giving the witness of anger, however justified, and violence, St. Joseph gave the example of humility and obedience. The Scripture is clear on how readily he responded: "He rose and took the child and his mother by night, and departed to Egypt, and remained there" (Matt 2:14–15). In fact, the Scripture demonstrates how closely St. Joseph listened and how carefully he was obedient to the angel's instructions after he awoke from each of his three dreams. In each case, the description of St. Joseph's actions followed the angel's instructions *word for word* (see Matt 1:24; 2:14, 21). In this, St. Joseph teaches us the power of true obedience. St. Benedict, in his Holy Rule, calls young men to this way of St. Joseph, that "armed with the strong and noble weapons of obedience [they may] do battle for the true King, Christ the Lord."[5]

Humility and obedience undo the sin of Satan and the sin of Adam. Satan resisted God and tried to overthrow Him, as the Prophet Jeremiah described: "For long ago you broke your yoke and burst your bonds; and you said, 'I will not serve'" (Jer 2:20). Adam and Eve abandoned the criteria for judgment that God had given them and invented their own: "The woman saw that the tree was good for food, and that it was a delight to the eyes, and that the tree was to be desired to make one wise" (Gen 3:6). In contrast, St. Joseph humbly accepted the designs of God and obediently carried out His will. We do not hear him questioning or applying creative interpretations. St. Joseph executed the will of God with accuracy, word for word. The result was that the Child was protected— from the wrath of Herod, from the wrath of Satan, and even from the wrath of an angry protector. St. Joseph was no angry protector, only a humble and obedient one.

In the liturgical tradition, as well as folk piety, Christians have seen how the humility and obedience of St. Joseph result in not only successfully evading danger but in bringing down idols as well, simply by bringing

---

[5] St. Benedict, *The Rule of St. Benedict in English*, trans. Timothy Fry, O.S.B. (Collegeville, MN: Liturgical Press, 2018), Prol 3.

the Infant Jesus into their midst.[6] Without chariots and armies, the humble Holy Family destroyed the ancient powers of Egypt and replaced them with the eternal power of love and truth. This was prophesied in Isaiah 19:

> Behold, the LORD is riding on a swift cloud
>   and comes to Egypt;
>
> and the idols of Egypt will tremble at his presence,
>   and the heart of the Egyptians will melt within
>   them. . . .
>
> In that day there will be an altar to the LORD in
> the midst of the land of Egypt, and a pillar to the
> LORD at its border. (Isa 19:1, 19)

According to the legends, this happened without any violence. The details of the flight into Egypt are not clearly elaborated, but many of the Fathers of the Church explained that the prophecy of Isaiah 19 was fulfilled by the journey of the Holy Family. In the first centuries of the Church, they could also point to the widespread and fervent faith that still existed in Egypt to the point that non-Christian worship had practically been eradicated.

As one telling of the story goes, when the Holy Family approached the city of Heliopolis (part of modern-day Cairo), the idols simply bowed down and crumbled. In

---

[6] Otto F. A. Meinardus, *The Holy Family in Egypt* (American University in Cairo Press, 1986). See also Sr. M. Danielle Peters, "Flight into Egypt," University of Dayton, accessed May 16, 2019, https://udayton.edu/imri/mary/f/flight-into-egypt.php.

their place, a fervent faith grew that continues to stand today with great courage against various violent forces that threaten it. The apocryphal accounts of the travels of the Holy Family through Egypt have been filled with supernatural wonders, but there is also a thread of humility and tenderness that flows through them. From a rock preserved with the footprint of a Child, to the basin in which Mary baked bread, to various trees that provided shade, to a rock, now used as an altar, on which the Infant slept—these legends present the humble Holy Family simple surviving as exiles, depending on the goodness of local people, and trying to live their daily lives in a transient existence.

These stories, drawn surely from some historical reality as well as from mystical visions and human imagination, invite us to approach St. Joseph in our own experiences of homelessness and feelings of exile. When we feel undefended, overwhelmed by the idols of popularity, power, riches, and worldliness, we can place ourselves in the midst of the humble and obedient St. Joseph and his Holy Family. As expressed by the prophet Hosea, they will draw us close with cords of compassion and bands of love and raise us like an infant to the cheek and bend down and feed us (see Hos 11:4). These acts of tender love, in themselves, drive away those loud and violent idols that seek to draw us in.

The Gospel passage on the flight into Egypt quotes from the prophet Hosea: "Out of Egypt have I called my son" (Matt 2:15). That passage from Hosea continues with a lament on how easily we turn from the Lord toward idols even though He has given us everything (see

Hos 11:2). He has taken us up into His arms and healed us, but we did not recognize it was Him (see Hos 11:3). But He affirms that He will continue to reach out to us, to bring us home. Like the Good Shepherd, who left the ninety-nine to find the one lost sheep, God sends the Infant Jesus, through the obedience of St. Joseph, into Egypt to rescue all those who have turned to idols. As soon as we find ourselves attached to idols, we can let St. Joseph bring Jesus and Mary to us to destroy those idols and bring us redemption and healing. God does not expect us to find our own way out of Egypt. He sends His Holy Family to find us and rescue us.

The quality of St. Joseph's obedience makes that rescue mission possible. His obedience moves him not only to act promptly (the Scripture emphasizes that he acted immediately after he awoke from the dream and departed with Mary and Jesus "by night") but also to wait patiently, obeying the command to "remain there till I tell you" (Matt 2:13). Such obedience is only possible for one who loves and trusts deeply. In St. Joseph's prompt action, as well as his patient long-suffering, we behold a heart that has truly become conformed to the Heart of God. Holy obedience is not the behavior of an automaton, and it does not come about by developing an iron will. The most meritorious response to God's will is a fully human response that engages sentiment, intellect, and will. Though our feelings are sometimes the last part of us to respond, in a fully ordered human heart, the emotions also align with the intellect and will. The angel's explanation of Herod's violent behavior satisfied St. Joseph's intellect, and his will resonated with the angel's nocturnal message well enough to be engaged. We can only presume that his prompt action gives a little window into his passionate heart as well. He desired to protect his wife and Child. He did not try to find a way to compromise for the sake of his own comfort. He acted immediately.

Such obedience must develop over time through a relationship. St. Joseph was not a robot, but a human being, acting in faith, in need of discernment. In the Ignatian spiritual exercises, St. Ignatius teaches that discernment to make a choice (an "election" in his vocabulary) comes through a process of first remembering the principle and foundation. We are made out of love and for love. Our identity comes from God's unconditional love for us, and our purpose is in glorifying Him with our lives. Then, there is a process of clearing away the obstacles of attachments and sin. Finally, when the heart is like a balance at equilibrium, willing to accept whatever God brings, it is possible to make the significant choices that set the direction for our lives. This is not a process of violently choosing something radically opposed to our desires, but gradually bringing our desires in conformity to God's will such that the choice becomes more fluid, heartfelt, and certain. "This election should emerge cleanly out of a unity between divine and human freedom: the whole purpose is to prepare ourselves. . . . This delicate consonance between God's most free offer and man's most free acceptance [is] a consonance that is 'clear and pure.'"[7]

---

[7] Jacques Servais, S.J., ed., *Hans Urs von Balthasar on the Ignatian Spiritual Exercises: An Anthology* (San Francisco, CA: Ignatius Press, 2019), 58.

What this teaches us about St. Joseph is the quality of his heart and his availability to God. His readiness to obey was a sign of how he kept his heart like a balance at equilibrium, ready to respond to God's call. Furthermore, he sustained that availability for years in Egypt, waiting until the angel told him to return. Although we are tempted to settle into patterns and places that free us from uncertainty and help us settle into a sense of control over our lives, St. Joseph maintained a heart that was docile to divine intervention and ready to respond. As Pope Francis described it:

> Even through Joseph's fears, God's will, his history and his plan were at work. Joseph, then, teaches us that faith in God includes believing that he can work even through our fears, our frailties and our weaknesses. He also teaches us that amid the tempests of life, we must never be afraid to let the Lord steer our course. At times, we want to be in complete control, yet God always sees the bigger picture.[8]

St. Joseph's life was defined by the certainty that God's ways are best and that God is infinitely trustworthy. It is for this reason that we, whose wills and hearts are more weak and fragile, can bring our vulnerability under St. Joseph's protection. We can trust him to hear God's will and to carry us to Egypt or to carry us home according to the calculations of divine timing that God alone

---

[8] Pope Francis, *Patris Corde*, §2.

knows. In the process, idols are destroyed and lost sheep are found and a little family grows closer together and closer to God under the influence of God's grace.

Tenderness

In one way, St. Joseph is like the archangel St. Michael, who was also charged with protecting the Child and His Mother: "The dragon stood before the woman who was about to bear a child, that he might devour her child when she brought it forth. . . . Now war arose in heaven, Michael and his angels fighting against the dragon" (Rev 12:4, 7). The imagery in the Book of Revelation implies violence and aggression as we picture St. Michael taking up spear and shield to destroy and cast down the devil and his apostate angels. Christian art has immortalized such images and impressed them into our Catholic imagination. Considering that St. Michael's greatest weapon is humility, which is inscribed in his name meaning "Who is like God?" in Hebrew, the reality may be a bit different, and even a bit more like the victory of St. Joseph. In any event, we know that St. Joseph did not raise up armies or wage violent war against Herod. His method was altogether different. Without stirring violence in his heart, he remained always tender toward his little family and presumably toward all whom they met along the way. The shepherds, the Magi, and the countless strangers on the way to Egypt and back would have been recipients of St. Joseph's tender love:

Here I would add one more thing: caring, protecting, demands goodness, it calls for a certain tenderness. In the Gospels, Saint Joseph appears as a strong and courageous man, a working man, yet in his heart we see great tenderness, which is not the virtue of the weak but rather a sign of strength of spirit and a capacity for concern, for compassion, for genuine openness to others, for love. We must not be afraid of goodness, of tenderness![9]

Pope Francis made similar observations about Our Lady: "Whenever we look to Mary, we come to believe once again in the revolutionary nature of love and tenderness. In her we see that humility and tenderness are not virtues of the weak but of the strong who need not treat others poorly in order to feel important themselves."[10] In the language of Pope Francis, St. Joseph and his Holy Family were the greatest revolutionaries in the Revolution of Tenderness. This is how they could praise the One who brings down the mighty from their thrones and lifts up the lowly.

As Pope Francis noted for both Joseph and Mary, tenderness is "not the virtue of the weak." The etymology of tenderness is from the Indo-European root *ten*,

---

[9] Pope Francis, Inaugural Homily on the Feast of St. Joseph, March 19, 2013, http://w2.vatican.va/content/francesco/en/homilies/2013/documents/papa-francesco_20130319_omelia-inizio-pontificato.html.

[10] Pope Francis, Apostolic Exhortation on the Proclamation of the Gospel in Today's World *Evangelii Gaudium* (November 24, 2013), §288.

which means "stretched." When we think of a "tendon," "tension," or "attention," we get a sense of the way that tenderness stretches the heart. The one who is tender does not act impulsively and snap but stretches in patience and waits on the one who is in need. The tender person does not defeat the enemy through reaction and revenge but patiently absorbs the violence like a house built on rock that weathers a storm. This is the father who holds a pouting child close to his heart while he absorbs the blows of pain and anger erupting from a frightened toddler. Slowly the anger plays itself out and the child collapses into arms of love. With more hardened violence and abusive evils, tenderness shields the innocent victim and stretches across the field of action, standing between predator and prey. Or, as in the case of the Holy Family, tenderness gathers up the little innocents and disappears into exile, following the directive of God's command. We must imagine that the tender heart of St. Joseph grieved mightily over those innocents that he could not gather up and take with him. Perhaps the angel's words about his Son were his consolation in that regard: "You shall call his name Jesus, for he will save his people" (Matt 1:21).

As St. Joseph courageously and tenderly led his little family into exile, we do not get the image of a weak man or an elderly, frail man, but rather a man of strength. Despite the descriptions of St. Joseph in some apocryphal literature that have passed on through the ages in Christian art as well, the head of the family who endured the rigors of exile needed strength, courage, and hope. His heart was stretched by the indefinite time given by the angel: "Remain there till I tell you" (Matt 2:13). He probably repeated those words

to himself a thousand times across the burdens of the long
journey into the strange land. While most people would
train and prepare for months before hiking the Appala-
chian Trail or the Camino de Santiago, St. Joseph had to
uproot his family and depart the same night in order to
survive Herod's insanity. This was not the task of one who
is physically weak, spiritually weak, or emotionally weak. It
was not a journey for the faint-hearted.

St. Joseph's tenderness lacked nothing in terms of
courage and hope. He faced many trials and persevered
through years of hardships. He never shut down his heart
in despair or gave up before powers greater than he could
handle. In this way, he exemplified Pope Francis's description of an "aggressive tenderness" that is needed also now
in our efforts for evangelization:

> One of the more serious temptations which stifles
> boldness and zeal is a defeatism which turns us
> into querulous and disillusioned pessimists, "sour-
> pusses." Nobody can go off to battle unless he is
> fully convinced of victory beforehand. If we start
> without confidence, we have already lost half the
> battle and we bury our talents. While painfully
> aware of our own frailties, we have to march on
> without giving in, keeping in mind what the Lord
> said to Saint Paul: "My grace is sufficient for
> you, for my power is made perfect in weakness"
> (2 Cor 12:9). Christian triumph is always a cross,
> yet a cross which is at the same time a victorious
> banner borne with aggressive tenderness against
> the assaults of evil. The evil spirit of defeatism is

brother to the temptation to separate, before its time, the wheat from the weeds; it is the fruit of an anxious and self-centred lack of trust.[11]

St. Joseph did not separate the wheat from the weeds, but tenderly cared for the Finest of Wheat that grew up in his home. That Finest of Wheat grew among the weeds in Nazareth who would not only not recognize His Divinity but also even try to throw Him headlong over a cliff (Luke 4:29)! As St. Joseph looked at the disorders in society and perhaps even bristled under the same hardness and rigidity of the Pharisees that his Son would later fight against, he could focus his energy on the boy entrusted to his tender care and make sure he grew up healthy, strong, and fully alive. He only had to return to the dream and remember the promise of the angel as he gazed on the Son he did not physically conceive and take comfort in the words "He will save his people" (Matt 1:21).

While St. Joseph hardened against the difficulties of the journey, he was always softened toward his bride and Son. He cared for them and absorbed as many of the hardships as he could. One film creatively depicted him as giving half his rations to Our Lady and the other half to the donkey who carried her.[12] For this reason, we can count on him to take care of us as well. St. Joseph is a father with great tenderness, who sacrifices to provide for those entrusted to his care. Furthermore, he does that regardless of our worthiness. It is enough that God has

---

[11] Pope Francis, *Evangelii Gaudium*, §85.
[12] *The Nativity Story*, directed by Catherine Hardwicke, 2006.

created us in the image of His Son, and he teaches us to do the same:

> Joseph's attitude encourages us to accept and welcome others as they are, without exception, and to show special concern for the weak, for God chooses what is weak (cf. 1 Cor 1:27). He is the "Father of orphans and protector of widows" (Ps 68:6), who commands us to love the stranger in our midst. I like to think that it was from Saint Joseph that Jesus drew inspiration for the parable of the prodigal son and the merciful father (cf. Lk 15:11-32).[13]

As members of the Church, he is our universal patron, and we have been entrusted personally to his patronage. He will care for all of us who come to him in need. If we are willing to be vulnerable with him, presenting our needs before him and asking him to provide for us and protect us, he will not fail to come to our aid:

> Remember, most pure spouse of Mary, ever Virgin, our loving protector, St. Joseph, that no one ever had recourse to your protection or asked your aid without obtaining relief. Confiding, therefore, in your goodness, we come before you and humbly implore you. Despise not our petitions, Foster-Father of the Redeemer, but graciously receive them. Amen.[14]

---

[13] Pope Francis, *Patris Corde*, §4.
[14] Memorare to St. Joseph.

We can imagine that if God was willing to entrust the care of His Son to St. Joseph on earth, He now entrusts him with at least as much in heaven. The Church's liturgy has applied the following words of the Lord to St. Joseph: "Who then is the faithful and wise steward, whom his master will set over his household, to give them their portion of food at the proper time? Blessed is that servant whom his master when he comes will find so doing. Truly I tell you, he will set him over all his possessions" (Luke 12:42–44).[15] Through the Church's logic, St. Joseph has all of God's possessions at his disposal, and so he can provide for us in any of our needs. Of course, the ultimate answer that St. Joseph provides for every prayer is the ultimate gift he can offer, namely, his Son, Our Lord Jesus Christ Himself. He provides that gift without fail to anyone who asks him.

Veils the Mystery

"Joseph did not wish to unveil (her mystery) . . ."[16]

In his excellent interpretation of various Marian scriptural texts, Ignace de la Potterie, S.J., argued that "unveil" best translates the Greek word *deigmatizo* in the context of what is being communicated in Matthew 1:19. Whether he knew exactly what was happening or was simply per-

---

[15] See also the Introit antiphon and Preface for the Solemnity of St. Joseph on March 19. This is also used for the versicle at the end of the Litany of St. Joseph.

[16] Ignace de la Potterie, *Mary in the Mystery of the Covenant*, trans. Bertrand Buby (New York: Alba House, 1992), 54–55.

plexed, or even if he truly suffered in the way supposed by
the less compelling suspicion theories, St. Joseph chose to
leave Mary's mystery beneath the veil. Rather than drawing
attention to it by exposing her, he planned to separate
himself from her quietly. In the end, the angel showed him
in the dream that the best way he could veil her mystery
would be by directing the eyes of suspicion toward himself.
His decision to remain with her told everyone that he was
going to accept the humble role of raising a baby conceived
in shameful circumstances—either through his own illicit
anticipation of having relations with Mary before moving
in together or in the immoral circumstances of another
man's involvement with his wife. In this way, he covered
her, not unlike the Holy Spirit, who had already "covered
her" with His shadow when she had initially conceived
the Son of God in her womb. Thus, through his obedience
to the angel and a humble acceptance of any false accusa-
tions, St. Joseph kept the mystery of Mary veiled beneath
his firm presence and loving care.

What was the mystery he was veiling? It is first of
all the mystery of the divine conception of the Incarnate
Word that had taken place in her womb. That mystery is
already infinite, and we could linger there indefinitely. But
we could also step back and take in the mystery of the
woman who could conceive Him. There again we have a
mystery that has already exhausted countless volumes as
we go ever deeper and yet still fail to sound its depths.
Centuries of reflection have led the Church to proclaim
four essential dogmas to describe how she is uniquely
blessed among women. We can pause and reflect on one
example that the Church's devotional life has offered to us

to summarize the Church's teaching, namely, the Immaculate Heart of Mary. The Immaculate Heart of Mary burns with love, radiates beauty, is tender and soft with feminine sensitivity, and aches and bleeds with compassion. No sin has touched that heart from the inside, although sin has pierced it from the outside. Pure love makes that heart hot with passion, full of life, and fiercely tender for her little ones. It is a generous and generative heart that is miraculously and superabundantly life-giving even though it remains forever virginal. That heart is also full of the mysteries of God, starting with those she witnessed during her life (see Luke 2:19, 51) and expanding to include all the mysteries of heaven in her bodily Assumption and coronation. The mystery of that Immaculate Heart was entrusted to the protective care of St. Joseph. He kept it carefully veiled beneath his loving, spousal care.

St. Joseph also veiled the mystery of the Incarnation and kept it hidden from all who would harm it, especially Satan and his apostate angels. This was explained in the second century by Origen, reflecting on a text of the great St. Ignatius of Antioch:

> I found an elegant statement in the writing of a martyr—I mean Ignatius, the second bishop of Antioch after Peter. During a persecution, he fought against wild animals at Rome. He stated: "Mary's virginity escaped notice of the ruler of this age." It escaped his notice because of Joseph, and because of their wedding, and because Mary was thought to have a husband. If she had not been betrothed or had (as people thought) a

husband, her virginity could never have been concealed from the "ruler of this age."[17]

This fits together nicely with the teaching of Pope
St. John Paul II on the importance of the marriage of
Joseph and Mary. Although the Church's teaching, liturgical prayers, and the writings of the saints have primarily
emphasized the importance of the virginity of Mary and
the miraculous, virginal conception, Pope St. John Paul II
insisted, "While it is important for the Church to profess
the virginal conception of Jesus, it is no less important to
uphold Mary's marriage to Joseph."[18] The reason he gave
was connected with the juridical fatherhood and the fulfillment of various promises that flowed through David's
line. The reason that Origen and St. Ignatius gave,
however, is also equally valid. The marriage itself was a
veil that diverted the devil's sights. The best he could
determine was through the testimony of the Wise Men
and then, by inciting Herod, he wiped out all the children in Bethlehem. He did not notice the one little family
that slipped away under the veil of St. Joseph, however,
because his attention was still focused on finding a single
virgin.

In this we gain a key insight about the importance of
marriage. Our Catholic imagination and attention have
naturally focused on the purely supernatural vocations
of priesthood and religious life, and the devil's attention

---

[17] Joseph T. Lienhard, trans., *Origen: Homilies on Luke*, Fathers of the
Church 94 (Washington, D.C., Catholic University of America Press,
1996), 24–25.
[18] Pope St. John Paul II, *Redemptoris Custos*, §7.

seems to have focused there as well. We must remember, however, that God hid His most sacred mysteries beneath the veil of a marriage. A family became the treasure trove that concealed all the Riches of Heaven in a humble little place on earth. In a sense, religious houses, with a chapel and tabernacle at their center, are only trying to imitate the family home of St. Joseph in Nazareth. Likewise, every parish priest who lives in a home attached to his parish church is a caretaker like St. Joseph, only imitating his family life which took place in the Real Presence of Jesus throughout each day. Ultimately, priests and religious learn to live better when they learn from marriages and families how they receive a baby and arrange everything in their lives around that little and helpless image of God. As the great geologist and father of modern tectonic theory, Xavier Le Pichon, recognized, the healthiest systems are those that are arranged around the weakest member.[19]

As we grow in our Catholic faith, the annual observance of Advent and Christmas, together with the regular prayer of the Joyful Mysteries of the Rosary, naturally leads us to wonder what life in the Holy Family was like. Some ancient, noncanonical apocryphal works guessed wrongly that there were externally spectacular events taking place, like Jesus breathing life into clay pigeons that He fashioned with His Hands.[20] The tradition of the

---

[19] Krista Tippett, "Interview with Xavier Le Pichon—The Fragility at the Heart of Humanity," The On Being Project, accessed May 14, 2019, https://onbeing.org/programs/xavier-le-pichon-the-fragility-at-the-heart-of-humanity/.

[20] Gospel of Thomas 2:3–5, in Rick Brannan, *Greek Apocryphal Gospels,*

Church, however, has upheld that life was wonderfully ordinary in the Holy Family, with the only extraordinary dimension being that it was free of sin. In this way, St. Joseph helps us understand that the most amazing life can be lived in the simple, tender love of the most humble circumstances. It also means that we can begin to pierce the veil of Nazareth quite fruitfully simply by reflecting on our own experiences of everyday life. The way that St. Joseph woke up in the morning, walked to work, ate lunch, interacted with customers, and taught his trade to his Son was completely the same as ours. This is the nature of the hidden life that served as a veil to protect the Incarnate Word and the Immaculate Conception from the devil's pride and hateful envy.

For our prayer, we can ask St. Joseph to share with us a glimpse behind the veil. A veil is a protection that only allows those to see who have eyes to see. "Blessed are the pure of heart, for they shall see God" (Matt 5:8). If we approach this mystery with impure hearts, out of mere curiosity, a desire to exploit, an intention for irreverence, or some other form of defilement, it will disappear like a mirage. If we approach this mystery with the vulnerability of God and the obedience and humility of St. Joseph, however, we will discover a mystical world that was already beneath our eyes, hidden from us only by the veil of St. Joseph.

Fragments, and Agrapha: A New Translation (Bellingham, WA: Lexham Press, 2017), 59.

Most Chaste

In addition to his obedience, St. Joseph also veils Mary's mystery with his heroic chastity, seen in both his modesty and his purity of heart. St. Joseph is hailed in the Divine Praises after Eucharistic Benediction as Mary's "Most Chaste Spouse." In seeing St. Joseph as "most chaste," we learn a great deal about the way he loves and serves his bride, as we can read in the *Catechism*'s description of chastity:

> Chastity means the successful integration of sexuality within the person and thus the inner unity of man in his bodily and spiritual being. Sexuality, in which man's belonging to the bodily and biological world is expressed, becomes personal and truly human when it is integrated into the relationship of one person to another, in the complete and lifelong mutual gift of a man and a woman. The virtue of chastity therefore involves the integrity of the person and the integrality of the gift.[21]

This gives us a picture of a man who has a deep inner unity with an integrated masculine sexuality. He is able to love and give himself in a complete and lifelong way. This accolade from the Church's prayer also lends credence to the widespread belief that St. Joseph was not an old man, withered and past his prime, but rather a vigorous, virtuous young man, full of passion, who was directed through

---

[21] *Catechism of the Catholic Church*, 2337.

hard-won self-mastery. In the words of Venerable Archbishop Fulton Sheen:

> But when one searches for the reasons why Chris-
> tian art should have pictured Joseph as aged, we
> discover that it was in order better to safeguard
> the virginity of Mary. Somehow, the assumption
> had crept in that senility was a better protector
> of virginity than adolescence. Art thus uncon-
> sciously made Joseph a spouse chaste and pure
> by age rather than by virtue. . . . To make Joseph
> appear pure only because his flesh had aged is like
> glorifying a mountain stream that has dried. The
> Church will not ordain a man to his priesthood
> who has not his vital powers. She wants men who
> have something to tame, rather than those who
> are tame because they have no energy to be wild.
> It should be no different with God. . . . Joseph
> was probably a young man, strong, virile, ath-
> letic, handsome, chaste, and disciplined; the kind
> of man one sees sometimes shepherding sheep,
> or piloting a plane, or working at a carpenter's
> bench. Instead of being a man incapable of loving,
> he must have been on fire with love. . . . Instead,
> then, of being dried fruit to be served on the table
> of the king, he was rather a blossom filled with
> promise and power. He was not in the evening of
> life, but in its morning, bubbling over with energy,
> strength, and controlled passion.[22]

---

[22] Archbishop Fulton J. Sheen, *The World's First Love*, 2nd ed. (San

Mary was all-beautiful, the finest flower of the race of Israel, pure as the driven snow. Such beauty is, by its nature, so vulnerable. St. Joseph's chastity was the protection that enabled her mystery to open and be seen. She knew that she could share the depths of her heart with him without fearing that he would use her or disregard her. She could expect the tender care of one who is pure of heart and who could see and reverence her Immaculate Heart. St. John Henry Newman acknowledged the depth and beauty of their relationship as being tied in with Joseph's sanctity:

> He is Holy Joseph, because according to the opinion of a great number of doctors, he, as well as St. John Baptist, was sanctified even before he was born. He is Holy Joseph, because his office, of being spouse and protector of Mary, specially demanded sanctity. He is Holy Joseph, because no other Saint but he lived in such and so long intimacy and familiarity with the source of all holiness, Jesus, God incarnate, and Mary, the holiest of creatures.[23]

In the language of the *Catechism*, the veil that St. Joseph used to cover Our Lady's purity is the veil of modesty. "Modesty protects the intimate center of the person. It means refusing to unveil what should remain

---

Francisco, CA: Ignatius Press, 2010), 92–93.

[23] St. John Henry Newman, *Meditations and Devotions of the Late Cardinal Newman*, 271.

hidden."[24] Modesty is not a prudish fear of things delicate and beautiful, but a prudential reverence for what is
beautiful in order to cherish it and protect it. "Modesty
protects the mystery of persons and their love.... It keeps
silence or reserve where there is evident risk of unhealthy
curiosity. It is discreet."[25] Here we can see even more
clearly the depiction of St. Joseph in Matthew 1:19 as
one who refused to unveil Mary's mystery. A master of
modesty does not exploit this mystery, nor expose this
mystery, nor run away from this mystery, but rather veils
the mystery with his love.

Furthermore, St. Joseph did not blindly veil the
mystery of Mary, but because of his own purity of heart,
from which flowed his virtue of chastity, he was able to see
God. Whether he saw God immediately, as St. Bernard
of Clairvaux contended, or whether he came to see God
only after the angel appeared to him in a dream, the fact is
that he was the first (except Mary) to see God in Mary's
womb. "[Purity of heart] enables us to see according to
God . . . ; it lets us perceive the human body—ours and
our neighbor's—as a temple of the Holy Spirit, a manifestation of divine beauty."[26] St. Joseph saw the body of
Mary as a temple of the Holy Spirit and also as a temple
of the Divine Son whom she carried in her womb. Mary
carried the most precious treasure the world had ever
known, and in her pregnancy, she became more fragile
and vulnerable each day. Although he considered himself

---

[24] CCC 2521.
[25] CCC 2522.
[26] CCC 2519.

unworthy at first, with the angel's urging, St. Joseph committed himself to protect this precious treasure for the rest of his life.

Even in his hesitation, St. Joseph is a good example for us. Perhaps we are too cavalier in the way we approach Jesus in the Blessed Sacrament or even the way we care for (or ignore) Jesus in the poor. In the minds of St. Bernard and St. Thomas Aquinas, St. Joseph hesitated in taking up care of Mary because he was aware of his own weakness in light of the greatness of this task. St. Bernard of Clairvaux wrote, "Why did he resolve to send her away? . . . He noticed that she was very obviously bearing the divine presence within her and it awed him. But not being able to penetrate this mystery, he resolved to send her away."[27] St. Thomas Aquinas reiterated this insight in his *Summa Theologica*: "Joseph wanted to give the Virgin her liberty, not because he suspected her of adultery, but out of respect for her sanctity he feared to live together with her."[28]

In addition to teaching us reverence, St. Joseph teaches us chastity and modesty and leads us to purity of heart. We can learn this first by letting ourselves be seen by him. As we entrust our own bodies and hearts to his loving, fatherly care, we can learn how he reverences us. He never

---

[27] St. Bernard of Clairvaux, "Homily *Super Missus Est*," in Bernard of Clairvaux, *Homilies in Praise of the Blessed Virgin Mary*, trans. Marie-Bernard Said, Cistercian Fathers Series, no. 18-A (Kalamazoo, MI: Cistercian Publications, 1993), 26–27.

[28] St. Thomas Aquinas, *The Summa Theologica of St. Thomas Aquinas*, trans. The Fathers of the English Dominican Province (London: Burns, Oates & Washbourne, 1920), Supplementum III, q. 62, a. 3.

beholds us with scorn or judgment. Even in our own failures in chastity or modesty, he covers our nakedness like
Noah's good sons (Gen 9:23). He does not control us
through shaming, but rather invites us to learn from him.
In his purity of heart, he was able to behold the mystery of
Mary. He could see her beauty, inside and outside. And in
her womb at first, and then in her arms, at her breast, and
in his company, he could see the mystery of the Incarnation. He beheld the mystery of God's love that became so
little, so fragile, and so vulnerable, trusting in human care
for everything. He teaches us this gaze and helps us move
from a pornographic culture that exploits and spoils what
is beautiful to a culture of reverence that sees God in all
beauty and then works to cherish it and protect it with the
veil of modesty and the tenderness of love.

Arrival in Nazareth

The Holy Family ended up in Nazareth because of
another one of Joseph's dreams. After spending their
whole married life in exile, the Holy Family finally came
to a place they could call a home. They were led there
by an angel in Joseph's fourth dream, guided to avoid
another murderous tyrant. In this case, St. Joseph heard
the bad news and first felt fear before the Lord redirected
him through the angel. The Scripture tells us:

> But when he heard that Archelaus reigned over
> Judea in place of his father Herod, he was afraid
> to go there, and being warned in a dream he with-

drew to the district of Galilee. And he went and dwelt in a city called Nazareth, that what was spoken by the prophets might be fulfilled. "He shall be called a Nazarene." (Matt 2:22–23)

St. Joseph's heart was chastened as he lived in obedient faith over so many years. The Lord gave him a few lights, though they could be considered a mixed blessing. One light that Joseph received was the spiritual consolation that came through a dream. We do not know exactly how he experienced his dreams, but we know that they were strong enough to move him to take radical steps in his life. We also know that St. Joseph was interiorly sensitive enough to detect those movements of the heart and understand them. As Pope Benedict XVI described it:

Whereas the angel "came" to Mary (Lk 1:28), he merely appears to Joseph in a dream—admittedly a dream that is real and reveals what is real. Once again this shows us an essential quality of the figure of Saint Joseph: his capacity to perceive the divine and his ability to discern. Only a man who is inwardly watchful for the divine, only someone with a real sensitivity for God and his ways, can receive God's message in this way. And an ability to discern was necessary in order to know whether it was simply a dream or whether God's messenger had truly appeared to him and addressed him.[29]

---

[29] Pope Benedict XVI, *Jesus of Nazareth: The Infancy Narratives*, trans. Philip Whitmore (New York: Image Books, 2012), 41.

St. Ignatius of Loyola described various qualities of spiritual consolation, and we could presume that one of these describes the experience of St. Joseph. St. Ignatius tells us that these bodily-spiritual experiences accompany the movements of the good spirit. They are the overflow of divine grace into our inner senses—our imagination, memory, and feelings.

Spiritual consolation sometimes feels like our hearts are on fire with love for our Creator and Lord, such that we feel lifted up above every other creature. Sometimes we experience the grace of God's closeness as tears that move us because we are overwhelmed by God's love in Christ's Passion or the other mysteries of His life or because we are moved to contrition for our sins, since we have offended such a loving God. Other times we are moved to an increase of the virtues of faith, hope, or love. An increase of faith could be described as really knowing what we already believe. For example, while we readily confess the Real Presence of Jesus in the Eucharist, an increase of faith could be the sudden, overwhelming certainty that that is really and truly Him! Likewise, an increase of hope could be a sudden confidence that things are going to work out, that God is going to come through, even when things are very, very bad. St. Ignatius also points to spiritual joy as a sign of God's commu- nication of grace, and lastly, he mentions peace and all interior stillness.[30]

We can suppose that St. Joseph awoke from his dream

---

[30] Ignatius of Loyola, *The Spiritual Exercises of St. Ignatius: Or Manresa*, (Charlotte, NC: TAN Books, 1999), no. 316.

with some tangible experience of spiritual consolation to make such a sudden, radical decision with a certainty that was clear and beyond doubt. He needed such a strong movement of the Holy Spirit to take such a drastic step. He received that clear guidance on four different occasions that are recorded in Scripture. At the same time, our dreams and even our spiritual experiences have a way of fading into the background. Remember that Jesus had to chastise the Church in Ephesus: "I have this against you, that you have abandoned the love you had at first" (Rev 2:4). Our first love often has to do more with His love for us, which intoxicates us (Acts 2:15). That love must be chastened by living it out. Joseph's love for God and his love for his wife and her Child were chastened over many years in Egyptian exile while he clung to the memory of a dream. His years in Nazareth were surely the same.

One thing that surely helped him was the way that his wife loved and trusted him. Mary believed him. She believed each one of his dreams. We have no reason to believe that she received any particular spiritual consolation herself. She simply trusted in the man God had sent into her life. And she trusted him completely—with her life and the life of her most precious Son. Chaste love is always sustained and strengthened by chaste love. Joseph's trustworthiness and fidelity were supported and strengthened by his wife's trust and faithfulness in return.

There is something powerful about mutual trust. The interlocking of mutual trust between two loving hearts is a three-ply cord that is hard to break from the outside (Eccl 4:12). Their mutual trust and love remained unbroken through all the trials of exile, the uncertainties of the journey, the hardships of finding a place to live, of navigating a new language, of adjusting to a foreign culture, of seeking out an unknown destination. On the other hand, there is something so fragile about such trust, because it is hypersensitive to the smallest acts of infidelity. Such trust allows the hands of another right inside the ribcage to touch the heart directly, and a small wrong movement can cause such great pain.

For this reason, Mary's radical trust in Joseph was a confirmation and strength for him, but also a reason for holy fear. Her trust let him all the way inside. A selfish decision, a callous word, or a harsh action could cause tremendous pain to that sensitive and vulnerable heart. Such vulnerability is necessary for true intimacy, but it takes a great risk. Mary and Joseph learned during years of exile to become even more perfectly attuned to each other until they landed in the place of their dreams—or at least the place of Joseph's dream: Nazareth.

Like Mary, we can discover the beauty of Joseph's heart by trusting in his dreams. Placing our trust in St. Joseph will not diminish our dignity or take away our autonomy. And when we trust in him, we can experience, like Mary did, Joseph's holy fear. He takes his responsibility very seriously, and he carries out his mission conscientiously. He knows the price of failure, and he makes a total personal investment to avoid it. This is the reason Pope Pius IX gave him the title Patron of the Catholic Church:

> As almighty God appointed Joseph, son of the patriarch Jacob, over all the land of Egypt to save grain for the people, so when the fullness of time

had come and He was about to send to earth His only-begotten Son, the Savior of the world, He chose another Joseph, of whom the first had been the type, and He made him the lord and chief of His household and possessions, the guardian of His choicest treasures.[31]

In doing this, Bl. Pius IX counts each one of us among God's choicest treasures and entrusts us to the care of St. Joseph.

A Prayer for Protection

This is a widely distributed prayer with a reputedly ancient origin whose popularity has led some to attach particular importance and various promises to it. It captures the strong and tender protection of St. Joseph:

O Saint Joseph, whose protection is so great, so strong, so prompt before the throne of God, I place in you all my interests and desires.

O Saint Joseph, do assist me by your powerful intercession and obtain for me from your divine Son all spiritual blessings through Jesus Christ, Our Lord, so that having experienced here below your heavenly power, I may offer my thanksgiving

---

[31] Pope Pius IX, Decree *Quemadmodum Deus* (December 8, 1870), https://osjusa.org/st-joseph/magisterium/quemadmodum-deus/.

and homage to the most loving of fathers.

O Saint Joseph, I never weary of contemplating you and Jesus asleep in your arms. I dare not approach while He reposes near your heart. Hold Him close in my name and kiss His fine head for me, and ask Him to return the kiss when I draw my dying breath. St. Joseph, patron of departing souls, pray for me. Amen.

Chapter Two

A FRIEND IN SILENCE

Silent

When the Magi entered into Jerusalem, they lost sight of the heavens and they turned to worldly power as they sought out Herod, the King of Judea. Perhaps they rationalized that they were looking for the newborn king and so they should ask the reigning king. Their mistake cost the lives of many innocents and led to the sorrow of many hearts. They should have kept their eyes on the heavens. Fortunately, they did not listen to Herod, who encouraged them to persist in their talkativeness. "Ask around," he instructed them: "Go and search diligently for the child, and when you have found him bring me word, that I too may come and worship him" (Matt 2:8). "Diligently" describes the way that St. Luke investigated his Gospel (see Luke 1:3), but "search" can also be translated as "ask around" or "interrogate." The talkative approach of Herod, searching in worldly ways, will not uncover St. Joseph. The Magi seemed to intuit this, and so they did not follow Herod's instructions, but left the city, or as the RSV translates it, "They went their way" (Matt 2:9).

They did not follow Herod's way of noisy inquiries, but they went *their* way and they were rewarded: "Behold, the star which they had seen in the East went before them" (Matt 2:9). Those who choose a path of silent seeking, looking up to the heavens, will be filled with great joy: "When they saw the star, they rejoiced exceedingly with great joy" (Matt 2:10).

In this chapter, we consider the path of silence. This is another path for drawing near to St. Joseph, and by approaching him, we approach Mary and Jesus as well. Although we fill these pages with words, the reader must not fall into Herod's trap and reduce the search for the Christ child to a collection of interrogations and gathering up the words of others. Words can only be pointers to a reality that presents itself ultimately in silence, in a place where words fall off and only love remains. It is the passionate hearts of the Magi that brought them beyond worldly advice to catch again the light of the star that led them silently to St. Joseph. We can imagine him standing at the door of the house, which is why he is not mentioned in the scriptural verse of their discovery: "And going into the house they saw the child with Mary his mother, and they fell down and worshiped him" (Matt 2:11). Their search led them to St. Joseph, and St. Joseph let them in to behold his wife and worship his Son.

St. Joseph was likely on guard, as any good father would be with his vulnerable wife and newborn son. Having experienced so much rejection, however, and aware of the infamous, erratic violence of Herod, St. Joseph was likely even more alert to protect his little family. Even though he had not yet been warned by the angel that Herod had particularly set his sights on the child, St. Joseph was thoughtful enough to be careful. For some reason, the Magi passed his test. Perhaps it was because they came in silence. He could see their depth, their seriousness, the intensity of their search, the many sacrifices that had been required of them to reach the Infant King. The words of this encounter between St. Joseph and the Magi are only presumed in Scripture, not recorded. Rather, we read only about their sincere and silent acts of worship: falling to the ground and presenting their gift. Like the Offertory Rite in the Holy Mass, the gifts are brought forward without a word exchanged between the givers and the one who receives them in the Person of Christ.

The Magi teach us how to find St. Joseph: With our eyes raised to the heavens, let the noise of the world fall away and let the advice of worldly power slip into the background. Then proceed in silence, led by the passion of the heart toward the most unlikely place, a little house where we find a humble man guarding his little family. St. Joseph is more readily found by those who choose silence because he was, himself, a man of silence.

Of course, we know that St. Joseph spoke. He was not afflicted with the muteness imposed for nine months on his wife's cousin Zechariah. In particular, we know he was the first to speak the greatest word ever spoken—the Name of Jesus. We know that he spoke when he professed his marriage vows and he spoke when he roused his bride and baby by night. Surely he spoke with the Magi and at other times with the shepherds and with innkeepers and neighbors and clients and rabbis and cousins. In fact, the

Scripture leaves it to our imaginations how he spoke with
Mary and later with Jesus. There must have been beautiful conversations that the angels liked to overhear.

But the most important witness St. Joseph gave was
not with words, and so no words of his are quoted in
Scripture. Even when he and Mary finally found their Son
in the Temple after three days, Mary spoke with Jesus on
behalf of them both, saying, "Your father and I . . . " (Luke
2:48). St. Joseph's most important witness was through his
actions and through his presence. We know that he taught
his Son his trade as a carpenter, because Jesus is referred
to in one place as "the carpenter's son" (Matt 13:55) and
in another place as "the carpenter" (Mark 6:3). That surely
required words, but also actions and example. The tacit
learning described by Michael Polanyi can inform our
imagination when we think of St. Joseph and Jesus in the
carpenter's shop.[1]

We also know that St. Joseph acted out his Fiat.
While Mary spoke her response to the angel, "Be it done
to me . . ." St. Joseph got up and moved into action, always
following the angel's instructions word for word. For all
these reasons, St. John Paul II called him a man of silence
and a master of the interior life.[2] Thus, if we want to draw
closer to St. Joseph and welcome his little family into our
hearts, we must learn to make a place for him in silence.
We must avoid the mistake of Herod, who advised talkativeness and continued interrogations. Likewise, we must

---

[1] Michael Polanyi, *The Tacit Dimension* (Garden City, NY: Doubleday
and Company, Inc., 1966).
[2] Pope St. John Paul II, *Redemptoris Custos*, §25–26.

avoid the mistake of the innkeeper, who was too busy or whose inn was too full to make room for God.

Now we will examine each of these themes and how they teach us a way to draw closer to St. Joseph and, in passing through his heart, to enter, like the Magi, into the house where Jesus and Mary dwell with him.

Tacit Knowledge

When we hear that a man has suffered greatly, a certain picture comes to mind. When we add that he has suffered in silence, it enhances our mental picture of him. Blaming and complaining are ways that we release mental anguish. When the pain is very strong, some even turn to yelling and cursing. The man who is able to suffer in silence, on the other hand, elicits the respect of others, including those who suffer with him and often even those who inflict suffering on him. Without uttering a word or a whimper, such a man demonstrates the state of his interior strength. Usually, we must use words to describe what is happening within us if we want others to understand. In the case of much suffering, however, a man could never describe in words the kind of interior strength that he demonstrates in silence.

The ultimate example of this was found in the Son of Man, who also, in His Passion, revealed Himself to be the Suffering Servant as He fulfilled the words of Isaiah's prophecy, "He was oppressed, and he was afflicted, yet he opened not his mouth; like a lamb that is led to the slaughter, and like a sheep that before its shearers is silent, so he opened not his mouth" (Isa 53:7). Perhaps, at a human level, He was inspired in silent suffering by His beloved father Joseph. It is not hard to imagine the suffering of St. Joseph in the various ways described in Scripture: for example, in his planned separation from Mary, his rejection in Bethlehem, his exile in Egypt, the slaughter of innocents whom he could not save, and in the prophecy of Simeon that he could not protect his bride and Son from terrible suffering. He faced it all with silent strength and simply took what actions he could to minimize the suffering of others.

Furthermore, we must not confuse such silent suffering in Jesus and Joseph as being merely the suppressed emotion often described as a "stiff upper lip." It is not a matter of stuffing the pain or numbing it with the resolve of an iron will. Those are defense mechanisms of a fallen nature that sometimes lead to depression or other psychological problems that tend to come out sideways. In the silent suffering of Jesus and Joseph, we know that they truly suffer. Jesus even eventually cries out on the Cross! Yet there is something else that keeps their heads just above the ocean of pain, their eyes still fixed on the love of the Father. It is a matter of heroic virtue rather than suppressed emotion. It is the anchor of trust in the Father's unconquerable love that keeps the gaze lifted up to heaven even as the suffering of earth weighs heavily on the heart and soul. As Pope Francis said:

> Joseph is certainly not passively resigned, but courageously and firmly proactive. In our own lives, acceptance and welcome can be an expression of

the Holy Spirit's gift of fortitude. Only the Lord can give us the strength needed to accept life as it is, with all its contradictions, frustrations and disappointments.[3]

Now let us imagine a man who does good for others. That gives us a certain mental picture. When we add that he always does good in silence, it enhances that image in our minds. There is a special quality in a man which makes him quiet and observant. He watches for the needs of others and finds ways to provide for them even without being asked. Sometimes he is so subtle that he can provide for every need without even being noticed. The desired object or service has simply appeared at hand, and it is not clear where it came from. This is the ideal that St. Benedict strove for in his monasteries. He conceived of such attentive service as a consequence of regular practice in being totally silent: "Let there be complete silence [at meals]. No whispering, no speaking—only the reader's voice should be heard there. The brothers should by turn serve one another's needs as they eat and drink, *so that no one need ask for anything*."[4]

This is the picture that we form in our minds of St. Joseph, who did good in silence and worked in silence. A man's silence might demonstrate an interior that is empty of thoughts or even paralyzed by fear. St. Joseph's silence was closer to the experience of a man in a foreign land who does not speak the language. He has many things

---

[3] Pope Francis, *Patris Corde*, §4.
[4] RB 38:5–6 (emphasis added).

to offer, but no way to put them into words that can be understood. His heart was filled with the greatness of his love, his insightful observations, his sensitivity to the needs of others, and his readiness to serve. He did not need to use up any energy to turn all that into words, and he could invest all that energy into even greater demonstrations of love. His Son did the same, as we know from St. Peter's simple summary of the kerygma: "He went about doing good and healing all that were oppressed by the devil, for God was with him" (Acts 10:38).

This exercise in imagination also applies to a man at prayer. A man who prays out loud may elicit a certain appreciation from others. In fact, it can be quite beautiful to hear the prayers that come forth from a man's heart. On the other hand, when we enter a chapel and see a man kneeling in prayer with head bowed or with his eyes fixed on a holy image or on the Eucharist, it has a different effect on us. There is a mystery in that man that we can only glimpse from the outside. If he does not know we are watching, we might be bold enough to watch him a little longer. Watching him makes us wonder all the more what secrets he holds in his heart; what sighs of love, what pleading for others, what intimate discourse takes place inside that man's silence before God? At a certain point, the man himself may not even know—it is only the Holy "Spirit [who] searches everything" (1 Cor 2:10) and then turns his interior into prayer with "sighs too deep for words" (Rom 8:26). We could summarize this with the profound words the peasant in Ars spoke to his pastor about his prayer: "I look at him and he looks at me."[5]

The Apostles had this experience of wonder when they saw Jesus at prayer, and so they asked Him to teach them. As the evangelist recorded it: "He was praying in a certain place, and when he ceased, one of his disciples said to him, 'Lord, teach us to pray, as John taught his disciples'" (Luke 11:1). They wanted to understand His experience from the inside. They wanted to replicate His silent discourse with the Father in their own hearts. In response, He directed their attention to the Father and taught them to pray, "Father, hallowed be your name" (Luke 11:2). He was directing their attention to the heavenly Father, of course, but is it possible that He originally learned such prayer as He grew up and watched His father Joseph? Pope Benedict XVI assured us that "Joseph fulfilled every aspect of his paternal role. He must certainly have taught Jesus to pray, together with Mary."[6] At least we know that Jesus's love for Joseph always led Him to lift His Heart to His Father in Heaven. Surely that was true in a special way when the eyes of Jesus as a little boy looked in love at his dear human father in prayer.

Altogether, this picture of St. Joseph's silence—in doing good, in prayer, and in suffering—fulfills the teaching given by his Son in the Sermon on the Mount: "When you give alms, do not let your left hand know what your right hand is doing, so that your alms may be in secret; and your Father who sees in secret will reward you" (Matt

[5] CCC 2715.
[6] Pope Benedict XVI, General Audience, December 28, 2011, http://w2.vatican.va/content/benedict-xvi/en/audiences/2011/documents/hf_ben-xvi_aud_20111228.html.

6:3–4). "When you pray, go into your room and shut the door and pray to your Father who is in secret; and your Father who sees in secret will reward you" (Matt 6:6). "When you fast, anoint your head and wash your face, that your fasting may not be seen by men but by your Father who is in secret; and your Father who sees in secret will reward you" (Matt 6:17–18). St. Joseph was a master of silence and carried out his goodness, prayer, and suffering in secret as his Son would later instruct us to do as well:

> In the course of that pilgrimage of faith which was his life, Joseph, like Mary, remained faithful to God's call until the end. While Mary's life was the bringing to fullness of that fiat first spoken at the Annunciation, at the moment of Joseph's own "annunciation" he said nothing; instead he simply "did as the angel of the Lord commanded him" (Mt 1:24). And this first "doing" became the beginning of "Joseph's way." The Gospels do not record any word ever spoken by Joseph along that way. But the silence of Joseph has its own special eloquence, for thanks to that silence we can understand the truth of the Gospel's judgment that he was "a just man" (Mt 1:19).[7]

In order to learn "Joseph's Way," we must draw close to him in silence. He will let us into the secret place from which he did good and suffered and prayed, but we must draw near and watch carefully. Learning from him

---

[7] Pope St. John Paul II, *Redemptoris Custos*, §17.

requires careful attention rather than volumes of instructions. It is apprenticeship rather than a recipe. It comes
from carefully watching the master in order to learn his
skill. As the psalmist instructs us, "Behold, as the eyes of
servants look to the hand of their master, as the eyes of a
maid to the hand of her mistress, so our eyes look to the
LORD our God, till he have mercy upon us" (Ps 123:2).

The philosopher Michael Polanyi described the fundamentally inexpressible part of knowledge as the "tacit
dimension" and concluded that such knowledge could
only be passed on through a form of interiorization and
indwelling:

> Consider the situation where two persons share
> the knowledge of the same comprehensive
> entity—of an entity which one of them produces
> and the other apprehends. Such is the case when
> one person has formed a message and the other
> has received it. But the characteristic features of
> the situation are seen more clearly if we consider
> the way one man comes to understand the skill-
> ful performance of another man. He must try to
> combine mentally the movements which the per-
> former combines practically and he must combine
> them in a pattern similar to the performer's
> pattern of movements. Two kinds of indwelling
> meet here. The performer co-ordinates his moves
> by dwelling in them as parts of his body, while the
> watcher tries to correlate these moves by seeking
> to dwell in them from outside. He dwells in these
> moves by interiorizing them. By such exploratory

indwelling the pupil gets the feel of a master's skill and may learn to rival him. Nor is the structural kinship between subject and object, and the indwelling of one in the other, present only in the study of bodily performance. Chess players enter into a master's spirit by rehearsing the games he played, to discover what he had in mind.[8]

In other words, through watching carefully, imitating, and rehearsing, we learn to take what is inexpressibly present in another person and reproduce it in ourselves. That is the process of apprenticeship by which Jesus presumably went from being a "carpenter's son" to being a "carpenter." It is the process by which we learn to do good and suffer and pray as well. And so we can continue to draw close to St. Joseph, observe his silent way of living, and try to imitate it and rehearse it in our own lives. We can observe more silence and practice Polanyi's concept of "indwelling" as we learn what silence feels like from the inside. In this way, we also learn a little better what Joseph feels like from the inside.

Action

It seems that "Joseph's Way" was also a way deeply appreciated by another Joseph—Joseph Ratzinger—in his adjustment of the ancient method of praying with Scripture. The classical method of praying with Scrip-

---

[8]   Polanyi, *The Tacit Dimension*, 29–30.

ture—which goes back to ancient times, was cherished by the Fathers of the Church, and is at the heart of monastic spirituality—is called *lectio divina*. After centuries of only being passed down from person to person, from master to apprentice, it was finally written down by Guigo the Carthusian and summarized in four steps: *lectio, meditatio, oratio,* and *contemplatio.*[9] This description was standard for a millennium until Pope Benedict XVI added a fifth step: *actio*. His reasoning was simple: "We do well also to remember that the process of *lectio divina* is not concluded until it arrives at action (*actio*), which moves the believer to make his or her life a gift for others in charity."[10]

This is not surprising, since we worship a God who is Love. Authentic communion with Love will always lead to love, and love requires an act of the will. As St. Thomas defined it, "Love wills the good of the other."[11] Thinking is important, and words are important. Transformational conversations can even lead to the structural development of changing our DNA,[12] but ultimately actions make us who we are. Our Fiat may begin with a word, like Mary's powerful self-offering to God through the archangel Gabriel, but it must resolve in action. In fact, as we grow in holiness and become more like God,

---

[9] Guigo II, *Ladder of Monks and Twelve Meditations*, trans. Edmund Collegde and James Walsh (Kalamazoo, MI: Cistercian Publications, 1981).

[10] Pope Benedict XVI, Post-Synodal Apostolic Exhortation on the Word of God in the Life and Mission of the Church *Verbum Domini* (September 30, 2010), §87.

[11] St. Thomas Aquinas, *ST* I-II, q. 26, a. 4, corp.

[12] Judith Glaser, *Conversational Intelligence: How Great Leaders Build Trust and Get Extraordinary Results* (New York: Routledge, 2016), 82.

all our words become more efficacious. We speak only the truth without any gloss. Our promise is a bedrock that others can build on. But it is possible to deliver our Yes without any words at all, simply by acting it out, as St. Joseph does.

One well-known psychologist, Dr. Jordan Peterson, hesitated to make a Christian profession of faith, fearing that he could not live up to its high standards. He stated unequivocally that creeds must be acted out. He did not want to claim something that he could not faithfully put into practice. It is good to learn how to think and speak so as to formulate our ideas. Indeed, we even discover the truth in the process of trying to express it, but ultimately it must be acted out in order to become part of us.[13]

We see this also in the teaching of Jesus: "If you love me, do what I command you" (see John 14:15). God's commandments direct our actions. The word "commandment" in Greek is ἐντολή, which comes from the verb ἐντέλλομαι, which is derived from the words "in" (ἐν) and "goal/completion/fulfillment/perfection" (τέλος). Thus, a "commandment" instructs us on how we can reach the goal of completion or perfection. Beginning with the moment of our conception, we are all a work in progress, or we could describe the condition of our life as being on a journey. In the words of Gabriel Marcel, we could be classified as *homo viator*, the itinerant man.[14]

---

[13] Dr. Jordan Peterson, interview with Bishop Robert Barron, *Word on Fire*, March 2019, https://www.wordonfire.org/peterson/.

[14] Gabriel Marcel, *Homo Viator: Introduction to the Metaphysic of Hope*, trans. Emma Craufurd and Paul Seaton, 1st ed. (South Bend, IN: St. Augustine's Press, 2010).

A commandment guides us on our path. This is true of all commandments, but different lawgivers lead us to different goals. Following the commandments of a just nation leads a man to the virtue of justice. Following the commandments of a master carpenter leads a man to become a master carpenter. Following the commandments of the Law of Moses raises a man to the heights of Mosaic righteousness, which was the high regard given to St. Joseph in Scripture: "[He is] a just man" (Matt 1:19). As he takes up the new commandments in the Order of the Incarnation, however, St. Joseph is led to the new level of holiness that is also prescribed for us. The commandments of Jesus lead us to become "like him, for we shall see him as he is" (1 John 3:2).

The path of holiness is the path of the commandments. That includes both the natural law confirmed by God to Moses and the new commandment given to us by Jesus. It is not always easy to know how to apply the commandments to the concrete situations of our lives, however. This was the dilemma faced by St. Joseph when he found Mary "with child of the Holy Spirit" (Matt 1:18). St. Joseph teaches us a path, however, that leads away from frenetic activity and opens us to the intervention of the good spirit, who can guide our discernment with spiritual consolation. When the spiritual consolation came as the good spirit spoke to St. Joseph in a dream, he acted immediately, wasting no more time for words or further discernment.

Sometimes it is also necessary to start without knowing exactly how a process will reach its consummation. The one who is willing to take the first step will always be accompanied by St. Joseph. A journey of a thousand miles begins with a single step. That's the step St. Joseph took when he obeyed the census of Caesar and took his bride to Bethlehem and so fulfilled the prophecy. St. Joseph took the long journey to Egypt by first getting out of bed in the middle of the night and then, with the Child and His Mother, stepping out into the darkness. Likewise, St. Joseph did not have access to a GPS to anticipate all the delays and accidents when he set out on his return journey to Nazareth. His travels to Jerusalem for the Presentation and the yearly feasts, likewise, involved one step after the next. In fact, whenever we encounter St. Joseph in the Scriptures, he is always going somewhere. Each journey required taking the first step and then letting the process unfold as the journey progressed.

Such first steps are part and parcel of our lives, and although the journey may seem daunting or even impossible, we get stronger as we move forward. We usually do not receive the grace to live marriage until we are married. We usually do not receive the grace to face martyrdom until we face martyrdom. Often, even healing simply happens on the way, as we see in the account of the ten lepers: "As they went they were cleansed" (Luke 17:14). In the movie *Forrest Gump*, the main character was hobbled with crutches and braces that hindered every movement. In one painful scene, some bullies set upon him and began pelting him with stones. His dear friend Jenny shouted compassionately, "Run, Forrest, run!" and Forrest began to move as quickly as possible despite his crippled condition. Slowly he dropped the crutches and the braces fell away, and Forrest narrated simply, "From that day on, if I was going somewhere, I was running!"

One way that we draw close to St. Joseph is in our willingness to act out our beliefs. Try it! Likewise, when we are willing to put a commandment into action, St. Joseph will be there to support us. As we see a long journey stretch out in front of us, even a journey of marriage or priesthood, of healing or of sobriety, or any other journey that is leading us to holiness, we will discover that St. Joseph is at our side to strengthen us, teach us, and accompany us to our destination, step-by-step, until we are like him.

Master of the Interior Life

The same aura of silence that envelops everything else about Joseph also shrouds his work as a carpenter in the house of Nazareth. It is, however, a silence that reveals in a special way the inner portrait of the man. The Gospels speak exclusively of what Joseph "did." Still, they allow us to discover in his "actions"—shrouded in silence as they are—an aura of deep contemplation. Joseph was in daily contact with the mystery "hidden from ages past," and which "dwelt" under his roof. This explains, for example, why St. Teresa of Jesus, the great reformer of the Carmelites, promoted the renewal of veneration to St. Joseph in Western Christianity.[15]

---

[15] Pope St. John Paul II, *Redemptoris Custos*, §25.

St. Teresa of Ávila wrote, "Contemplative prayer
[*oración mental*] in my opinion is nothing else than a
close sharing between friends; it means taking time fre-
quently to be alone with him who we know loves us."[16]
This description gives us a beautiful picture of the relationship between Jesus and St. Joseph. We are invited to
imagine the kind of sharing that happened in their work
together or in the quiet of the evening. Although Mary
and Joseph were surprised to find Jesus in the Temple
after He went missing for three days, when they found
Him in the Temple, they did not express any surprise at
His wisdom or the way He instructed the teachers. We
can envision an atmosphere of deep sharing in the House
of Nazareth and in the relationship of Joseph and his precious Son:

> Contemplative prayer seeks him "whom my soul
> loves." It is Jesus, and in him, the Father. We seek
> him, because to desire him is always the begin-
> ning of love, and we seek him in that pure faith
> which causes us to be born of him and to live in
> him. In this inner prayer we can still meditate, but
> our attention is fixed on the Lord himself.[17]

In this description from the *Catechism*, we can again
see a description of St. Joseph as a contemplative. He

[16] St. Teresa of Jesus, *The Book of Her Life*, 8.5, in *The Collected Works of St. Teresa of Avila*, trans. K. Kavanaugh, O.C.D., and O. Rodriguez, O.C.D. (Washington DC: Institute of Carmelite Studies, 1976), 1:67, quoted in CCC 2709.

[17] CCC 2709.

placed Jesus at the center of his life and lived, worked, ate, slept, spoke, and did everything with Him or for Him. Although we do not get the details of this hidden life, the glimpses we are given are enough for Pope St. John Paul II to assert that St. Joseph's life, shrouded in silence, has "an aura of deep contemplation." His silence was a contemplative silence, not empty of meaning, but so full of meaning that it was beyond words. "Contemplative prayer is silence, the 'symbol of the world to come' or 'silent love.' Words in this kind of prayer are not speeches; they are like kindling that feeds the fire of love."[18] Too many words only cheapen the times of great love.

"Contemplative prayer is the poor and humble surrender to the loving will of the Father in ever deeper union with his beloved Son."[19] From St. Joseph's first silent response to the angel in taking Mary and the fetal Jesus into his home, his daily surrender to the Father's will did indeed lead to a deeper union with His beloved Son. This was a union that provides a model for us in that it persisted throughout his daily life. As Pope St. John Paul II said it, "Joseph was in daily contact with the mystery 'hidden from ages past,' and which 'dwelt' under his roof."[20] Contemplation, unlike meditation, is the form of prayer that can persist throughout all our activities: "One cannot always meditate, but one can always enter into inner prayer, independently of the conditions of

---

[18] CCC 2717.
[19] CCC 2712.
[20] Pope St. John Paul II, *Redemptoris Custos*, §25.

health, work, or emotional state."[21] Thus, St. Joseph lived a contemplative life, remaining in the presence of Jesus throughout each day, whether eating or sleeping, working or conversing, in sickness and in health.

We don't know specifically how St. Joseph maintained his awareness of the presence of God. We know he often had the opportunity to speak the Name of Jesus, however, as he spoke to his Son throughout each day. We could see him as the first practitioner of the "Jesus Prayer." The Jesus Prayer developed throughout many centuries and was popularized through the Russian classic, *The Way of the Pilgrim*.[22] It tells the tale of a Russian pilgrim who set out to learn and practice the apostle's commandment to pray without ceasing. The path he found was through repeating the Jesus Prayer thousands of times a day: "Lord Jesus Christ, Son of God, have mercy on me, a sinner." For St. Joseph, these little acts of recollection and refocusing his heart on the Son of God may have consisted of a glance in the direction of his Divine Son, or a hand on His Shoulder or a caress of His Arm. Likewise, the young man may have come up next to him at times when he was too intense in his work or tempted to frustration and prevented His dear father from sinning by the loving reminder of His presence.

When we think of such touching experiences, we might protest that St. Joseph had an unfair advantage over us and we could not possibly imitate his continu-

---

[21] CCC 2710.

[22] Faith Annette Sand, *The Way of a Pilgrim and the Pilgrim Continues His Way*, trans. R. M. French, 2nd ed. (Pasadena, CA: Hope Publishing House, 1989).

ous state of recollection. On the other hand, it was not merely the physical presence of Jesus, but also St. Joseph's righteousness that made him sensitive to the presence of God, and his silence predisposed him to be aware of the slightest movements of Jesus. These aspects of St. Joseph can be imitated by us. Furthermore, St. Joseph did not have a St. Joseph to help him, and in that sense, we are the ones with the advantage. St. Joseph will help all those who try to silence their interior and make room in their hearts for Jesus. Whether we take the Name of Jesus on our lips and let it continue to resonate in our hearts, or whether we take the verse of a psalm to recollect our faculties or some other word or phrase from our *lectio divina*, St. Joseph wants to help us create an aura of contemplation and remain always close to his Son and his Son's eternal Father.

"Those souls most sensitive to the impulses of divine love have rightly seen in Joseph a brilliant example of the interior life."[23] Dr. John Crosby defined interiority according to Karol Wojtyla in the following way:

> By this he means the subjectivity of each human being. But what does he mean by subjectivity? I would explain it like this: through my subjectivity I exist as a subject and not just as an object. As subject I live my being from within, and do not just encounter it from without as an object. Of course I can cognize my being from without; this happens when I see myself as others see me.

---

[23] Pope St. John Paul II, *Redemptoris Custos*, §27.

But there is an experience of myself from within that only I can have; we can call it "my presence to myself." When I see myself as others see me, I then become a public object, to which they and I have equal access. But in my self-presence, in my subjectivity, I am withdrawn from public view, for I alone have access to myself from within. Another person would have to be me in order to be present to me as I am present to myself. Here we are led to speak of the "interiority" of the person who is present to himself. Interiority is in fact almost interchangeable with subjectivity. My subjectivity is simply me living out of my inner center.[24]

Our inner center is the most vulnerable part of ourselves. That is where we are most truly ourselves. That is the naked truth of our existence, the core of our being. We all create personas to hide behind. We show to others what we believe is more acceptable rather than what we actually experience inside ourselves. The more these personas distort the view of our interiority, the less transparent we are. The more we let others see us as we truly are inside, the more naked and vulnerable we feel. When we stop using words to justify ourselves or to make excuses for our behavior; when we stop our superficial chatter, whether interior or exterior; when we let ourselves fall totally silent inside and outside, we come into

---

[24] Dr. John Crosby, "On the Difference Between the Cosmological and Personalist Understanding of the Human Being," *Quaestiones Disputatae* 9 no. 2 (2019): 113.

touch with our deepest selves. Or perhaps we never reach our deepest selves, but at least we can go deeper into our interiority and face some of the naked truth of our own dependent being and even our own sinfulness. This is what some spiritual masters have called the "abyss of our nothingness."[25]

The *Catechism* describes this process as purification and self-offering: "We let our masks fall and turn our hearts back to the Lord who loves us, so as to hand ourselves over to him as an offering to be purified and transformed."[26] This purification is always painful, because we not only create personas to fool others, but inevitably we fool ourselves as well. There is a process of disillusionment that unfolds as we allow ourselves to enter more deeply into silence and allow ourselves to be poor and naked in the presence of God. While it can be painful and even unbearable at times, it is also beautiful and fruitful and leads to a deeper, abiding union with God: "In this silence, unbearable to the 'outer' man, the Father speaks to us his incarnate Word, who suffered, died, and rose; in this silence the Spirit of adoption enables us to share in the prayer of Jesus."[27]

When we set out to enter into such a profound silence and undergo that painful purification, we will always have a friend and traveling companion in St. Joseph. He will help our silence to be fruitful and our lives to become

---

[25] For example, *Heaven in Faith* no. 4, in *The Complete Works of Elizabeth of the Trinity*, vol. 1, trans. Sr. Alethea Kane (Washington, D.C: ICS Publications, 1984).
[26] CCC 2711.
[27] CCC 2717.

more contemplative. He will help us to keep the Name of Jesus on our lips and the presence of God in our hearts. He will help us to live out our active lives with a more contemplative spirit, thus making all our activities not only useful for this world but also eternally fruitful in building up the kingdom of his Son. St. Joseph was successful enough in his work to provide for his family, but he was never famous for the products of his carpenter shop.[28] Rather, he fulfilled the simple and profound insight of St. Thérèse of Lisieux and St. Teresa of Calcutta by doing ordinary things with extraordinary love and little things with great love.[29]

Pope St. John Paul II summarized this, saying, "Furthermore, in Joseph, the apparent tension between the active and the contemplative life finds an ideal harmony that is only possible for those who possess the perfection of charity."[30] In our own efforts to live the truth in love and be faithful to our daily duty while never losing sight of the Lord, but always depending on His help, we look to St. Joseph to guide us. This will always involve leading us into deeper interior and exterior silence, as Cardinal Robert Sarah beautifully summarized:

> Interior silence is the end of judgments, pas-

---

[28] No trace of his work has been passed down. There was even debate among the Fathers of the Church about the meaning of his occupation (described with the Greek word *tekton*).

[29] St. Teresa of Calcutta and Brian Kolodiejchuk, *Where There Is Love, There Is God: A Path to Closer Union with God and Greater Love for Others* (New York: Image, 2012), 325.

[30] Pope St. John Paul II, *Redemptoris Custos*, §27.

sions, and desires. Once we have acquired interior silence, we can transport it with us into the world and pray everywhere. But just as interior asceticism cannot be obtained without concrete mortifications, it is absurd to speak about interior silence without exterior silence. Within silence there is a demand made on each one of us. Man controls his hours of activity if he knows how to enter into silence. The life of silence must be able to precede the active life.[31]

Making a Place

St. Luke recorded, almost in passing, a surprising and painful reality that challenged poor St. Joseph to find a place for his wife to give birth: "There was no place for them in the inn" (Luke 2:7). The fact that St. Joseph was returning to the city of David, specifically because it was the city of his forefathers and likely the city of his living relatives as well, makes this lack of room even more painful. Pope Benedict XVI took up this verse in a Christmas homily in 2012 and applied it to us in a very challenging way:

> Inevitably the question arises, what would happen
> if Mary and Joseph were to knock at my door.
> Would there be room for them? And then it

---

[31] Robert Cardinal Sarah and Nicolas Diat, *The Power of Silence: Against the Dictatorship of Noise* (San Francisco: Ignatius Press, 2017), no. 19.

occurs to us that Saint John takes up this seemingly chance comment about the lack of room at the inn, which drove the Holy Family into the stable; he explores it more deeply and arrives at the heart of the matter when he writes: "he came to his own home, and his own people received him not" (Jn 1:11).[32]

When we speak of making room for the Word, that necessarily involves silence. To receive the Word, we must stop competing by producing our own words. We must learn to make room in our hearts by quieting or silencing our inner dialogue so that we can receive from the outside. "He came to his own . . . " and truly our hearts are made for him. As St. Augustine famously exclaimed, "You have made us for yourself, and our hearts are restless and will not rest until they rest in Thee!"[33] We make room in our hearts for so many things that do not satisfy us, but we busy ourselves and fill ourselves so there is nothing left for God:

> Do we really have room for God when he seeks to enter under our roof? Do we have time and space for him? Do we not actually turn away God himself? We begin to do so when we have no time for God. The faster we can move, the more effi-

---

[32] Pope Benedict XVI, Homily for Mass at Night for the Lord's Nativity, December 24, 2012, http://www.vatican.va/content/benedict-xvi/en/homilies/2012/documents/hf_ben-xvi_hom_20121224_christmas.html.

[33] St. Augustine, *Confessions*, bk. I, chap. 1, no. 1.

cient our time-saving appliances become, the less
time we have. And God? The question of God
never seems urgent. Our time is already completely full.[34]

St. Joseph continually made room for God. He first
made room for Mary in his life and accepted her as his
bride. Although the language is unclear to modern ears,
his "betrothal" in the Jewish law was a genuine marriage.
The Fathers of the Church were clear on this point.[35] The
lifelong commitment was made, and the legal bond was
formed. Joseph and Mary were committed to each other
for life. As Pope St. John Paul II explained, "According to
Jewish custom, marriage took place in two stages: first,
the legal, or true marriage was celebrated, and then, only
after a certain period of time, the husband brought the
wife into his own house. Thus, before he lived with Mary,
Joseph was already her 'husband.'"[36] When things became
more complicated due to Mary being with child of the
Holy Spirit, St. Joseph again made room for the mystery
and dedicated his life to carefully veiling that mystery
(Matt 1:24). Like Abram, St. Joseph became a homeless
man for God's sake, indefinitely leaving homeland and
extended family when commanded by an angel (Gen
12:4, Matt 2:14).

---

[34] Pope Benedict XVI, Homily for Mass at Night for the Lord's Nativity, 2012.
[35] Joseph Lienhard, *St. Joseph in Early Christianity: Devotion and Theology: A Study and an Anthology of Patristic Texts* (Philadelphia: St. Joseph's Press, 1999).
[36] Pope St. John Paul II, *Redemptoris Custos*, §18.

Each of those steps required St. Joseph to silence any interior protests or complaints. Even if he was sinless (as some Doctors of the Church have claimed[37]), he was still human, and the prospects of welcoming the Incarnate God into his life or leaving everything by night to depart for a foreign land were no less daunting for him than for any other human being. The temptations to fear, the lies that throb in our minds arising from our weaknesses or insecurities, or the feeling of powerlessness before powerful worldly forces were enough to create noise in any heart, but amazingly, St. Joseph was able to make room for God in the midst of it all. He was able to silence the competing interior voices so that he could hear the Word of the Lord:

used in intro

> In silence, man conquers his nobility and his grandeur only if he is on his knees in order to hear and adore God. It is in the silence of humiliation and self-mortification, by quieting the turmoil of the flesh, by successfully taming the noisy images, by keeping at a distance the dreams, imaginations, and roaring of a world that is always in a whirl, in order to purify himself of all that ruins the soul and separates it from contemplation, that man makes himself capable of looking at God and loving him.[38]

---

[37] Reginald Garrigou-Lagrange, *The Mother of the Saviour: And Our Interior Life*, trans. Bernard J. Kelly (Charlotte: TAN Books, 2012), 277–9.

[38] Sarah and Diat, *The Power of Silence*, no. 66.

Our unwillingness to make a place for Christ is even more painful when we realize that He has lovingly gone ahead to prepare a place for us: "In my Father's house are many rooms; if it were not so, would I have told you that I go to prepare a place for you? And when I go and prepare a place for you, I will come again and will take you to myself, that where I am you may be also" (John 14:2–3). These words are extremely comforting when we inevitably face our finitude and ultimate homelessness in this world. When we experience the tenuousness of our material possessions because of a natural disaster or financial collapse, we realize we are only pilgrims in this world and the things of this world are passing away. Likewise, after the loss of a loved one or a near encounter with death, we realize that we are not destined for this world, but we are "strangers and exiles on the earth" (Heb 11:13).

Interestingly, Jesus's work to go ahead and prepare a place for us is at the same time creating a place within us where He Himself lives. St. Teresa of Ávila interpreted this passage from the Farewell Discourse as referring to the Interior Castle that exists in the inner recesses of the human soul.[39] By drawing us deeper within, through purifications and dark nights, through surrender and silent love, the soul's interior is opened up and the one praying is drawn closer to the Trinity Who wishes to abide forever and rule in the very center of our souls. In light of this, we see that making room for God is not even something we

---

[39] Teresa of Ávila, *The Interior Castle*, 1.1.1, trans. Kieran Kavanaugh, O.C.D., and Otilio Rodriguez, O.C.D., The Classics of Western Spirituality (Mahwah, NJ: Paulist Press, 1979), 35.

need to do actively so much as it is something the Lord is already doing within us if we will only let Him.

Here again St. Joseph wants to help us. As he demonstrated in Bethlehem, he is the master of finding any opening, any space for the Divine Nativity to take place. In the original Divine Nativity, the place he found was simply a feeding trough. Though we often translate it as "manger" and we think of the manger as being the whole stable, the word in Greek is φάτνη, which refers specifically to the trough from which the animals ate (Luke 2:7). When Mary had her baby, St. Joseph was ready to make a little nest for their Precious Infant in the feeding trough of an animal. Symbolically, we could connect the feeding trough with the hunger in our own hearts and interpret this to mean that he can find a place for Jesus in our desires. Even our animal hunger can be an opening for the Divine Nativity. St. Joseph will work with our desires to expand them and little by little to make room for God to grow. Ultimately, every desire actually points to God as its fulfillment. Even when he finds in us that the inn is full, he makes his way into a poor little desire in us that is good enough to grow steadily into the full stature of Christ (see Eph 4:13). What began in Infancy in Bethlehem became full grown in Nazareth under St. Joseph's care. The key is for us to make at least that little desire available to him. When we can recognize how full our hearts and our lives are but turn over to him our little desire for God to grow in us, he can work with that to make a place for Christ in our souls.

As a final image, we can consider the room that St. Joseph made in his arms for Jesus. He set down his tools and stopped his productivity and simply held his baby. This is adoration. It is not efficient or productive. It is a simple act of love that says it is enough that you exist and that I exist and that we can be together. Let us spend a few moments reflecting on St. Joseph holding the Baby Jesus in his arms and gazing on his sleeping Son. The longer he looks, the more love fills his heart. Everything else melts away, and there is only this Infant. In that moment, St. Joseph knows that he is fulfilling the highest purpose of his existence. This is a model for us that we can take into our own prayer and especially our time in Eucharistic adoration. As we gaze on the very same Infant who comes to us in the form of bread, we are fulfilling our highest purpose. We are made to adore Him, and it will be the eternal orientation of our hearts, our beatific vision.

A Prayer for Interior Life

We conclude this chapter with a prayer for consecration to St. Joseph. It is notable for including a particular request that St. Joseph help us obtain a fervent love of the interior life:

> Be pleased, O dear Saint Joseph, to accept the consecration which I now make of myself to you. I dedicate myself wholly to you, that you may always be my father, my patron, and my guide in the way of salvation. Obtain for me a great purity of heart, and a fervent love of the interior life. Grant that following your example, I may direct

all my actions to the greater glory of God, in union with the Divine Heart of Jesus, with the Immaculate Heart of Mary, and with you. Finally, pray for me, that I may share in the peace and joy which you possessed in your holy death. Amen.[40]

[40] Francis L. Filas, *Joseph: The Man Closest to Jesus: The Complete Life, Theology and Devotional History of St. Joseph* (Boston: St. Paul Editions, 1962), 640.

Chapter Three

A FATHER TO
LITTLE ONES

Unless You Become Like This Child

Gazing on Jesus in the arms of Joseph also prepares us
for our next consideration. As we place ourselves in the
position of Jesus in Joseph's arms, we can learn the greatest
experience of fatherhood. We learn from St. Joseph what
it means to be unconditionally loved. It is an invitation to
be little and childlike, and when we take the risk of being
vulnerable like a child, we get a taste of divine love and we
experience a father's tenderness for his Son:

> As the Lord had done with Israel, so Joseph did
> with Jesus: he taught him to walk, taking him by
> the hand; he was for him like a father who raises
> an infant to his cheeks, bending down to him and
> feeding him (cf. Hos 11:3–4). In Joseph, Jesus saw
> the tender love of God: "As a father has compas-
> sion for his children, so the Lord has compassion

for those who fear him" (Ps 103:13).[1]

Jesus warned us that "unless you turn and become like children, you will never enter the kingdom of heaven" (Matt 18:3). Furthermore, he emphasized that "whoever humbles himself like this child, he is the greatest in the kingdom of heaven" (Matt 18:4). "This child" clearly refers to the child that he placed in the midst of the disciples (Matt 18:2), but we could also interpret "this child" to refer to Jesus Himself, who is always the eternal child of the heavenly Father and is clearly the greatest in the kingdom of heaven. He reinforced his identification with the child in his next statement by saying, "Whoever receives one such child in my name receives me" (Matt 18:5). Jesus wants us to learn to be like Him, particularly in childlikeness and humility.

There is little recorded in Scripture of the childhood of Jesus. We can presume that this is because it was quite a normal childhood, since Scripture generally records only the extraordinary data of revelation. We know from Scripture that Jesus grew up for a period of time in Egypt and the rest of His childhood was in Nazareth. We know they had a poor, simple life, because we know Mary and Joseph were too poor to afford a lamb and so had to make the offering of two turtledoves for Mary's purification and the redemption of the firstborn in the Temple (Luke 2:24; Lev 12:8). We know Joseph was a carpenter and so taught his trade to his Son. From this we can surmise that Jesus had the experiences of dependency, discovery, hard

---

[1]   Pope Francis, *Patris Corde*, §2.

work, and learning that are distinctive of childhood.

One of the great qualities of childhood is a sense of awe and wonder. The human knowledge of Jesus grew through experience, and so we can imagine that He experienced the wonder of a child and He delighted in His first discoveries. It is wonderful to think of how St. Joseph would have prepared such discoveries for his Son. There is something different about discovering new wonders from the arms of our father. Joseph had the opportunity to take Jesus to the Sea of Galilee, He could hold Him up to pet a camel, He helped Him use the tools of the carpenter's trade, and He could share the joy of His first wooden creation. Perhaps even more mysteriously, Joseph could introduce Jesus to the Temple, where Jesus always felt at home. Joseph could have described for Jesus what was in the sanctuary and the hidden mysteries of the holy of holies even as he led his Son through the prayers of the Jewish high feasts. He could show Him the lambs and explain the meaning of the sacrifices.

We can let St. Joseph be a father for us as well. He wants to introduce us to the natural wonders of the world around us as well as the mysteries of the Jewish and Christian faith. We just have to be willing to be little children. We can ask Jesus to renew our sense of childlike wonder as we look at our churches, the sacraments, and even the world's natural wonders with the new eyes of a child. We can imagine ourselves being carried through our parish church by St. Joseph, who can point out the mysteries to us and lift us to touch the Stations of the Cross or see the stained glass more clearly. He can teach us the Sign of the Cross or guide our hand into the holy water font. We can also invite him into our workplaces to help us with our tasks and celebrate our successes. And we can explore the natural wonders of the world with him as well.

Without a father to help us, new things can feel threatening or overwhelming or simply confusing. A child experiences the world differently when he is in the arms of his father. Unexpected threats from a hissing swan or a snorting bull cause a child to bury his head in the neck of his father. A strange woman in the Temple can be more safely observed from behind the leg of a father. The violence of the sacrifices could be better absorbed with a father's reassuring explanation of their meaning in light of history and God's law.

In all of it, Jesus had a loving guide in St. Joseph. At the same time, Joseph likely learned as much from his Son, who had an intuitive knowledge and a deeper insight into the meaning of everything, even if He could not always articulate it. The questions He asked or the things He was attracted to would reveal those things with the deepest meaning. What is ordinary for us becomes extraordinary again when we see it through the eyes of a child. This would be particularly true for the one who could see through the eyes of the Divine Child. In this way, we see the childlikeness of St. Joseph as well. He provides an example of never being too old for discovery.

Furthermore, this helps us to glimpse the child-likeness of the heavenly Father as well. After all, Jesus completed His teaching on childlikeness by saying, "Whoever receives me, receives not me but him who sent me" (Mark 9:37), and so we see that receiving a child leads us to the heavenly Father, who is in some way like that child. Perhaps it is in the way that G. K. Chesterton described:

> Because children have abounding vitality, because they are in spirit fierce and free, therefore they want things repeated and unchanged. They always say, "Do it again"; and the grown-up person does it again until he is nearly dead. For grown-up people are not strong enough to exult in monotony. But perhaps God is strong enough to exult in monotony. It is possible that God says every morning, "Do it again" to the sun; and every evening, "Do it again" to the moon. It may not be automatic necessity that makes all daisies alike; it may be that God makes every daisy separately, but has never got tired of making them. It may be that He has the eternal appetite of infancy; for we have sinned and grown old, and our Father is younger than we. The repetition in Nature may not be a mere recurrence; it may be a theatrical encore.[2]

There is a logic to nature that can best be understood in this childlike way. After all, the Scriptures described the act of creation as play: "When he fixed the foundations of earth, then was I beside him as artisan; I was his delight day by day, playing before him all the while, Playing over the whole of his earth, having my delight

---

[2] G. K. Chesterton, *Orthodoxy* (New York: John Lane Company, 1909), 108–109.

with human beings" (Prov 8:29b–31, NABRE). And the word "artisan" here could also be translated as "little child."

There is an oldness and cynicism that can come with age, but if we can let St. Joseph be a father for us, it may restore our childlike sense of awe and wonder. We can remember that Jesus was never too old to delight in children or to praise His Father with awe and wonder (Matt 11:25). He called the Apostles "little children" (John 13:33), and St. John followed that example many times in his letters.

St. Joseph Re-Parents Us

Many saints, even those with loving parents, found an even more perfect father in St. Joseph. St. Teresa of Ávila developed a devotion to St. Joseph when she faced her biological father's limitation, namely, his mortality. As wonderful as our parents may be, they are limited in various ways, not the least of which is death. Their limitations are not necessarily sinful or blameworthy, and could merely be the fact that they were not there for every moment of our lives or they could not read our minds or they had their own weaknesses that prevented them from understanding us fully. From these honest limitations to much more severe deficiencies, our own parents did not parent us in all the ways we needed. That is to say, they were not able to reflect God's love perfectly for us at each moment of our childhood. For this reason, there are aspects of God's love that we missed as children. The good news is that God wants us to recover all these aspects, and part of our healing journey of grace is to recover some of those aspects as adults. It is as if He saved up the graces we missed and He finds others ways to communicate His love to us through human relationships and also through prayer.

Many times the human limitations or even deficiencies of our parents are filled in by other parental figures in our lives. That continues to be true as we move into adulthood. We can usually name coaches, teachers, priests, uncles, grandfathers, and neighbors who played a partial paternal role in our lives. We are fathered by these wonderful and loving people. Through the combined love of so many father figures, we begin to glimpse the face of the heavenly Father. All the father figures ultimately point to Him. At the same time, it can help us to have a perfectly loving father in St. Joseph, who can meet us and form us in prayer. In particular, a simple prayer practice for healing consists of revisiting childhood wounds and allowing St. Joseph to re-parent us.

Unfortunately, childhood is not only a time of delight and discovery, but also a time when we have been wounded by our experience of this fallen world that is too affected by man's sin. Our fathers can protect us from some of this evil, but ultimately every father is limited. No father can be with his child at each moment or understand everything that is happening in him. Even the best fathers cannot protect their children from every wound of this fallen world. When we first experience the pain of broken trust, disappointed expectations, or personal failures, it leaves a mark on us. We might call these "traumas" (simply coming from the word for "wound" in Greek) with a lowercase "t." They form some of the fabric of our growing up. When we are able to process and digest these experiences with our parents, it is a great help for us. Many parents have helped their children make sense of their first experiences of the pain and cruelty of this fallen world. At the same time, most of us have had experiences that left a deep mark, but for various reasons were never fully processed.

There are many times that we can trace back patterns of dysfunction in our lives to our childhood and discover that if our fathers had acted differently, the patterns may have developed differently. The good news is that it is possible to receive some healing for those areas of our interior life. Memories live in us dynamically and represent more than simply a page of history, and sometimes we can replay some iconic scenarios in a new way that opens us to a grace of healing. In this regard, St. Joseph can "re-parent" us and help those childlike parts of us that otherwise may remain burdened and weigh us down.

Our childhood experiences form patterns of feeling, thinking, and acting that are so significant that they have been described in some psychological models as "sub-personalities." In our early years, we learn responses to difficult situations that tend to repeat themselves in analogous situations later in life.

We can think of a child named Jack who was hurt at a young age. Due to a misunderstanding, a friend's father yelled at him, claiming that Jack had bullied his son, when in fact Jack had tried to protect him from the bullies. He was terrified at being accused and felt helplessly misunderstood. His response at the time was to withdraw into himself and never share his experience. For the next several decades of his life, any time he was accused of something, it triggered a disproportionately high amount of pain and a repeated response of shutting down.

As Jack recognized this pattern, he could identify in himself an accused little boy as well as another part that acted as a protector and tried to reduce the pain by shutting down. To seek some healing for this foundational childhood experience, he shared the memory with his spiritual director. His spiritual director guided him to enter into the memory in prayer. As he prayed, he called to mind the memory vividly enough to experience the feelings and the thoughts he'd had as a little boy. The protector tried to interfere, but gently he was able to help the protector step aside and give him access to the vulnerable, hurt child. The next step was to invite St. Joseph to be a father for him in that experience. As he let St. Joseph into his prayer, he felt the protection of that loving father. St. Joseph came to stand next to him, endured the false accusation with him, and stood up for him against the friend's father. The little child felt new security and strength after that prayer experience. Furthermore, when he experienced some accusation after that and felt the protector start to shut him down, he was able to return to the memory of St. Joseph standing up for him and draw new strength and confidence into that area of his heart.

As another example, there was a man named Alex who struggled with getting into verbal battles. When someone brought up a controversial topic or made claims that were not accurate, Alex immediately pounced and began to debate the point. He became very energized and focused and felt a strong need to be right and to win. He became quite intimidating when he behaved in this way, and it was a scary contrast to his normally peaceful disposition.

When Alex took this experience to prayer and asked himself what he was afraid would happen if he didn't engage so fiercely in such discussions, the answer came to him that he was afraid he would be left behind. That brought up a memory of intense debates between men of his family, which he had experienced from a young age. He was the youngest of the men in his family, and their way of bonding was to debate various points quite vigorously. Although it was contrary to his natural disposition, Alex felt deeply that he needed to learn that form of interacting or he would be left behind. Alex took that memory into prayer, allowed himself to enter back into the scene, and asked St. Joseph to re-parent him.

When he entered into his younger self to the point that he could feel the fear of being left behind, he let St. Joseph into the memory. St. Joseph stood behind him and put his arm around him and reassured him that he loved him and he would never leave him behind. That gave Alex the peace and assurance he needed to modify the memory. This time, in his imagination of the memory, he did not enter into the debate with the men of his family. Alex found healing in the flow of love and acceptance from God through St. Joseph into that feeling of fear. Through his imagination in prayer, he was able to revisit that experience several times after that and continue to allow the healing process to unfold.

To be certain, Alex's wound was quite minor. It was

definitely not a serious trauma, even though it had a lasting negative impact on his life. With more serious wounds with much stronger emotions attached to them, one must be careful of stirring up too much pain and getting overwhelmed. If we are gentle and careful interiorly, we usually know when a door is opening for us. For example, the emergence of a memory can be a sign that we are ready to enter into that memory in prayer and find healing. Sometimes we cannot even access the memories from deeper wounds because the pain is simply too strong and we are not ready for it. Developing a relationship of childlike trust in our loving father St. Joseph can strengthen us and prepare us for deeper healing.

These simple examples illustrate a concrete way that St. Joseph wants to be a father for us. It is worth pointing out that such healing experiences with St. Joseph should not be considered a replacement for the experiences of "re-parenting" that can happen through our human relationships. By having the chance to retell her story, an individual sometimes re-experiences a childhood wound. When that happens, a loving, attentive counselor can respond in a tender way, bringing God's merciful love to that individual as a parent could have done in the original childhood experience. When there is a sufficient foundation of human love, however, we can elaborate these experiences in prayer, and St. Joseph can be a particularly loving father for us (with Mary serving as a particularly loving mother).

With these points in mind, we can start to see that there is always a little child in us that can be hurt and triggered by painful and difficult experiences. In fact, at some level we are all just little children pretending to be grown-ups. We tend to hide the more vulnerable and sensitive parts of ourselves, especially those parts that were wounded in the past by cruelty or misunderstanding. We hide those little parts behind our strengths. Some of us defend ourselves with our intellects, others with our muscles, others with our achievements. Some hide behind to-do lists and productivity, while others daydream of a better future in order to escape the present. Some defenses cause us more trouble, such as hatred, blame, and vengeance. We also numb our pain and hide behind chemicals ranging from sugary foods to alcohol or even narcotics.

In those moments when we start engaging our defense of choice, we would do well to find the child in us that is feeling hurt and invite St. Joseph in to take care of us. Sometimes the very moment of our struggle is too intense and we identify too much with our defense, but in those cases, we can look back on the experience and try to rediscover the child who was afraid and the protective defense that rose up to limit its pain. As we let ourselves feel the pain of our inner child and learn to bring that pain to the loving care of our father St. Joseph, we can receive a deep consolation that may even heal that wound or at least start to form a new pattern for us in integrating and accepting that little child as a good and important part of our interior life.

This brings out a valuable way to approach prayer. We always do best to approach prayer in the vulnerability of littleness. If we try to impress God with our strengths and hide behind our achievements, we will feel like He is absent because we do not receive the response we were hoping for. If we come before God with the open hands of a little child, we will find a Father who likes to fill our hands with His gifts. If we know that anything we present to Him is more like the scribbling art of a child rather than the Mona Lisa, we will better be able to receive His delight in us. When we run into struggles and feel that our prayer is useless or we feel incompetent, we can humbly ask like the Apostles, "Lord, teach us to pray" (Luke 11:1), and we can be sure that He will. In fact, He will remind us to start our prayer with "Father" (Luke 11:2). In so doing, He reminds us to be little children. And whenever we say "Father," we always think of the heavenly Father, but we can also think of the human father, St. Joseph, who helps us to be human children like Jesus.

St. Thérèse's Insight

St. Thérèse of Lisieux was made a Doctor of the Church and is best known for her teaching on the little way of spiritual childhood. On her deathbed, she explained what she meant by littleness: "It is to recognize our nothingness, to expect everything from God as a little child expects everything from her father; it is to be disquieted about nothing, and not to be set on making our [own] living."[3] Here St. Thérèse connects littleness and fatherhood. She acknowledges that one cannot be little without the

---

[3] August 6, 1897, entry no. 8, in *St. Therese of Lisieux: Her Last Conversations*, trans. John Clarke (Washington: ICS Publications, 1977), 139.

knowledge that there is a good father who can and wants
to provide everything we need. She spoke here of God's
fatherhood, but as we have discussed at length, God also
likes to mediate His fatherhood through the fatherhood
of St. Joseph. St. Thérèse herself knew that and acknowledged the important fatherly role of St. Joseph in her life:
"I prayed specially to St. Joseph to watch over me; from
my childhood, devotion to him has been interwoven with
my love for our Blessed Lady. Every day I said the prayer
beginning: 'St. Joseph, Father and Protector of Virgins'...
so I felt I was well protected and quite safe from danger."[4]

In order to be little, St. Thérèse instructed us first to
recognize our nothingness. One of the most basic ways
to do this is by looking at the dependency we have in our
very existence. Our fathers are a constant reminder that
we were not conceived by our own power. The intimate
union of our parents that was blessed by the gift of God
was necessary for our creation. And so, when we look
at our father, we are reminded of our utter dependency
for the most basic reality of our life: our existence itself.
When we realize that everything depends on existence
and we can take absolutely no credit for our existence, we
see how fundamentally we are nothing. "What have you
that you did not receive? If then you received it, why do
you boast as if it were not a gift" (1 Cor 4:7)?

In addition to the utter dependency of our existence
that we remember by looking to our biological parents,
we can also discover our utter dependency on the gift of

Thérèse of Lisieux, *The Story of a Soul*, trans. T. N. Taylor (London:
Burns, Oates & Washbourne, 1912), 90.

salvation in looking to Mary and Joseph. When we look to St. Joseph, we can be reminded of the gift of his and Mary's faith that cooperated with God's plan to bring about our redemption. As we said earlier, St. Joseph's faith to enter into marriage with Mary was necessary for the conception of Jesus. As the Fathers of the Church saw it, Jesus was a fruit of their marriage even if not a fruit of their physical conjugal union. After all, our redemption was even more important than our creation: "Our birth would have been no gain had we not been redeemed."[5]

These are two simple steps we can take to enter into a deeper awareness of our own nothingness and to receive anew the gift of our existence and the gift of our redemption. It is an utterly gratuitous gift that should move us to awe and wonder: "O wonder of your humble care for us! O love, O charity beyond all telling, to ransom a slave you gave away your Son!"[6] When we take this approach and recognize our nothingness, we can also discover the joy of being a child who receives everything from the hands of a loving father. This is an especially touching way to approach St. Joseph. If his cooperation with the plan of God helped to bring about our redemption, what other wonderful gifts does he have in store for us? After all, since he gave his life for our salvation, should we not expect that he will continue to help us receive all the fruits of that salvation and sanctification won for us on the Cross of his Son? And so, recognizing how dependent we are on others for the most fundamental things, let us

---

[5]   Easter Vigil, The Exsultet
[6]   Easter Vigil, The Exsultet.

not be afraid to approach St. Joseph with the open hands of a beggar and the hopeful heart of a child before her father.

St. Thérèse said that littleness is to be "disquieted about nothing." What are the things that cause us to be disquieted? Let us think about the young Jesus, who had His first project in carpentry. In His humanity, we can presume He had to learn the trade. Even if He picked it up faster than any other human being, there is always a learning curve, even at the level of having hands big enough, sufficient physical strength, or adequate dexterity to perform a task. God was not afraid to become little and need to grow and learn! Jesus had an advantage, however, that He also wants to share with us: He always had the help of St. Joseph. When He had to learn a new skill or practice, when He had to meet a deadline or face a difficult customer, He always had St. Joseph at His side to support Him and even teach Him.

This is the way that we can be "disquieted about nothing," as St. Thérèse said. When we have confidence that we have a father who provides for us, then it gives us the courage to be like children and ask for whatever we need. We can find peace and strength in the loving fatherly presence of St. Joseph, who helps us just as he helped Jesus. There are so many things we do not ask for, though! We take for granted that we can earn our own living, that we can provide our own food, that we can make our own friends. We trust in our own efforts and our own plans to achieve everything for ourselves. A sign that we are overextending ourselves is the feeling of stress and anxiety. Although there are other reasons for experiencing those feelings, one reason is that we put too much pressure on ourselves to be self-sufficient. We develop the cognitive dissonance of knowing that we are limited but imagining that everything depends on our own efforts. How much easier it becomes when we can admit that we are limited, ask our father St. Joseph for help, and move forward as a little child, always learning how to do our best with St. Joseph's help in his workshop.

St. Thérèse observed:

> Even among the poor, they give the child what is necessary, but as soon as she grows up, her father no longer wants to feed her and says: "Work now, you can take care of yourself." It was so as not to hear this that I never wanted to grow up, feeling that I was incapable of making my [own] living, the eternal life of heaven.[7]

St. Thérèse knew that she could not make her own living in the heavenly kingdom, or, in other words, that she could not redeem herself. She was aware of this aspect of her nothingness. She gave that as the explanation for why she did not want to grow up. She did not want to hear the words, "Work now, you can take care of yourself." St. Thérèse had a great insight into how fundamental our dependency is. It is not a stage that we work through or a grade that we graduate from. Sometimes we accept that we were dependent as babies, but now we reason that

---

[7] August 6, 1897, entry no. 8, in *St. Therese of Lisieux: Her Last Conversations*, 139.

we have grown up and we should provide for ourselves. In some human measures like food and shelter this is true, but even then it is only partially true. In fact, we are incredibly dependent on an extensive chain of dependencies. One man explored how many people it takes to put a cup of coffee on his breakfast table and discovered it required thousands![8] Just think of how many people it took to maintain the electrical grid, computer systems, and printing presses to create this book! And just as we should never stray too far from a proper gratitude toward those who work to provide the basic necessities for sustaining our existence, so also we should stay close to the one who plays such a fundamental role in providing for our redemption.

Fortunately, to answer St. Thérèse's concern about being told to make her own living, we never find St. Joseph to be a begrudging provider. He always brings us joyfully to his Son, our Redeemer. It only requires that we let ourselves be little, recognize our helplessness in redeeming ourselves, and turn to him for his fatherly care. St. Joseph will never turn us away. The time will never come when "her father no longer wants to feed her."

Children Need Grandparents

Throughout the centuries, St. Joseph has been pictured

---

[8] A. J. Jacobs. "My Journey to Thank All the People Responsible for My Morning Coffee," TED Salon: Brightline Initiative, June 2018, https://www.ted.com/talks/a_j_jacobs_my_journey_to_thank_all_ the_people_responsible_for_my_morning_coffee.

as an old man. This seems to have developed as a protective measure because the miraculous conception of Jesus
in the Virgin Mary and her lifelong virginity were such
important Christian doctrines. Thus, the logic is that
Joseph was an old man and thus no "threat" to Mary's
virginity. This picture of St. Joseph has various problems.
The two most significant are that there is no precedent
for such an old man to marry a young virgin, and that
it is highly unlikely that such an extraordinary event
would not be mentioned or explained in the Scripture.
The other problem is that while an old man might not
threaten Mary's virginity,[9] he would also be less helpful in
protecting her on her long journey to Bethlehem or even
more so in the exile into Egypt. The logic of St. Josemaría
Escrivá is also helpful on this point:

> You don't have to wait to be old or lifeless to
> practice the virtue of chastity. Purity comes from
> love; and the strength and gaiety of youth are no
> obstacle for noble love. Joseph had a young heart
> and a young body when he married Mary, when
> he learned of the mystery of her divine mother-
> hood, when he lived in her company, respecting
> the integrity God wished to give the world as one
> more sign that he had come to share the life of
> his creatures. Anyone who cannot understand a
> love like that knows very little of true love and is

---

[9] However, that is a dubious conclusion because old age did not prevent
the old men in the Book of Daniel from lusting after Susannah (see
Dan 13).

a complete stranger to the christian meaning of chastity.[10]

Having said that, we might wonder why the Holy Spirit allowed the image of St. Joseph as an old man to become so widespread in Christian art, literature, and even apologetics. One reason may be that there is something touching about the image of an old man cradling a baby with such tenderness. Another is that St. Joseph represents God the Father, who is also depicted as the "Ancient of Days." And lastly, these depictions of St. Joseph may be alluding to his wisdom, which normally comes from old age. In other words, St. Joseph serves not only as a father figure but also as a grandfather figure.

Pope Francis has spoken quite extensively about the importance of the elderly in the lives of the young. They provide roots and carry in their hearts the memory of a people:

> The elderly have dreams built up of memories and images that bear the mark of their long experience. If young people sink roots in those dreams, they can peer into the future; they can have visions that broaden their horizons and show them new paths. But if the elderly do not dream, young people lose clear sight of the horizon. Perhaps our parents have preserved a memory that can help us imagine the dream our grandparents dreamed

---

[10] St. Josemaría Escrivá, Homily for the Solemnity of St. Joseph, March 19, 1963, https://stjosemaria.org/in-st-josephs-workshop/.

for us. All of us, even before our birth, received, as a blessing from our grandparents, a dream filled with love and hope, the dream of a better life. Even if not our grandparents, surely some of our great-grandparents had that happy dream as they contemplated their children and then grand-children in the cradle. The very first dream of all is the creative dream of God our Father, which precedes and accompanies the lives of all his children. The memory of this blessing that extends from generation to generation is a precious legacy that we should keep alive so that we too can pass it on.[11]

In this description given by Pope Francis, we see the connection between the dream of a grandparent and the dream of God the Father. We can also detect in an elderly St. Joseph the way that Israel had become old, but she had not lost her dream. St. Joseph carried the dream of King David forward as a faithful descendent who never forgot his royal heritage. The grace of the Old Covenant was wearing thin, but the promise of the Messiah's coming kept hope alive. In that way, we could imagine a harmony of the young and old images of St. Joseph. Namely, we could imagine that St. Joseph began as an old man, but that his encounter with Mary and Jesus began to renew his youth. Of course, this would only be a symbolic inter-

---

[11] Pope Francis, Post-Synodal Apostolic Exhortation to Young People and to the Entire People of God *Christus Vivit* (March 25, 2019), §193–94.

pretation, but may serve to harmonize the young and old images of St. Joseph.

In any event, we can certainly recognize the importance of grandparents. The elderly St. Joseph evokes images of a grandfather who holds and cares for a new grandchild. That image is full of love and tenderness, and there is a youthfulness that shines from the elderly face as a new hope is embraced in the divine baby.

To develop this point a bit further, let us consider again the challenging critique of Venerable Archbishop Fulton Sheen, who protested Christian art favored the lack of vitality in old age over the tamed vigor of virtuous youth. He explained that these traditional images depict Joseph as tired and tame by depicting him as old. In my interactions with older men, however, I have not necessarily found that tired, tame, and old actually go together.

Sheen makes compelling points of course, but we could also apply his own logic to the image of the old Joseph by recognizing that an old Joseph could have a virtue that is tried and true. It is like the difference between an old priest or bishop, who has been tried over many years and has perfected the virtue of chastity. The virtue of chastity should be contrasted with mere abstinence. A chaste man does not love less. He loves more! He does not see less. He sees more! He does not necessarily have less passion in his heart, but could even have more, although it is fully under the direction of his reason and thus perfectly subject to the will of God. Seen in this light, an old Joseph could have been a man who cherished Mary deeply because of his many years of self-mastery and virtue, seeing her beauty more clearly and reverencing her deeply in the light of who she is in the eyes of God.

Furthermore, in regard to Joseph as a protector, we have marveled on many occasions at old men, even octogenarians, who have kept up their youthful strength. More than one has completed an Ironman Triathlon, a feat that is beyond the capacity of many younger men. Whether the trip to Bethlehem or the Flight into Egypt, perhaps an old Joseph, even more than a young one, could have retained the strength and additionally profited from more decades of wisdom, to accompany Mary and Jesus lovingly along these long and treacherous journeys.

In the end, I believe the Holy Spirit allows some ambiguity in the age of St. Joseph so that we can imagine that he beautifully embodies this fullness of masculinity that has qualities of both young and old. He can be imagined with the virginal strength, energy, and ideals of a young man along with the virtue, wisdom, and dreams that come with old age. In this way, he offers to us a more perfect image of God the Father.

Littleness of Daily Life

We can draw close to St. Joseph by sharing with him the littleness of everyday life. Most of the life of Jesus, the Incarnate Son of God, does *not* appear in Sacred Scripture. In fact, the *vast* majority of His life does not appear in Sacred Scripture. Rather, in the ordinary littleness of everyday life, He simply shared life with Mary and Joseph. In this way, St. Joseph appears as the father of the littleness of ordinariness. He was willing to be there with Jesus in countless experiences that would be lost to history. This encourages us to find St. Joseph as a father and friend in the ordinariness of our own lives. "Each of us can discover in Joseph—the man who goes unnoticed, a daily, discreet and hidden presence—an intercessor, a support and a guide in times of trouble. St. Joseph reminds us that those who appear hidden or in the shadows can play an incomparable role in the history of salvation."[12]

Especially since the Church added a memorial to the liturgical calendar for "St. Joseph the Worker," many have pointed out how St. Joseph is close to ordinary workers. St. Joseph shares our daily work with us, even when it often feels like a drudgery. We can turn to St. Joseph for help with that work. Perhaps more importantly, we can find in St. Joseph a faithful companion in that work. No worker labors alone. And especially when we feel the pinch of littleness in the ordinariness of our work, St. Joseph appears to us as a father of that ordinariness, and as a good father, he encourages us and strengthens us to persevere. We can ask him whether our work matters and hear that he is proud of us. He reminds us that like his time with Jesus in Nazareth, it is all an essential part of sanctifying this world and preparing it for the kingdom.

We can also turn to St. Joseph in the ordinary tasks that also contain the unknown. St. Joseph had to do many things that were ordinary for the human race but absolutely new for him. Presuming he never had children, the basic tasks of raising a son were new to him. For that,

---

[12] Pope Francis, *Patris Corde*, Introduction.

he had to trust the teaching of the law and the experience of those who had come before him. He did that faithfully, as the Scripture records for us. He circumcised Jesus, he gave Him the name the angel had revealed, he took Him to the Temple for the presentation of the first-born, and he brought Him again at age twelve, which was the normal time for a bar mitzvah. Considering how strangely everything started out after the betrothal, one can imagine that Joseph was always wondering what else would change, but without receiving further instructions, he simply carried out the expected tasks.

In fact, it is striking that such an extraordinary man in such extraordinary circumstances actually lived such an ordinary life. Pope Francis saw that as normative for the young:

[In the Presentation of Christ in the Temple] it is not young people who are creative: the young, like Mary and Joseph, follow the law of the Lord, the path of obedience. The elderly, like Simeon and Anna, see in the Child the fulfilment of the Law and the promises of God. And they are able to celebrate: [they] are creative in joy and wisdom. And the Lord *turns obedience into wisdom* by the working of his Holy Spirit. At times God can grant the gift of wisdom to a young person, but always as the fruit of obedience and docility to the Spirit. This obedience and docility is not something theoretical; it too is subject to the economy of the incarnation of the Word: docility and obedience to a founder, docility and obedience to a

specific rule, docility and obedience to one's superior, docility and obedience to the Church. It is
always docility and obedience in the concrete.[13]

Pope Francis recognized the docility and obedience
that are the necessary path for the young to be open to
the wisdom that comes as a gift of the Holy Spirit. Joseph
and Mary guide us along this path and accompany us in
our own path. We can risk remaining little, remaining
docile and obedient, when we can turn to Joseph and
Mary for their love and support.

Why is it so hard for us to walk this path of docility and obedience? Perhaps it is related to Pope Benedict
XVI's observation about the way sin poisons our thinking:

We all carry within us a drop of the poison.... We
call this drop of poison "original sin." Precisely on
the Feast of the Immaculate Conception, we have
a lurking suspicion that a person who does not sin
must really be basically boring and that something
is missing from his life: the dramatic dimension
of being autonomous; that the freedom to say no,
to descend into the shadows of sin and to want
to do things on one's own is part of being truly
human; that only then can we make the most of
all the vastness and depth of our being men and
women, of being truly ourselves; that we should

---

[13] Pope Francis, Homily for the Feast of the Presentation, February 2, 2015,
http://www.vatican.va/content/francesco/en/homilies/2015/docu-
ments/papa-francesco_20150202_omelia-vita-consacrata.html.

put this freedom to the test, even in opposition to God, in order to become, in reality, fully ourselves. In a word, we think that evil is basically good, we think that we need it, at least a little, in order to experience the fullness of being.[14]

When we set out on the sinless path of Mary and Joseph, living in docility and obedience, we risk living a repetitive, boring life that seems that it will not arrive at the fullness of being. Or conversely, when we are living such an ordinary life, we can look to our right and our left and discover Mary and Joseph walking alongside us.

In the end, the path of docility and obedience should be seen as a relief. We do not have to create new adventures every day. We do not have to invent new patterns of behavior every day. We do not need to come up with a new law or a new worship or a new plan or a new world. By simply living in the world God gave us and according to the law He taught us and by practicing the religion He revealed in Christ, we have everything we need to make the ultimate journey to the fullness of being and eternal happiness. Most of that journey consists of simply living out each day in docility and obedience, following the schedule, fulfilling our duty, growing in our relationships, and drawing closer to God. If we are living that way, then when God interrupts our plan and calls us in a new direction, we will be alert and ready to respond.

---

[14] Pope Benedict XVI, Homily for the Solemnity of the Immaculate Conception, December 8, 2005, http://www.vatican.va/content/benedict-xvi/en/homilies/2005/documents/hf_ben-xvi_hom_20051208_anniv-vat-council.html.

A Prayer for His Fatherly Care

This prayer was composed by Pope Francis for the Year of
St. Joseph. He asks simply for St. Joseph to show himself
a father to us little ones:

> Hail, Guardian of the Redeemer,
> Spouse of the Blessed Virgin Mary.
> To you God entrusted his only Son;
> in you Mary placed her trust;
> with you Christ became man.
> Blessed Joseph, to us too,
> show yourself a father
> and guide us in the path of life.
> Obtain for us grace, mercy, and courage,
> and defend us from every evil. Amen.[15]

---

[15] Pope Francis, *Patris Corde*, §7.

Chapter Four

HIDDEN WITH ST. JOSEPH

The Hidden Kingdom

St. Joseph "became a unique guardian of the mystery 'hidden for ages in God' (Eph 3:9)."[1] In this statement, St. John Paul II directs our attention to the hiddenness of Jesus and the way that Joseph guards that hiddenness. He also references St. Paul's teaching that hiddenness is something God Himself cherishes and maintains, even for ages at a time. Jesus repeatedly used images of hiddenness to describe the kingdom of God: leaven hidden in the dough (Matt 13:33), a treasure hidden in the field (Matt 13:44), a pearl that hides inside an oyster (Matt 13:45), a seed that is hidden and grows underground (Mark 4:26–29).

This also echoes the teaching of St. John at the conclusion of his Prologue: "No one has ever seen God; the only-begotten Son, who is in the bosom of the Father,

---

[1] Pope St. John Paul II, *Redemptoris Custos*, §5.

he has made him known" (John 1:18). All together this gives us the image of a God who holds a precious secret, namely, His only-begotten Son. He holds that secret close to His Heart, in His bosom. He cherishes and loves that secret in a divine way, in fact in a divine Person whom we name the Holy Spirit. And in the fullness of time, He finally lets one person in on that secret. With her permission, He shared His secret and entrusted His Son from His bosom into a new humanity in her womb.

Before sharing His secret with her, He hid her under the loving care of St. Joseph. As mentioned earlier, St. Joseph veiled the virgin through their marriage, protecting her from the eyes of the Enemy. Then the Father shared His secret with St. Joseph through the angel in a dream. In this way, the hidden Son of the Father was made flesh and entered into time and space, moving from the hiddenness of His divine Father to the hidden womb of His human mother, who was hidden under the care of her loving spouse. Mary and Joseph are masters of hiddenness, because they themselves lived hidden lives. They are king and queen of a hidden kingdom. In fact, it was specifically in discovering and caring for God's secret that they, too, became part of God's secret, God's hidden kingdom, as parents of the King, their lives hidden with Christ in God (Col 3:3). In this way, they are also a model for us.

God wants to share His secret with us. He places His secret presence within us at Baptism and gives His secret to us hidden under the appearance of bread in the Eucharist. For us to see, however, requires us to enter into our inner room and pray to the Father in secret (Matt 6:6).

When we enter into our inner room, there is a part of us that becomes hidden. We draw close to the Lord in faith, and it cannot be communicated except in a language of faith to a person of faith. This is what Joseph and Mary also experienced. Who could understand? So, they simply guarded the mystery and remained hidden, overlooked by everyone, except a few people with whom God also shared the mystery. There were shepherds and Magi, an old priest and a prayerful widow. Only a few had the eyes to see. Only a few had entered into that hidden place where they could share in the ancient secret.

One prominent example of a woman who entered into hiddenness and then had eyes to see the Hidden One was Elizabeth. The Scripture tells us, "Elizabeth conceived, and for five months she hid herself, saying, 'Thus the Lord has done to me in the days when he looked on me, to take away my reproach among men'" (Luke 1:24–25). Here we see that Elizabeth was a hidden woman for many years as she was buried under the reproach of others. They looked on her barrenness with scorn, and then they overlooked her as one who was cursed. When she conceived, she probably became the talk of the town. Thus she hid herself for five months to remove herself from the gossip. It was this hidden place that Mary entered into, bearing her own secret. The hidden Elizabeth was alerted to Mary's secret by her own secret, her hidden son, John, who danced when the New Ark of the Covenant entered the house (see Luke 1:41; 2 Sam 6:14). And Elizabeth rejoiced at the secrets that were being revealed in her hidden home in Ain Karem:

She exclaimed with a loud cry, "Blessed are you among women, and blessed is the fruit of your womb! And why is this granted me, that the mother of my Lord should come to me? For behold, when the voice of your greeting came to my ears, the child in my womb leaped for joy. And blessed is she who believed that there would be a fulfilment of what was spoken to her from the Lord." (Luke 1:42–45)

The Carmelite Doctors help us to understand the hiddenness that is required when we seek to uncover the hidden mystery. St. John of the Cross wrote, "If you want to find a hidden treasure you must enter the hiding place secretly, and once you have discovered it, you will also be hidden as the treasure is hidden."[2] St. Thérèse put this in her own words in a letter to her sister Celine: "Jesus is a hidden treasure, an inestimable good which few souls can find, for it is hidden, and the world loves what sparkles. . . . To find a hidden thing one must hide oneself; our life must then be a mystery."[3] This describes beautifully what took place with St. Joseph. His love was completely submerged into the mystery of God's secret, hidden for all ages.

---

[2]   John of the Cross, *The Complete Works of Saint John of the Cross of the Order of Our Lady of Mount Carmel*, trans. David Lewis, vol. 2 (London: Longman, Green, Longman, Roberts, & Green, 1864), 17.

[3]   Letter 145, in *Letters of St. Thérèse*, vol. 2, *1890–1897*, trans. John Clarke, O.C.D. (Washington, D.C.: ICS Publications, 1988), 808.

Speaking of secrets in this way can start to sound like Gnosticism. The proponents of Gnostic heresies claimed an elitism that came from secret knowledge, accessible only to a few. We know there are also evil secrets that create bonds of power among men of malice. Gnostic secrets, mafia secrets, and secret societies are the devil's distortion and lead to enslavement, exclusion, and corruption. That includes the secret of Herod, who "summoned the Wise Men secretly and ascertained from them what time the star appeared" (Matt 2:7). This does not describe the secret of St. Joseph, however, who wanted all to know his beloved son. His secret was never a matter of exclusion or elitism. In fact, it is often the child who most easily comes to discover the secret. The baptized infant is filled with God's secret, as is the small child who receives Holy Communion. St. Thérèse likewise gave testimony to the loving knowledge that is made available to the one who opens her heart to God:

> Ah! had the learned who spent their life in study come to me, undoubtedly they would have been astonished to see a child of fourteen understand perfection's secrets, secrets all their knowledge cannot reveal because to possess them one has to be poor in spirit!

As St. John of the Cross writes in his Canticle:
... with no other light or guide
Than the one that burned in my heart.
This guided me
More surely than the light of noon

> To where he was awaiting me
> —him I knew so well . . . (Dark Night stanza
> 3, 4)[4]

And so it is also true for us that to draw close to St. Joseph, we must enter into the hidden place, that inner room Jesus spoke of (Matt 6:6). We must step out of the glamor of the world and make our home in that hidden kingdom that the world considers irrelevant, namely, the invisible reality of faith. We must be willing to die to our vanity as we disappear from the city and head into the hill country. It is only there in hiding that we can peek into the hidden encounter of Mary and Elizabeth, who sang songs of praise at the invisible encounter of two infants who were out of sight in their mothers' wombs.

On the other hand, for those who already feel hidden, or even abandoned, forgotten, and left behind, a simple glance can reveal the companionship of St. Joseph. As the reproaches against Elizabeth drove her into hiddenness and Mary found her in her home in the hill country, so also St. Joseph has a way of finding the exiles and the lost ones and joining them in that hidden place of reproach and abandonment. Whether it was due to the critical glances he received from those who thought he had relations with Mary before they lived together, or whether it was the suspicion with which this foreigner was viewed in Egypt, he was familiar with the hiddenness felt by the

---

[4] Guy Gaucher, *John and Thérèse: Flames of Love: The Influence of St. John of the Cross in the Life and Writings of St. Thérèse of Lisieux* (Staten Island, NY: Alba House, 1999), 19.

rejected and abandoned. He draws close to those who feel unimportant, irrelevant, or simply left behind in this fast-paced world. Rather than trying to keep up, we can instead lean back and find that the strong and loving St. Joseph is right there with us to hold us and help us feel less alone.

A Master of the Darkness

St. Joseph is presented to us in Scripture as a Master of the Darkness. This might account for one of his titles, "Terror of Demons." At least it should be an encouragement for us to seek him when we are faced with night and darkness. That certainly applies to physical night and darkness, but also to spiritual night and darkness. St. Joseph can protect us and guide us if we turn to him in our own times of darkness. He can help us to hear God in the darkness through dreams, and he can help us to persevere in the darkness of our spiritual journey. When we are faced with the spiritual darkness which is a necessary part of advancing in the spiritual life, we will find a father and helper in St. Joseph.

Normally, darkness is the domain of the Enemy. Jesus taught us to walk in the day: "If any one walks in the day, he does not stumble, because he sees the light of this world. But if any one walks in the night, he stumbles, because the light is not in him" (John 11:9–10). St. Paul likewise warns Christians against the darkness, saying, "Once you were darkness, but now you are light in the Lord; walk as children of light" (Eph 5:8). St. Paul taught the Thessalonians on this point at even greater length:

> You are not in darkness, brethren, for that day to
> surprise you like a thief. For you are all sons of
> light and sons of the day; we are not of the night
> or of darkness. So then let us not sleep, as others
> do, but let us keep awake and be sober. For those
> who sleep sleep at night, and those who get drunk
> are drunk at night. But, since we belong to the
> day, let us be sober, and put on the breastplate of
> faith and love, and for a helmet the hope of salva-
> tion. (1 Thess 5:4–8)

Clearly there is a symbolic, spiritual level to this
teaching, but definitely also a straightforward, literal level
as well. Most crimes take place at night. City streets are
less safe at night. Intoxication generally takes place at
night. Darkness covers illegal activities. A friend in Alco-
holics Anonymous once said that several AA members
often lovingly remind each other, "Nothing good happens
after midnight."

Fortunately, God redeems the night. The great Easter
hymn, the Exsultet, eloquently hails the Night of the Resurrection, first connecting it to the night of Passover and
the Exodus, the pillar of fire, and the distinctive Easter
worship of Christians, and then celebrates the night's
hidden knowledge:

> O truly blessed night,
> worthy alone to know the time and hour

when Christ rose from the underworld![5]

The hymn then proceeds to acknowledge the victorious power of the Easter Night that brings an end to the dominion of night and also overcomes the destructive consequences of the darkness we described earlier:

> This is the night
> of which it is written:
> The night shall be as bright as day,
> dazzling is the night for me,
> and full of gladness.
>
> The sanctifying power of this night
> dispels wickedness, washes faults away,
> restores innocence to the fallen, and joy to
> mourners,
> drives out hatred, fosters concord, and brings
> down the mighty.[6]

This hymn celebrates the victory of light over darkness, of life over death, and of mercy over sin. And since the Resurrection, the night gains a new meaning, no longer limited to evil deeds of darkness. Because the Resurrection inserted light into the night, St. John of the Cross can also speak of the Dark Night and of the special lights that become possible only in that night. These

---

[5] *The Roman Missal*, trans. The International Commission on English in the Liturgy, 3rd typical ed. (Washington, DC: United States Conference of Catholic Bishops, 2011), 355.
[6] *The Roman Missal*, 355.

lights are the beginnings of deeper contemplation in the night of the senses.

St. Joseph guides us through the night in two different ways. First, he is open to God's symbolic communication given through dreams. God always speaks in symbols, in obscure ways that He makes accessible to anyone who will receive His gift of faith. Jesus taught the Apostles in parables and recognized that not everyone had eyes to see or ears to hear. This symbolic language came through many times in dreams. St. Joseph was a Master Dreamer, and he can help us navigate the dreams of God that come in our sleep. We will consider this further in the next section.

St. Joseph was also able to be awake and act by night. He departed for Egypt after awaking from a dream. The evangelist is sure to point out that he led Mary and Jesus out "by night" (Matt 2:14). It is for this reason that St. Joseph is often pictured with a lantern. He is able to carry light into the darkness. If we invite St. Joseph into our darkness, he is the one who can lead us through the paths of deeper prayer. We will consider this further in the section "A Lantern in the Night."

Dreams: Hope in the Night

Likewise, we can find in St. Joseph a man who is able to receive special light in the night. In particular, St. Joseph received divine communication in dreams by night. Scripture remembers four dreams that guided St. Joseph. Dreams are an important part of the person of St. Joseph and also provide a connection between the St. Joseph of the New Testament and the patriarch Joseph of the Old Testament.

Dreams redeem the night. Dreams come after the lights go out and we make the decision to let go of this life and slip into the surrender of unconsciousness. Sleep is an analogue for death, and while we do not get to practice dying well, God gives us the daily practice of falling asleep, in part as a preparation for death. It is not surprising that the Church's liturgical night prayer concludes with the blessing, "May the all-powerful Lord grant us a restful night and a peaceful death."

Dreams communicate to us in symbols. Coming from the Greek, *symballo*, meaning "to throw together," symbols throw many events, faces, objects, and ideas together in a single image. Symbols are the language of God, who always wants to say more to us than can be captured in a single thought or idea. He says a multitude of things through a single figure or through a single story. The woman of Revelation 12 can be simultaneously Israel, Mary, and the Church. David can represent each one of us in both our greatness and our sinfulness and can show us the pathway to mercy. The love story of the Song of Songs is the love story of mankind, of Israel, of the Church, and of each one of us. As we read in Sacred Scripture, God has a way of communicating to every generation through the symbols of a single narrative.

The wise are those who put on the mind of Christ and learn to interpret the symbols of God. The wise patriarch Joseph interpreted the symbols of his own dreams and also the symbols of others' dreams. The prophet Daniel was also able to read the symbols of dreams and gave us a clear promise of the Savior's first coming. Joseph, son of David, was able to interpret the symbols of dreams to distinguish the fanciful movements of the subconscious from the divine communications given through angels. This enabled him to receive the woman who took all the symbols and pondered them—literally "symbolled" them or "threw them together"—in her heart (Luke 2:19). Her heart is the place where all of God's symbols were collected, and Joseph is the one chosen to guard that heart, filled with the stuff of dreams. Ultimately, what collected in her heart, the very dreams of God, became Incarnate in her womb and was born into the loving care of the man of dreams.

Dreams allow us to experience the impossible. The physics of dreams follow the metaphysics of the subconscious with unexpected connections and a strange stream of thoughts and images. This makes it possible to dream of things that have never existed and to dream of a future that is impossibly better than the present. At the same time, dreams are built from memories. The fragments that come together to make up our dreams are cobbled together from memories both recent and long past. The more developed our imagination and the more memories we have, the richer our dreams will be. Perhaps that is why the Lord spoke especially of the dreams of the elderly that would be inspired through the Spirit (Joel 2:28).

It is also the memory of promises that gives us the courage to have hope and dream of a better future. It is the memory of our first encounter with the Lord that helps us dream of His second coming and His first coming to others. At the beginning of the Synod on the topic of young people, Pope Francis addressed the Synod Fathers:

> We ask the Paraclete to help us preserve the memory of the Lord and rekindle in us his words that have made our hearts burn (cf. Lk 24:32). A Gospel ardour and passion which lead to an ardour and passion for Jesus. A memory that can rekindle and renew in us the capacity to dream and to hope. For we know that our young people will be capable of prophecy and vision to the extent that we, who are already adult or elderly, can dream and thus be infectious in sharing those dreams and hopes that we carry in our hearts (cf. Joel 2:28).[7]

In Mary and Joseph, we have memory and dreams, fulfillment and promise. They make it possible for us to surrender to the night, to entrust our lives to the unconsciousness of sleep under their watchful care. They help us to face the darkness of failure and sin while preserving the light of hope and even fostering dreams of a better future. St. Joseph knows that there are Herods out there prowling in the darkness to destroy small children because he hears God's angels, and so he protects God's children. He dreams of God's kingdom, and he helps children to find it. When we entrust our lives to St. Joseph, he can help us

---

[7] Pope Francis, Homily for the Opening of the XV Ordinary General Assembly of the Synod of Bishops, October 3, 2018, http://w2.vatican.va/content/francesco/en/homilies/2018/documents/papa-francesco_20181003_omelia-inizio-sinodo.html.

to understand the Scriptures, written in God's symbolic dream language, he can protect us from our enemies who prowl in the darkness, and he can help us to hear the angels who communicate God's loving care for us.

A Lantern in the Night

The night is an image that describes a deprivation of the senses. The senses are the natural initial path for our learning. Normally, we receive the material world through our external senses, which is then gathered together by our internal senses. Our unique powers of abstraction then draw out the essence of things as we tease out spiritual knowledge from material realities. This raises us through our natural operations to the knowledge of God, who is the essence of all essences. The senses operate normally in the light.

Some knowledge cannot be communicated naturally, however. There is more to God than can be derived from sensory abstraction and rational deduction. God is like every beautiful thing, but infinitely more beautiful. God is revealed in every good deed, but He is infinitely more good than every good deed. God is like a friend, but infinitely more than a friend. God is like a father, but infinitely more than a father. This supernatural knowledge of God can only be received through faith, and it appears to our senses as darkness.

The same is true for receiving grace of union in God's love. Grace is normally communicated through sensory realities. The highest form of this is in the sacraments, but through the Incarnation, many realities have become sacramental. There are the formal sacramentals of the Church, such as holy water, blessed candles, and holy images. We receive these material realities through our senses, and they communicate grace to our souls. Consequently, our spiritual growth goes hand in hand with the development of our interior and exterior senses. It aids our prayer to look at sacred images, smell incense, and hear sacred music. Likewise, we do well to use our inner senses for prayer, including our imagination and our memory.

At the same time, there is a point at which God also communicates grace to us beyond that which can be communicated by our exterior or interior senses. Our senses seem to go dark, plunged into the night, and yet there is a supernatural knowledge and grace of union that continues to flow into our souls. This is a critical transition in the spiritual life. Paradoxically, while one would normally consider someone who passes through this night to be a master, the passage can only occur by becoming a child. Jesus's warning, "Truly, I say to you, unless you turn and become like children, you will never enter the kingdom of heaven," applies here (Matt 18:3). The reason is that we can only receive all that God wants to give by choosing to trust Him completely. We must embrace the openness, helplessness, and trust of a child to let God lead us in this new way. St. Joseph presides over this intentional surrender to childlike obedience. To say it simply, in order to become a spiritual child, we need two spiritual parents to care for us.

This transition through the night into childlike surrender takes place in St. Teresa's fourth mansion.[8] The night is the experience of disorientation that necessarily takes place. After developing our interior and exterior senses and feeling that we have some control in our lives of prayer, we face the wall of darkness in which all our skills fail to produce fruit. Our meditations become dry and dull. Our prayers feel dissatisfying. Furthermore, for those living active lives, the night is experienced as the limits of our human powers. The words of preachers fall short, the efforts of entrepreneurs meet obstacles and fall through, the confidence of mothers fails as they face problems in their children that go beyond their understanding.

The experience of reaching our limits, of entering into the night of powerlessness and failure, is always painful, but can also be blessed. It is always a departure from the safety of our birthplace. As we grow up, our birthplace becomes threatened by Herod, who is a symbol of our pride and control. St. Joseph holds the lantern for us that can help us navigate this night. He knows what it is like to wander without a map, to surrender to a plan that is beyond anyone's imagination, to receive grace that could never be limited to the senses. He gives us the protection we need to become childlike. We can find in him a loving father, a human sign of the heavenly Father. He leads us by this lantern into an exile that is uncomfortable, but it is safe from the murderous Herod of our self-sufficiency.

In addition to the Matthean image of St. Joseph carrying a lantern through the dark night, Fr. Andrew Doze saw this role of St. Joseph in the Lucan image of Jesus's

---

[8]   Teresa of Ávila, *The Interior Castle*, 67.

going down to Nazareth after the Finding in the Temple (Luke 2:41–52). After reaching the maturity of adulthood, able to hold His own with the Teachers of the Law, Jesus did not rely on the power of human wisdom, even wisdom aided by divine grace. Instead, He submitted Himself to the darkness of obedience. He became obedient to parents who were less than He was, choosing now to become a child in their home. He was given to them as a child, but now He chose childlike obedience in a new way, with His mature human freedom. We did not originally choose childhood, but our growth in the spiritual life requires the free choice to turn and become like a child in order that we may receive the grace of heaven (see Matt 18:3):

> What Teresa of Avila calls the fourth Mansion is this central experience that can be lived in thousands of ways. It often is a difficult ordeal; man gives up his limited human logic, his thoughts as man, as Jesus says to Peter, his self-sufficiency as an adult, to open himself to the radically new experience which comes from God, this childlike trust that the genius of Therese of the Child Jesus expressed better than anyone else. Jesus had gone up to the temple; he comes down from it. . . . The fourth Mansion is the descent, disconcerting, very trying at times, but which bears incomparable fruit as one moves from one state into the other. The descent of the head into the heart![9]

---

[9] Andrew Doze, *Saint Joseph: Shadow of the Father*, trans. Florestine Audett (Staten Island, NY: Alba House, 1992), 87.

St. Joseph receives us into this new way of life that operates more from divine logic than human logic. It is a kind of new birth. To conclude this section with a third image, we can think of St. Joseph as the one who delivers us into this new way of life. St. Louis de Montfort saw consecration to Mary as a way of living in the womb of Mary, drawing all our nourishment from her: "St. Augustine even says that, during their present life, all the elect are hidden in Mary's womb and that they are not truly born until the Blessed Mother brings them forth to life eternal."[10] As we know, eternal life begins now (see John 17:3), and this life begins especially as we enter into the fourth mansion. St. Joseph is the one who delivers us into this new life from the womb of Mary. As Jesus was initially received at His Birth into the arms of Joseph, so we are received in our spiritual rebirth into the arms of Joseph. The gentle voice of that loving father that Jesus heard from His mother's womb also beckons us as we dwell in her womb in this life to come forth through the darkness into a new spiritual reality that is beyond the life of the senses.

Following a Star

As we continue our journey of drawing close to St. Joseph, we can learn from the Wise Men, who found him by following a star. The Wise Men found their des-

---

[10] Louis de Montfort, *The Secret of Mary*, (Charlotte, NC: TAN Books, 2013), 13.

tination by gazing on lights that shone only at night. They spent countless hours in the night, gazing upon the stars. Though the language was obscure, they discerned a meaning from the stars that one day moved them to make a journey. Surely the Magi were already men of restless hearts, but their hearts were ignited by the sighting of a new star. "They had long peered into the great book of the heavens, seeking an answer to their questions—they had restless hearts—, and at long last the light appeared. That star changed them."[11]

Their journey was guided primarily by the obscure lights that shone in the darkness until they drew close to the great city, and it drew them in and they started to lose their way. "Above the great city the star disappears, it is no longer seen. What does this mean? In this case too, we must interpret the sign in its depth. For those men it was logical to seek the new king in the royal palace, where the wise court advisors were to be found."[12] When we are looking for St. Joseph, who is always found with Jesus, we must be careful not to fall into worldly logic and be misled by worldly ways. "God's criteria differ from human criteria. God does not manifest himself in the power of this world but in the humility of his love, the love that asks our freedom to be welcomed in order to transform us

---

[11] Pope Francis, Homily for the Solemnity of the Epiphany, January 6, 2016, http://www.vatican.va/content/francesco/en/homilies/2016/documents/papa-francesco_20160106_omelia-epifania.html.

[12] Pope Benedict XVI, Homily for the Solemnity of the Epiphany, January 6, 2011, http://www.vatican.va/content/benedict-xvi/en/homilies/2011/documents/hf_ben-xvi_hom_20110106_epifania.html.

and to enable us to reach the One who is Love."[13]

The world is so loud and so often and so easily leads us astray. We are distracted by the glimmer of fame, by the limelights of TV networks and movie productions. The lifestyles of the rich and famous appear before us as the glamorous goal that will make life easy and enjoyable. When children play at being princes and princesses, what starts as an attraction to what is beautiful and noble can quickly descend into dreaming of money and grasping after power. If we wish to find St. Joseph, we must have the conversion of the Magi: "They realized that power, even the power of knowledge, sometimes blocks the way to the encounter with this Child. The star then guided them to Bethlehem, a little town; it led them among the poor and the humble to find the King of the world."[14]

The Wise Men are contrasted with Herod in this passage of Matthew's Gospel. Herod never found Joseph. When the Magi asked Herod about the newborn King, he was troubled and he went immediately into frenzied activity, assembling *all* the chief priests and scribes of the people to inquire about the birth of the Christ (Matt 2:3–4). This was no small number of people, who were not easy to gather together at a moment's notice. This action reveals the frenzied desperation of Herod. Upon getting an answer, he then instructed the Wise Men to behave similarly: "Go and *search diligently ...*" (Matt 2:8). The word for "search" here has the sense of interrogating or questioning. Herod told them to go and ask around.

[13] Pope Benedict XVI, Homily for the Solemnity of the Epiphany, 2011.
[14] Pope Benedict XVI, Homily for the Solemnity of the Epiphany, 2011.

While it is valuable to seek wisdom from others, it is a common temptation that can keep us on the surface. There are some who have asked everyone about prayer, about Jesus, about St. Joseph, but have never slowed down, stepped out of the city lights, and sought Him themselves.

The Magi "went their way" (Matt 2:9). They did not go Herod's way, but instead departed the city and saw again the light of the star. They followed it until it "came to rest" (Matt 2:9). Matthew uses the same verb here as John uses to describe Mary at the foot of the Cross. It gives us the sense of standing still, of stability. This is what we must learn in prayer—to go out into the night, to follow the dim light of a star until we come to rest and remain steadfast in the darkness of the mystery. The star here symbolizes the mysteries of faith. For those with eyes to see, they are bright and beautiful, providing a lifetime of nourishment. The mysteries of the life of Christ revealed in the Word of God and made present in the Sacraments of the Church are a banquet to nourish our hearts and a bright star to lead us along the path of salvation. As our eyes of faith adjust to the night sky, we experience a joy with triple emphasis: we "rejoice exceedingly with great joy" (Matt 2:10) like the Magi as we follow the mysteries to the place where they rest at the house of Joseph. This is the only time in the Scriptures that "exceedingly" is used to modify "joy." In the other cases, it is only used to modify "fear" or "distress."

As the Magi came to the house, they surely met St. Joseph first. Following the star into the night to the place of its rest brought them to Joseph at the doorway of the house. The Scripture does not tell us of what that encounter consisted, but Joseph must have recognized that they were safe. In fact, it turns out that they were dreamers like himself (Matt 2:12). They shared their treasures, symbolizing the transformation of their lives and revealing to us a path to transformation as well. Pope Francis explained the gifts beautifully:

> *Gold*, the most precious of metals, reminds us God has to be granted first place; he has to be worshiped. But [to] do that, we need to remove ourselves from the first place and to recognize our neediness, the fact that we are not self-sufficient. Then there is *frankincense*, which symbolizes a relationship with the Lord, prayer, which like incense rises up to God (cf. Ps 141:2). Just as incense must burn in order to yield its fragrance, so too, in prayer, we need to "burn" a little of our time, to spend it with the Lord. Not just in words, but also by our actions. We see this in the *myrrh*, the ointment that would be lovingly used to wrap the body of Jesus taken down from the cross (cf. Jn 19:39). The Lord is pleased when we care for bodies racked by suffering, the flesh of the vulnerable, of those left behind, of those who can only receive without being able to give anything material in return. Precious in the eyes of God is mercy shown to those who have nothing to give back.[15]

---

[15] Pope Francis, Homily for the Solemnity of the Epiphany, January 6,

The Magi help us to find the hidden Joseph by departing from worldly logic and following the logic of the heavens: "God's power is revealed in quite a different way: in Bethlehem, where we encounter the apparent powerlessness of his love. And it is there that we must go and there that we find God's star."[16]

Hidden behind Weakness and Poverty

St. Teresa of Calcutta famously spoke of Jesus as being hidden behind the distressing disguise of the poorest of the poor. In this way, we can say that there are those who proclaim the Gospel by *being* Jesus. Jesus identified Himself with the hungry, the thirsty, the sick, the imprisoned, the naked, and the homeless (see Matt 25:31–46) to the extent that He equates caring for them with caring for Him: "Truly, I say to you, as you did it to one of the least of these my brethren, you did it to me" (Matt 25:40). That verse prompted Mother Teresa to hold up her open hand and say, "Remember the five fingers!" and count on her fingers to five as she spoke each word: "You did it to me." She wanted her sisters and the volunteers to remember the presence of Jesus in the poor as readily as they remembered their own hands. She even included this truth in the Divine Praises recited after Eucharistic Benediction: ". . . Blessed be Jesus in the Most Holy Sacrament of the Altar.

2019, http://w2.vatican.va/content/francesco/en/homilies/2019/documents/papa-francesco_20190106_omelia-epifania.html.

[16] Pope Benedict XVI, Homily for the Solemnity of the Epiphany, 2011.

Blessed be Jesus in the poorest of the poor . . ."

Pope Francis repeatedly reinforced this message in his own magisterium. He challenged the young people of the Philippines to remember not only what they did for the poor but the special gift that the poor give to them— Jesus. He asked, "Do you let yourself be evangelized by the poor, by the sick, by those you assist?"[17] On his visit to the United States, he specifically identified poverty with St. Joseph. Not only do the poor bring us Jesus, but they also bring us St. Joseph. St. Joseph, who was a son of David and thus the nobility of Israel, was hidden in the distressing disguise of a homeless man. Pope Francis said to the homeless at a soup kitchen in Washington, D.C.:

> Here I think of a person whom I love very much, someone who is, and has been, very important throughout my life. He has been a support and an inspiration. He is the one I go to whenever I am "in a fix." You make me think of Saint Joseph. Your faces remind me of his. . . . The Bible is very clear about this: there was no room for them. I can imagine Joseph, with his wife about to have a child, with no shelter, no home, no place to stay. The Son of God came into this world as a home-less person. The Son of God knew what it was to start life without a roof over his head. We can imagine what Joseph must have been thinking.

---

[17] Pope Francis, Address to Young People in Manila, January 18, 2015, http://www.vatican.va/content/francesco/en/speeches/2015/january/documents/papa-francesco_20150118_srilanka-filippine-incontro-giovani.html.

How is it that the Son of God has no home? Why are we homeless, why don't we have housing?[18]

Like Mother Teresa and Pope Francis, we can learn to draw near to Jesus and St. Joseph by drawing near to the poor. He is hidden behind their faces and in their hearts. Furthermore, without too much effort, we can learn to see our own poverty and discover that St. Joseph is already there. It's easy to imagine that the homeless in Washington, D.C., were quite surprised that their faces reminded the pope of St. Joseph. Hopefully, they felt a little more dignity in knowing that they had a special access to St. Joseph, a share in his interior experience and a companion with them in the most painful part of their lives. We can discover the same truth for ourselves. We have a special access to the experience of St. Joseph as we tap into the areas of our own poverty.

In Christianity, we learn that "[God's] power is made perfect in weakness" (2 Cor 12:9). Divine power is hidden beneath the covering of human weakness. This was a discovery of the great evangelizer, St. Paul. After all his efforts of evangelization, he found that the power was always hidden in his weakness, and so he could boast of his weakness and embrace the thorn in his side. He learned that "the foolishness of God is wiser than men, and the weakness of God is stronger than men," so God chose the weak to shame the strong and the foolish to

---

[18] Pope Francis, Address to the Homeless at the Charitable Center of St. Patrick in Washington, D.C., September 24, 2015, http://www.vatican.va/content/francesco/en/speeches/2015/september/documents/papa-francesco_20150924_usa-centro-caritativo.html.

shame the wise (see 1 Cor 1:25–29).

From St. Paul we learn that the source of power for evangelization is always hidden. Just as the power of the body is hidden in the heart, the power of the Body of Christ is hidden in poverty and weakness:

> The power of the word does not depend above all on our action, on our means, on our "doing," but rather on God, who hides his power behind signs of weakness, who becomes present in the gentle morning breeze (cf. 1 Kings 19:12) and is revealed on the wood of the cross. We must always believe in the humble power of the word of God and let God act![19]

From this perspective, we can understand the way that Bishop Bossuet praises the hidden life of St. Joseph in his first panegyric, as he spoke of that life's nobility and grandeur. He explained it in contrast to the vocation of the Apostles, who received God's revelation in order to proclaim it, while Joseph received it in order to hide it. In this, St. Joseph remained unknown and for centuries even hardly revered, and Bossuet points out the value of this example for us who are so tempted to believe in worldly ways of exaltation. "He who glorifies the Apostles in the renown of their preaching glorifies Saint Joseph in the

---

[19] Pope Benedict XVI, Address on the Occasion of the International Conference Organized by the Pontifical Council for Promoting the New Evangelization, October 15, 2011, http://www.vatican.va/content/benedict-xvi/en/speeches/2011/october/documents/hf_ben-xvi_spe_20111015_nuova-evangelizzazione.html.

humility of his silence; and from that we have to learn that the glory of the Christian lies not in distinguished achievements and offices, but in doing what God wills."[20]

This contains a beautiful message of hope, showing us that the homeless man is not less than the rich man in view of the kingdom of heaven. The housewife and the CEO have the same opportunity to live the Gospel in obedience to their personal calling and become holy. The same glory applies to the hidden life as to the apostolic life, and if anything, we could say of the apostolic life that it is more dangerous: "How hard it is for the rich man to enter the kingdom of heaven!" (see Matt 19:24). The apostle's temptation to pride and vanity are greater than those called to lives of hidden, humble service like St. Joseph. And so, for those whose names will not be found in Wikipedia, who are hidden from public acclaim, they can find a special friend and guardian in St. Joseph, who likewise walked the path of hiddenness in his poverty and weakness.

Cloak of St. Joseph

Pope Leo XIII wrote the first encyclical on St. Joseph. In it he concluded, "It is, then, natural and worthy that as the Blessed Joseph ministered to all the needs of the family at Nazareth and girt it about with his protection, he should now cover with the cloak of his heavenly patronage and defend the Church of Jesus Christ."[21] The pope offers the

---

[20] Rondet, *Saint Joseph*, 120.
[21] Pope Leo XIII, *Quamquam Pluries* (1889), §3.

image of St. Joseph hiding us under his protection and claiming us as his own. This image calls to mind similar biblical images.

One image comes from the psalms: "He who dwells in the shelter of the Most High, who abides in the shadow of the Almighty, will say to the LORD, "My refuge and my fortress; my God, in whom I trust . . . he will cover you with his pinions, and under his wings you will find refuge" (Ps 91:1–2, 4). God hovers over us and covers us under his wings.

Another Scripture that teaches us the significance of covering with a man's garment is from the Book of Ruth:

> At midnight the man [Boaz] was startled, and turned over, and behold, a woman lay at his feet! He said, "Who are you?" And she answered, "I am Ruth, your maidservant; spread your garment over your maidservant, for you are next of kin." (Ruth 3:8–9)

The expression "spread your garment" here is literally "spread your wing." There are layers of meaning to this action. The primary meaning is one of protection:

> Ruth's request that Boaz "spread his wing" over her has a deeper meaning in the canonical context. Earlier, Boaz blessed her for seeking refuge under the "wings of the LORD." By repeating the key word "wing" (Hebrew *kanaph*), the sacred author shows that the "wing" (protective power) of the Lord will actually be manifested by Boaz's "wing."

Boaz will be the one through whom God will grant protection to Ruth.[22]

This explanation applies immediately to our experience of St. Joseph. He wants to hide us under his cloak, under his wing. He wants to shelter us and be a manifestation of the Lord's protective power. As he hid the Baby Jesus away from Herod's wrath, so he will hide us. As Boaz hid Ruth under his wing and ultimately brought her into his own family, so St. Joseph likewise does that for us when we draw close to him and ask him for this favor. This is especially true for those who feel like Ruth—widowed and alone with no control over her future. She was willing to accept the "bitterness" (Ruth 1:13) of her mother-in-law Naomi's circumstance out of charity, remaining faithful to her even after the death of their husbands. For those who feel helpless and accept bitterness out of charity, they can find a protector in St. Joseph, who is willing to spread his cloak over each one who comes to him.

We see a further meaningful detail that connects this action of Boaz with St. Joseph in the mysterious midnight conversation of Ruth and her desired husband:

> What are we to make of this mysterious exchange between a man and a woman in the middle of the night? The key to answering these questions lies in the words of Ruth, when she asks Boaz to

---

[22] John Bergsma and Brant Pitre, *A Catholic Introduction to the Bible: The Old Testament*, vol. 1 (San Francisco: Ignatius Press, 2018), 344.

"spread your garment over your maidservant"—
in Hebrew, literally, "spread your wing [of your
garment] over your maidservant." The "spreading
of the wing" of the garment was a betrothal ritual in
ancient Israel that carried connotations of marital
intimacy (see Ezek 16:8). Had Boaz decided to
consummate on the threshing floor, Ruth would
have become his wife by that act (cf. Ex 22:16).
However, such an action would have been lacking
in propriety, a breach of social custom. Although
clearly attracted to Ruth, Boaz refuses to pursue
this attraction in a disordered way. He insists on
following law and proper custom, which dictated,
among other things, that a closer male relative
have the first right to wed Ruth.[23]

In this, we understand that St. Joseph's cloak is also
an image of chaste betrothal, and we are reminded of the
way that St. Joseph protected Mary, his betrothed, in her
time of need, and also always remained chaste with her.
He brought her into his family and legally extended his
lineage and his inheritance to her Son. He does this also
with the Church, as Pope Leo XIII taught us. He protects
her and provides for her needs as he hides her under the
cloak of his heavenly patronage. As he does this for the
Church, we see that he also does it for each one of us who
asks him. It remains up to us whether we will allow ourselves to be hidden with him in this way.

We can think of this as St. Joseph's "cloaking device."

---

[23] Bergsma and Pitre, *A Catholic Introduction to the Bible*, 344.

And we can go deeper into it as we bring each of the poor, little, threatened, weak, and hurting parts of our lives to him. Like Ruth placing her broken past and her hopeless future under the cloak of Boaz, we can do the same with St. Joseph, and he will never fail to respond in the same way as Boaz did—chastely, lovingly, and faithfully.

Using an even simpler image, we can think of how children who are scared awake by a nightmare run under the covers with their parents. St. Joseph lifts the covers for his little ones to draw close to him, to feel the strength and warmth of his protection, and to hide from the monsters that lurk in the darkness. These may be the monstrous insults we have received, the monstrous fears that taunt us, the monstrous enemies that threaten our peace and happiness, or any other monsters that rear their ugly heads. St. Joseph never turns us away. He never dismisses us as being too childish or too needy. He makes room for us, even allowing his own peaceful rest to be interrupted so that we will know we are safe in his care.

A Prayer to Hide in His Cloak

There is a traditional devotion to the Cloak of St. Joseph that can help us turn these sentiments into prayer. The prayers consist of several pages of text, but even just the final section is beautiful and edifying:

O Glorious Patriarch St. Joseph, you who were chosen by God above all men to be the earthly head of the most holy of families, I ask you to

accept me within the folds of your holy cloak, that
you may become the guardian and custodian of my
soul. From this moment on, I choose you as my
father, my protector, my counselor, my patron and
I ask you to place in your custody my body, my
soul, all that I am, all that I possess, my life and
my death. Look upon me as one of your children;
defend me from the treachery of my enemies,
invisible or otherwise, assist me at all times in all
my necessities; console me in the bitterness of my
life, and especially at the hour of my death. Say but
one word for me to the Divine Redeemer Whom
you were deemed worthy to hold in your arms,
and to the Blessed Virgin Mary, your most chaste
spouse. Request for me those blessings which will
lead me to salvation. Include me among those who
are most dear to you and I shall set forth to prove
myself worthy of your special patronage. Amen.

St. Joseph wants to include us among those most dear
to him. He wants to be our patron, father, and even counselor. He wants to defend us and care for us. Finally, the
prayer recognizes that he does not only offer this to the
perfect, but even to those who have bitterness in their
lives, to those who face visible and invisible enemies,
and to those who are not worthy of his special attention.
And the prayer also recognizes that when we receive such
loving care from St. Joseph, we find the desire to live up
to that special patronage we receive in him.

Chapter 5

STEADFAST
IN SUFFERING

The preceding qualities are chosen—vulnerability, little-ness, hiddenness, and silence. We come now to a quality that is not chosen but leads us to make a choice. When we face evil, we are sometimes confronted with fear and despair. When we suffer the presence of evil, we may make a bad decision to run away or to fight. In these cases, we can seek the intercession of St. Joseph. St. Joseph teaches us the way of constancy and perseverance. St. Joseph provides for us through his prayer and his strong, loving presence.

Fullhearted Man

As we approach Jesus and Mary through the heart of St. Joseph, what qualities do we find in that heart? Clearly we find the heart of a father, and so we find the heart of a man. He is a man who endured suffering and persevered in his duty, and so we find a heart marked by the virtue of constancy. Although he did not confront the devil with sword and shield, like St. Michael, but rather with humility and obedience, that does not mean he did not have the strength or stamina of a warrior. St. Joseph was not a fearful man who shrank away from a challenge or ran from any sign of danger. He was a courageous man who had the boldness to carry out the will of God, Who has a tendency to call us to impossible tasks.

To carry out the will of God, St. Joseph had to be a man of passion. He was a man with a supple heart who could be deeply moved to do what is right, to be faithful to his bride and Son, and to fulfill his commitments to the Lord our God. In responding obediently to God's will, St. Joseph did not exercise a mechanical obedience, but a fullhearted obedience complete with the passions of the irascible appetite that he needed in order to resist the great evil that threatened his family and to achieve the arduous good that he sought in his faithfulness to God's call.

St. Thomas Aquinas provides a beautiful teaching on our humanity in his Treatise on the Passions in the *Summa Theologiae*. Divided into two categories, "concupiscible" and "irascible," the passions are the internal movements that direct us toward the good and move us to resist evil. The concupiscible appetites include pleasure at the presence of the good and sadness at the presence of evil. A man is more fully humane who can enjoy the good and appropriately suffer pain at what is wrong. The irascible appetites give us energy to pursue the good that is difficult to achieve and fight the evil that is hard to resist. A fullhearted man is one who has the sensitivity to humanely savor goodness and suffer the loss of or absence of goodness, and has the energy to pursue great things and fight against evil.[1]

Joseph is a fullhearted man who did not shrink from suffering and who readily pursued hard tasks at God's command. This is in contrast to some caricatures of masculinity and fatherhood that appear in our world. On the one hand, we see exaggerated images of men who lack the humane emotions and are insensitive to suffering as well as to the good. They carry on a kind of brutish, almost unfeeling, existence and make for overbearing fathers who are more inclined to intimidate and control than to foster their children's growth. Perhaps they have strong irascible appetites with anger and audacity, but they are unable to suffer with their children or enjoy a relaxing evening with friends or appreciate a beautiful sunset.

On the other hand, we see images of men who are sensitive but lack an appropriate audacity to pursue great things or the anger to resist present evils. Underlying those emotions are a lack of hope and the greatness of heart called magnanimity. These men shrink in fear or hide in the shadows. They let the great challenges of their age pass them by, and they give in to fear rather than strive to lead their own families and fulfill whatever other responsibilities God entrusts to them. As described

---

[1] The renaming of the concupiscible appetites to "humane" and the irascible appetites to "energy" comes from the great work combining psychology and Thomistic anthropology by Anna Terruwe and Conrad Baars, as found in *Psychic Wholeness and Healing: Using All the Powers of the Human Psyche*, ed. Suzanne M. Baars and Bonnie N. Shayne, 2nd ed. (Eugene, OR: Wipf and Stock Publishers, 2016).

earlier, Joseph was a man of hiddenness who veiled the mystery of his Holy Family, but it was not because he was paralyzed by fear. Perhaps he would have taken up arms against Herod, but God had a different design—"Rise, take the child and his mother, and flee to Egypt, and remain there till I tell you" (Matt 2:13).

As St. Thomas describes at length in his Treatise on the Passions, it is one thing to have passion, but another thing for that passion to be permeated with reason and develop into virtue. Heroic virtue is the mark of the saints and the key criterion for the Vatican's investigation in their cause for canonization. Joseph was a saint. He was a just man, a virtuous man, and his strong passions were also permeated with reason and infused with grace. He placed his passionate heart in the service of God to care for his family, and he faithfully carried out God's will even in the face of great adversity. He was also able to enjoy the goodness, the beauty, and even the sweetness of his wife and their Son. His sensitive heart could suffer at the murder of the innocents in Bethlehem, and his identification with their suffering could spur the energy of anger and hope. Perhaps there was an internal struggle in knowing they would suffer for the sake of his Son. And perhaps he was consoled by remembering that God told him to name his Son "Jesus" for a reason: God saves. And Jesus would save His people. Joseph had hope in that.

The fact that Joseph had a sensitive heart, able to suffer and feel sadness over evil, and the fact that he could still have hope that God could overcome the evil, are the prerequisites for a righteous anger.[2] That anger is the passion that could drive his late-night departure and get his family to safety. It could also drive his prayer for God's salvation and his entrustment of the innocents into God's hands. Although the passion of Joseph's anger would more normally be moderated by the virtue of gentleness, that anger over injustice at the venomous rage of Herod would be well justified. Jesus expressed such anger at length (for thirty-six verses!) in His admonition of the Pharisees (Matt 23:1–36) and then expressed the simultaneously felt sadness over Jerusalem in sentiments He may have even witnessed in His beloved earthly father: "O Jerusalem, Jerusalem, killing the prophets and stoning those who are sent to you! How often would I have gathered your children together as a hen gathers her brood under her wings, and you would not! Behold, your house is forsaken and desolate. For I tell you, you will not see me again, until you say, 'Blessed is he who comes in the name of the Lord'" (Matt 23:37–39).

Constancy and Perseverance

The virtuous man exhibits an integration of the passions through reason. The virtues of patience, perseverance, and gentleness demonstrate a virtuous integration of the

---

[2] "Anger (ira) is the fifth irascible passion and the most complex: caused by sadness, it reaches out in hope for the elimination of that sadness," as expressed in the excellent work by Nicholas E. Lombardo, O.P., *The Logic of Desire: Aquinas on Emotion* (Washington, D.C.: Catholic University of America Press, 2011), 65.

concupiscible and irascible appetites. These virtues were heralded by St. Francis de Sales in his great, final sermon on St. Joseph: "What courage and strength does he not evidence in his victory over our two great enemies, the devil and the world?"[3] Likewise, the Church's officially approved Litany of St. Joseph is a positive theological declaration and includes a list of St. Joseph's virtues and a number of patronal titles. This makes it possible for Fr. Francis Filas, S.J., the great father of Josephology in the twentieth century, to write:

> The Litany of St. Joseph is a prolonged tribute to Joseph's sanctity. In it he is invoked as exercising particular virtues in an outstanding degree: justice, chastity, prudence, bravery, obedience, and faith; and his patronage indicates further virtues of his life: patience, poverty of spirit, industriousness, family care, protection from sin, sympathy for the afflicted and dying, hatred of the devil, and staunch guardianship of the Church.[4]

The virtues are a middle way between two extremes in the passions. Courage (or "bravery") is the median between cowardice and foolhardiness. These virtues are not merely badges of honor to exalt St. Joseph, but the titles in the litany show how they are oriented to works of mercy in "family care, protection from sin, sympathy for

---

[3] Francis de Sales, *Sermon Texts on Saint Joseph*, ed. and trans. Joseph F. Chorpenning, Peregrina Translations Series (Toronto: Peregrina, 1999), 121.

[4] Filas, *Joseph*, 397.

the afflicted and dying," and so on. Furthermore, these strengths in St. Joseph were perfected by his dependence on God, as the litany describes with his "poverty of spirit." Finally, St. Francis de Sales teaches us that St. Joseph's greatest weapon was humility. That's what gave him the power to conquer the devil's pride and to overcome the world's arrogance.[5]

St. Joseph exhibited perseverance in his endurance of great suffering: "With regard to perseverance, the opposite of that interior enemy which is the weariness that comes over us from the continuation of despicable, humiliating, and painful things, of misfortunes if we must speak, or from the various accidents that happen to us: oh how greatly was this saint tried by God and by men in his journey!"[6] St. Joseph endured all this for the sake of God and to prevent his family from suffering it. His humble steadfastness in the face of great trials demonstrates a vigor that is a model for all fathers. He neither exercises vainglorious bravado toward his enemies nor withers under the burdens of his unique vocation. To the contrary, he sustains the middle way of virtue.

"St. Joseph's virtues are those especially of the hidden life, in a degree proportioned to that of his sanctifying grace: virginity, humility, poverty, patience, prudence, fidelity, simplicity, faith enlightened by the gifts of the Holy Ghost, confidence in God, and perfect charity. He preserved what had been confided to him with a fidelity

---

[5] Francis de Sales, *Sermon Texts on Saint Joseph*, 121.
[6] Francis de Sales, *Sermon Texts on Saint Joseph*, 121.

proportioned to its inestimable value."[7] The inclusion of "perfect charity" at the end of the list is the most important of these virtues to notice, and it is precisely through charity that all the virtues are harmonized with the will of God. In fact, it helps us to consider St. Joseph's virtues of courage and perseverance in the light of charity as expressions of those divine qualities of faithful, covenant love captured by the Hebrew word *hesed*.

Pope Francis described *hesed* as the "masculine" form of mercy:

> Mercy, seen in feminine terms, is the tender love of a mother who, touched by the frailty of her newborn baby, takes the child into her arms and provides everything it needs to live and grow (*rahamim*). In masculine terms, mercy is the steadfast fidelity of a father who constantly supports, forgives and encourages his children to grow. Mercy is the fruit of a covenant; that is why God is said to remember his covenant of mercy (*hesed*).[8]

St. Joseph is a man of the covenant, and his steadfast fidelity mirrors that of the heavenly Father. Of course he never needed to forgive Jesus, but he certainly supported Him and encouraged Him to grow. And for those of us

---

[7] Reginald Garrigou-Lagrange, *Mother of the Saviour*, 286.

[8] Pope Francis, First Meditation of a Spiritual Retreat Given for Priests in the Year of Mercy, June 2, 2016, http://www.vatican.va/content/francesco/en/speeches/2016/june/documents/papa-francesco_20160602_giubileo-sacerdoti-prima-meditazione.html.

who accept St. Joseph as a spiritual father, we appreciate
his forgiveness as well. St. Joseph is an image of the heavenly Father, and his vocation is to live out that image for
the sake of the formation of the Incarnate Son's humanity. So we find in St. Joseph the covenant faithfulness of
the heavenly Father. What are the qualities of the Father's
faithfulness?

Abbot Bernard Bonowitz, O.C.S.O., reflected on this
point about St. Joseph in an unpublished retreat he gave
for clergy. He tapped into his Jewish heritage by starting with the translation for *hesed* as "utmost dedication"
or "absolute devotion." Then he outlined the qualities
of God's *hesed*. It is provident—not only providing for
our needs (see Ps 104:10–13), but also providing for the
most important need, which is His Presence, by coming
to meet us (see Exod 33:14). It is vigilant, educative, and
maturing (see Deut 32:10–11; Ps 144:1). It is strong and
mighty and delivers us from our foes (Exod 15:11). It is
self-giving as He reveals His law to Israel (see Exod 20)
and ultimately reveals His inmost secret to us (John 1:18).
It is also costly and suffers the brokenness of the relationship: "[They] provoked the Holy One of Israel" (Ps
78:41). Still God responds with tender mercy (*rahamim*).
His constancy is firm, but not rigid. His steadfast faithfulness always has an outer lining of tender mercy. It is
everlasting: "With everlasting mercy [*hesed*] I will have
compassion [*rahamim*] on you" (Isa 54:7–10).

St. Joseph is a man of the covenant after the Father's
heart. His *hesed* was at the heart of his virtuous fidelity
and was expressed in his marital covenant with Mary and
his fatherly role for Jesus as well as his faithfulness to his

people and their God of the covenant. All these covenants stretched him and caused him an excess of joy and sorrow that he bore with inner strength and absolute devotion.

In this way, we can depend on St. Joseph as a steadfast father and protector. We can bring him our fears, lean on him in our suffering, and count on him to provide for us. His virtuous strength is not merely a demonstration of some personal achievement, but it is a strength in relationship, permeated with love. He is a father who listens to God and does not give up. He goes beyond his own strength by counting on God's providence. He mirrors the Father's steadfast love for us and helps us find a reason for hope.

A New Abraham

St. Paul described Christ as a New Adam (see Rom 5:12–21), and St. Irenaeus described Mary as the New Eve.[9] In a mystical way, Mary represents the Church, and so she takes the position of the Bride of the Risen Christ and the Mother of the Redeemed. Seen in another way, she is Mother of the Head of the Mystical Body of Christ and so of course she is also Mother of the Body, that is, all the baptized. This beautiful theological formulation leaves out St. Joseph. Where does he fit in? Again, his role is over everything, like a veil that covers the mystery. He is the man of the covenant, and according to the genealogy of St. Matthew's gospel (Matt 1:1–15), is the one who

---

[9] See Adv. Hereses III.22.

inserts the Son of Mary into the covenant of Abraham and David. As the genealogy states, Jesus is son of David and son of Abraham (Matt 1:1). This makes Jesus a new Isaac, and it makes Joseph a new Abraham.[10]

First, we find in Joseph the just man, a man of the covenant. Pope Benedict XVI described this beautifully:

> The designation of Joseph as a just man (*zaddik*) extends far beyond the decision he takes at this moment: it gives an overall picture of Saint Joseph and at the same time it aligns him with the great figures of the Old Covenant—beginning with Abraham, the just. If we may say that the form of piety found in the New Testament can be summed up in the expression "a believer," then the Old Testament idea of a whole life lived according to sacred Scripture is summed up in the idea of a "just man."[11]

Furthermore, St. Joseph was a man who was rooted in the revealed word of God, like the man of Psalm 1: "Blessed is the man . . . [whose] delight is in the law of the LORD, and on his law he meditates day and night" (Ps 1:1–2):

> Psalm 1 presents the classic image of the "just" man. We might well think of it as a portrait of

---

[10] This idea of Joseph as a new Abraham comes from the retreat conferences of Abbot Bernard Bonowitz, O.C.S.O.

[11] Pope Benedict XVI, *Jesus of Nazareth*, 39.

the spiritual figure of Saint Joseph. A just man, it tells us, is one who maintains living contact with the word of God, who "delights in the law of the Lord" (v. 2). He is like a tree, planted beside the flowing waters, constantly bringing forth fruit. The flowing waters, from which he draws nourishment, naturally refer to the living word of God, into which he sinks the roots of his being. God's will is not a law imposed on him from without, it is "joy." For him the law is simply Gospel, good news, because he reads it with a personal, loving openness to God and in this way learns to understand and live it from deep within.[12]

Although Abraham did not have any written words from God to sink the roots of his being into, he clung to the word God spoke to him and the covenant God made with him: "Abraham believed God, and it was reckoned to him as righteousness" (Rom 4:3, quoting Gen 15:6). Abraham clung to the word God spoke to him as Joseph clung to the words spoken to him in the dreams. Even more impossible than the conception granted to Abraham, who was beyond childbearing age, God made a special covenant with Joseph to be the father of one son whom he would not be involved in conceiving in his virginal wife. Joseph was faithful to that covenant that was made with God in a dream through the intervention of an angel, not unlike the covenant God made with Abram while he was in "a deep sleep" (Gen 15:12). Furthermore,

---

[12] Pope Benedict XVI, *Jesus of Nazareth*, 39–40.

from the Son of Joseph, like the son of Abraham, there came forth blessings for all nations and descendants as numerous as the stars: "From one man, and him as good as dead, were born descendants as many as the stars of heaven and as the innumerable grains of sand by the seashore" (Heb 11:12).

The parallels of Isaac and Jesus are clear and give us another insight into the faith of Joseph, who "sacrificed" his Son with faith analogous to Abraham's. His ritual offering of Jesus in the Temple was a kind of reiteration of the offering of Isaac on that same mountain. And we can imagine the suffering he bore in the anticipation of the future offering he would make in not being able to protect his Son from being a sign of contradiction (see Luke 2:34).

Like Abraham, Joseph was called by God to make a great journey to an unknown land for an unspecified amount of time:

> By faith Abraham obeyed when he was called to go out to a place which he was to receive as an inheritance; and he went out, not knowing where he was to go. By faith he sojourned in the land of promise, as in a foreign land, living in tents with Isaac and Jacob, heirs with him of the same promise. For he looked forward to the city which has foundations, whose builder and maker is God. (Heb 11:8–10)

In Joseph's obedience, like in Abraham's, we find a man of tremendous interior strength and faithfulness. To return to the description offered by Pope Benedict XVI, we can see that this strength derived from being rooted in the word of God. The words spoken by an angel to Joseph in a dream were finally written down decades after they were spoken. Like Abraham, he must have repeated them to himself over and over, especially when the journey was tiring and the nights grew very dark.

Seeing St. Joseph as a new Abraham can also help us reconcile the image of an old Joseph with the image of a youthful one. Abraham was truly an old man and yet, even at one hundred years of age, he was fruitful in begetting a son and vigorous in raising him. There was nothing listless, lazy, or lifeless about him. This was the strength of Joseph's righteousness and obedience:

> It is important to underline that Joseph's obedience is not passivity. He is not ruled by fear; he is not resentful of God for what has been asked for him. He is not a person lacking in energy or creativity who accepts the divine initiative because he's too lazy or uninventive to come up with a life-plan for himself. To "hear the voice of the Lord and to love him with all one's heart, soul, strength and mind"—and to express this love consistently in all one's actions and decisions—this is supreme activity. [13]

It is this faithful, covenant love, this *hesed*, that St. Joseph can help us with as well. When our spirit grows

---

[13] Unpublished retreat conference of Abbot Bernard Bonowitz, O.C.S.O.

tired, when our suffering increases, when our fears and doubts begin to mount, St. Joseph can provide the strength and reassurance that we need to persevere in our own covenant with God that was made through the Blood of his Son.

Demons and Death

Two of the most fearful realities we regularly face are demons and death. St. Joseph's passionate, strong, faithful love comes to our aid against these enemies with a particular effectiveness. He is a shelter for us in our fears of these two great enemies, who are beyond our natural powers to overcome.

Terror of Demons

One of the titles from the Litany of St. Joseph that people find particularly intriguing is "Terror of Demons." It is not entirely clear where this title came from. As expressed earlier, St. Joseph and St. Michael both protected Mary and Jesus from demonic fury, but St. Michael was more likely to do that in a terrifying way (see Rev 12). St. Joseph preferred the hiddenness of humility, silence, and obedience. He was more inclined to use a cloaking device than take up swords and spears. He was an expert at protecting the Holy Family in such a firm but gentle way that he didn't scare the Baby.

Perhaps this is what is so terrifying to the demons. The stealth of St. Joseph veils us and hides us from their sight.

They do not know when we are slipping past them and simply evading their snares. St. Joseph was threatened by the demonic fury of Herod, but he slipped away. St. Joseph evaded the demonic hatred of Antipas by hiding with his little family in Nazareth. In their hidden life in Nazareth, which they lived under Joseph's care in an unremarkably ordinary way, they remained hidden for thirty years from the devil's rage. It is in these hidden, humble, obedient ways that St. Joseph terrorizes the demons. They cannot find him, let alone touch him. And they never know when he is raising up saints for the Kingdom. By placing ourselves under his paternal care, we can benefit from his protection like Mary and Jesus did.

In the next chapter, we will explore some connections between St. Joseph and St. Benedict. One of the connections was this power for protection against evil. In several episodes of his life, St. Benedict and his monks were attacked by the devil's disturbance. Unafraid because he was confident in God's power, St. Benedict expelled demons repeatedly through the Sign of the Cross, exposed demonic illusions through humble prayer, repaired damage caused by the devil through miraculous interventions, and freed a possessed seminarian through a simple command. His ministry against evil continues in the form of his intercession obtained through Benedictine medals that are marked with his Sign of the Cross.[14]

St. Joseph and St. Benedict help us to realize that the

---

[14] The letters CSPB on every Benedict medal signify the Latin phrase *Crux Sancti Patris Benedicti*, meaning "The Cross of Holy Father Benedict."

devil has more reason to be afraid of us than we of him. With the help of St. Joseph, Terror of Demons, we can trust in God's tender care for us to protect us, hide us, and deliver us from evil.

Patron of a Happy Death

St. Joseph also plays an important role at the end of our life. One might say that this is the most important service that any saint could offer: to assist us in having a happy death. We repeatedly ask Mary to pray for us at the "hour of our death," and according to pious traditions, St. Joseph was the happy recipient of this grace. In fact, St. Joseph's own death was so blessed by the Presence of his Son, who is the Son of God, and his wife, who is the Immaculate Virgin Mary, that he has been widely revered as the patron of a happy death. St. Alphonsus reasoned it out in this way:

> Since we all must die, we should cherish a special devotion to St. Joseph, that he may obtain for us a happy death. All Christians regard him as the advocate of the dying who had honored him during their life, and they do so for three reasons: First, because Jesus Christ loved him not only as a friend, but as a father, and on this account his mediation is far more efficacious than that of any other Saint. Second, because St. Joseph has obtained special power against the evil spirits, who tempt us with redoubled vigor at the hour of death. Third, the assistance given St. Joseph at

his death by Jesus and Mary obtained for him the right to secure a holy and peaceful death for his servants. Hence, if they invoke him at the hour of death he will not only help them, but he will also obtain for them the assistance of Jesus and Mary.[15]

Death has a terrifying quality to it because it is a journey we only make once, and it takes us into a place from which we never return. Although we get daily practice through that approximation of death which we call "sleep," and while Christian piety has encouraged the practice of reflecting daily on our death—*memento mori*—we do not naturally become comfortable with such an unnatural end to our earthly life. Although everyone dies, it cannot be called natural, since "God did not make death, and he does not delight in the death of the living" (Wis 1:13).

Death is especially tragic for those who seem to have more life left in them, more promise, more to accomplish. Accidental deaths are so painful and so hard for the survivors to recover from. Even for those advanced in years, there are dreams that remain unfulfilled. A classic example of this is St. Francis Xavier, whose life was prolific but fell short of his dream of reaching China. Pope Francis reflected:

I have always liked to dwell on the twilight of a Jesuit, when a Jesuit is nearing the end of life, on

---

[15] St. Alphonsus Ligouri, CSsR, quoted in José A. Rodrigues, *St. Joseph: Son of David* (Victoria, BC: First Choice Books, 2014), 108.

when he is setting. . . a classical image, that of St
Francis Xavier looking at China. Art has so often
depicted this passing, Xavier's end. So has literature, in that beautiful piece by Pemán. At the end,
without anything but before the Lord; thinking of
this does me good.[16]

Knowing how to pass on the mantle is part of a happy
death. It was the death of Simeon, who saw the salvation
he was promised (Luke 2:29–32), and the death of Moses,
who saw the promised land (Deut 34:1). It was the death
of Elijah, who passed on the mantle to his successor,
Elisha (2 Kgs 2:11–12), and the death of Paul the hermit,
who first beheld his successor, the great St. Anthony.[17]

Awareness of our death helps us to live more fully, and
so St. Benedict counsels us to keep death daily before our
eyes.[18] St. Benedict himself was blessed with a happy death
and is therefore invoked as patron of a happy death. With
the help of his brothers, he was able to move from his
bed to the chapel and die with his arms upraised in praise
to God. Although the devil tries to use the fear of death
to keep us bound, Jesus destroys the devil and the power
of death through His Cross and Resurrection (see Heb
2:14–15). This makes it possible for Christians to enjoy a

---

[16] Pope Francis, Homily on the Occasion of the Feast of St. Ignatius, July
31, 2013, http://www.vatican.va/content/francesco/en/homilies/2013/
documents/papa-francesco_20130731_omelia-sant-ignazio.html.

[17] St. Jerome, "Life of St. Paul the First Hermit," in *Early Christian
Biographies*, ed. Hermigild Dressler and Roy J. Deferrari, trans. Marie
Liguori Ewald, Vol. 15, The Fathers of the Church (Washington,
D.C.: Catholic University of America Press, 1952), 229.

[18] RB 4:47.

happy death, knowing that for them life is changed, not ended, as it says in the Preface of the funeral Mass.

This allows the Christian tradition to describe death in more positive terms as a birth, and so the death date of saints can be celebrated as their birthday into heaven. In fact, as described earlier, St. Augustine made this even more explicit and described baptism as an entrance into the womb of Mary until the Christian is born into eternal life.[19] We can see this birth as we described it earlier—a birth into a new way of living in Christ—but we can also look at it in its definitive form as our entrance into eternity. This drastically changes the way we view death. Although every baby experiences a form of trauma in passing through the birth canal, there is something so wonderful about the new life that opens up postpartum. Similar to babies, whose world radically changes after their departure from their mother's womb, our life will radically change after our departure from this world. The good news is that, thanks to Christ, we can have confidence that we will be passing into something better, and just as St. Joseph initially received Christ from the womb of Mary, we pray he will be there to receive us in our new birth into eternity as well.

A Prayer of Entrustment to the Sleeping Joseph

When we are feeling weak, or when we are suffering or fearful, we can find strength from St. Joseph by simply

[19] Quoted in Louis de Montfort, *The Secret of Mary*, 1998.

turning to him in prayer. There are many devotional prayers
of the Church that have grown throughout the last centuries from the lived faith of the many little ones who
have looked to St. Joseph as a father and friend. Fr. Filas
collected many of the officially approved prayers of the
Church in his great work on St. Joseph.[20] Fr. Calloway likewise gathered many of the beautiful prayers to St. Joseph in
his book on consecration to St. Joseph.[21]

In this section, we mention just one devotion that is
particularly tender and offer one prayer that could help us
entrust ourselves to St. Joseph's loving care in our times
of fear and suffering. The devotion is to the Sleeping
Joseph. Knowing that St. Joseph took his cares to bed
with him and received divine illumination in the night
helps us lay down our troubles so that we can enter into
sleep. Nighttime is particularly difficult for us, and the
anxieties of the day can interfere with our rest. That only
leads to further troubles as sleep deprivation makes us
even less able to handle the anxieties of a new day. Likewise, as we mentioned earlier, there is a kind of death that
takes place in sleep as we give up our consciousness and
hand over the control of our lives. We will have to leave
some things unfinished at the end of the day and likely
also at the end of our lives. St. Joseph longed to see the
salvation of the whole world, but he had to entrust its
final accomplishment to his Son without his further help
during His earthly life.

For all these reasons, St. Joseph can help us surrender

[20] Filas, *Joseph*, 637–652.
[21] Calloway, *Consecration to St. Joseph*, 233–248.

the anxieties of the day. The devotion that has developed and has been especially embraced by Pope Francis is to place our anxieties and petitions beneath an image of the Sleeping Joseph. When we have troubles that we cannot overcome or puzzles that we cannot solve, we can write them on a little piece of paper and place them under the Sleeping Joseph. Having entrusted them to him, we can let them go and try to enter into sleep ourselves.

Although it can seem trite or simplistic, there is something profound at work in this devotion. We are often plagued by unnamed anxieties that we do not acknowledge. Sometimes it is too hard to acknowledge them or we avoid them because we are afraid they will overcome us and expose our powerlessness. Consciously or unconsciously, we activate the protectors of denial or avoidance.

On the other hand, when we know that St. Joseph is able to handle our fears, doubts, anxieties, and sufferings, it can give us courage to face what is troubling us and entrust it to him. Then we can even acknowledge it and write it down and get it outside of ourselves. That already gives us a feeling of making it smaller by making it fit on a piece of paper. And we can even make it disappear in a small way as we place it under the little statue of the Sleeping Joseph.

Perhaps this explains why, when Pope Francis requested only a very few items be sent to him from Buenos Aires after he was elected pope, he included his statue of the Sleeping Joseph. He spoke about this to families in his Apostolic Journey to the Philippines:

I would also like to tell you something very personal. I have great love for Saint Joseph, because he is a man of silence and strength. On my table I have an image of Saint Joseph sleeping. Even when he is asleep, he is taking care of the Church! Yes! We know that he can do that. So when I have a problem, a difficulty, I write a little note and I put it underneath Saint Joseph, so that he can dream about it! In other words I tell him: pray for this problem![22]

A prayer that we can offer when we make this act of devotion is:

O St. Joseph, you are a man greatly favored by the Most High. The angel of the Lord appeared to you in dreams, while you slept, to warn you and guide you as you cared for the Holy Family. You were both silent and strong, a loyal and courageous protector. Dear St. Joseph, as you rest in the Lord, confident in his absolute power and goodness, look upon me. Please take me into your heart, dream of it, and present it to your Son (*mention your request*). Help me then, good St. Joseph, to hear the voice of God, to arise, and to act with love. I praise and thank God with joy. Saint Joseph, I love you. Amen.[23]

---

[22] Pope Francis, Address at a Meeting of Families in Manila, January 16, 2015, http://www.vatican.va/content/francesco/en/speeches/2015/january/documents/papa-francesco_20150116_srilanka-filippine-incontro-famiglie.html.

[23] Calloway, *Consecration to St. Joseph*, 247.

Chapter Six

Joseph Option

At this point, I hope the reader has been blessed with a greater closeness to Jesus through the heart of St. Joseph by traveling along the pathways of vulnerability, silence, littleness, and hiddenness. When we are blessed, we spontaneously want to share the blessing. We can obviously do that through witnessing to our experience. Pope St. Paul VI observed the importance of witnesses in our time when he taught, "Modern man listens more willingly to witnesses than to teachers, and if he does listen to teachers, it is because they are witnesses."[1] In addition to encouraging others to follow these pathways by witnessing to our personal experience, it is also possible to cultivate an environment in which others could encounter St. Joseph more easily. Such environments could have a powerful influence on individuals and could even become a leaven for a renewal of culture and society. We could call this the Joseph Option.

St. Joseph cultivated Nazareth, and the Joseph Option

---

[1] Pope St. Paul VI, Apostolic Exhortation on Evangelization in the Modern World *Evangelii Nuntiandi* (December 8, 1975), §41.

is the decision to cultivate Nazareths in our own lives. We learn this by taking the time to visit Nazareth in our prayer, in all the ways we have described in the preceding chapters. We need to spend time in the midst of the Holy Family. We do that best by becoming like them in silence and hiddenness and by becoming receptive to their love through vulnerability and littleness. Although we detailed some of their extraordinary experiences earlier in the book, following them to Bethlehem, Egypt, and Jerusalem, here we bring the qualities of the Holy Family into our daily lives by following them into Nazareth.

From one perspective, Nazareth was so completely uninspiring that Nathaniel could exclaim, "Can anything good come out of Nazareth?" (John 1:46). To reinforce this perspective, we can see that Nazareth was so plain that the Scripture offers us no details of the life there. The ordinariness of the Holy Family's life in Nazareth was also acknowledged by townspeople who were shocked at Jesus's supernatural mission (let alone His divine nature!). In fact, they expressed their surprise by referencing His relationship to Joseph as if that were enough to prove their point: "Is not this Joseph's son?" (Luke 4:22; see also John 6:42, Matt 13:55). Jesus and Joseph apparently lived very ordinary lives in Nazareth.

The ordinariness of Nazareth gives us the courage to believe that we could truly cultivate our own Nazareths. This is not only for the rich, the famous, or the highly skilled. It is for everyone. We can choose the Joseph Option. We can develop an environment and live in it in a way that helps others to encounter Jesus and Mary through the heart of St. Joseph.

Why call it "The Joseph Option"? There is an intentional connection between the Joseph Option and Rod Dreher's *The Benedict Option*. *The Benedict Option* looked to the example of St. Benedict as a model for Christian living in our own time. Dreher proposed that especially in these post-Christendom times, Christians could find inspiration and direction from the Patriarch of Western Monasticism, who also became a father of Western civilization. His insights encourage us to build a new Christian culture from the ground up, similar to the way St. Benedict did.[2]

I would like to propose that St. Benedict was just living out the Joseph Option. The original model for the sanctification of daily life and love was in Nazareth under the headship of Joseph. St. Joseph was the abbot of a very small monastery. We will see a number of connections between the monastic life of Benedict and the home life of Joseph. Thus we can see that St. Benedict was simply showing one way to implement the Joseph Option. At the same time, since Nazareth was not actually a monastery but was rather the home for a family, we can connect monastic life and family life through the heart of St. Joseph.

St. Benedict's "School": Another Nazareth

St. Benedict described the monastery as a school:

---

[2] Rod Dreher, *The Benedict Option: A Strategy for Christians in a Post-Christian Nation* (New York: Sentinel, 2017).

Therefore we intend to establish a school for the Lord's service. In drawing up its regulations, we hope to set down nothing harsh, nothing burdensome. The good of all concerned, however, may prompt us to a little strictness in order to amend faults and to safeguard love. Do not be daunted immediately by fear and run away from the road that leads to salvation. It is bound to be narrow at the outset. But as we progress in this way of life and in faith, we shall run on the path of God's commandments, our hearts overflowing with the inexpressible delight of love. Never swerving from his instructions, then, but faithfully observing his teaching in the monastery until death, we shall through patience share in the sufferings of Christ that we may deserve also to share in his kingdom. Amen.[3]

A school is where we grow in knowledge and virtue. In St. Benedict's school, we learn about the Lord and about how to serve Him. We learn about the good of others. We grow in virtue as we cultivate that good and also as we restrain ourselves in order to amend faults. We learn to face our fears with the virtues of hope and courage as we progress in life and faith. We learn patience and perseverance in suffering, and as we continue on the path, we come to taste the inexpressible delights of love.

Pope St. Paul VI described Nazareth in a similar way when he visited there in 1964:

---

[3] RB Prol 45–50.

Nazareth is the school in which we begin to understand the life of Jesus. It is the school of the Gospel. Here we learn to observe, to listen, to meditate, and to penetrate the profound and mysterious meaning of that simple, humble, and lovely manifestation of the Son of God. And perhaps we learn almost imperceptibly to imitate Him. Here we learn the method by which we can come to understand Christ.[4]

The Pope inspires us to understand and imitate Christ by visiting Nazareth spiritually and mystically. We learn about the Lord there through this method: "observe," "listen," "meditate," and we will "penetrate" the mystery. That mystery is clothed in a "simple," "humble," and "lovely" veil. We slowly start to imitate Christ "almost imperceptibly" as we take up residence in this school. Mary and Joseph were the first two who learned to imitate Christ. Interestingly, Jesus's human formation also included imitating them, and as we form our own Nazareths, we will almost imperceptibly imitate Mary and Joseph as well.

Joseph and Mary also had to face their fears, and Nazareth was for them a school of patience and perseverance. They knew their Son's destiny to suffer and be a sign of contradiction at a global level (see Luke 2:34). They knew that their Son was free and ultimately beholden only to

---

4 Pope St. Paul VI, Homily in the Basilica of the Annunciation in Nazareth during His Pilgrimage to the Holy Land, January 5, 1964, https://www.papalencyclicals.net/paul06/p6reflect.htm.

the heavenly Father, despite the anxiety this might cause
them (see Luke 2:48–49). They never knew when Joseph
would have another dream and they would have to flee
from another murderous tyrant. Mary and Joseph learned
to love their Son with open hands. They could not cling to
Him as He made clear when He declared in the Temple,
"Did you not know that I must be in my Father's house?"
(Luke 2:49b).[5] Nazareth was a school of daily trust, of
accepting each day on its own terms with gratitude.

St. Benedict's Rule is a mixture of Christian instruction and rules for daily life. There are only three chapters
dedicated to specific virtues, and they are obedience (RB
5), silence (RB 6), and humility (RB 7). These virtues are
foundational and essential for monastic life. They are also
the virtues that we encounter in the life of Joseph and
Mary, as we have already seen in earlier chapters. As St.
Benedict teaches in the Rule, all three are interrelated.
For example, silence and obedience are important aspects
of humility. St. Benedict says that obedience is the third
step of humility, and the ninth step is restraint of speech.
A humble monk does not raise his voice in protest against
his abbot, for example. Likewise, silence and humility are
important attitudes for living out obedience, since true
obedience is not merely external conformity but also a
humble, silent, internal acceptance.

We choose the Joseph Option when we cultivate
these three virtues and create environments formed in

5   For a beautiful account of Joseph's share in the Paschal Mystery, see
Frederick L. Miller, *St. Joseph: Our Father in Faith* (New Haven, CT:
Catholic Information Service, 2008), 25–30.

these virtues. The more that we can bring silence, obedience, and humility into our daily lives, the more we will create environments of reverence, tenderness, patience, and love. Like Benedictine monasteries have done for centuries, these environments help visitors to meet Jesus in the faces, presence, docility, gentleness, and hospitality of those who imitate the virtues of St. Joseph. By building a school for the Lord's service in which the virtues of St. Joseph are practiced, St. Benedict implemented the Joseph Option.

Tender Authority

What does authority look like in the Joseph Option? Pope Francis gave a picture of this when he described Nazareth as the School of St. Joseph: "During the hidden years in Nazareth, Jesus learned at the school of Joseph to do the will of the Father. That will was to be his daily food (cf. Jn 4:34)."[6]

Joseph had no small task. It was his responsibility to teach Jesus to do the will of the Father! At first, that seems overwhelming, but as we press into it, we discover how ordinary God's will really is. When Joseph asked Jesus to do His chores and complete certain tasks necessary for their carpentry projects, when he asked Him for a cup of cold water, or when they went together to visit a sick neighbor, in each case they were doing the will of the Father. At the same time, we know that Joseph

---

[6] Pope Francis, *Patris Corde*, §3.

would not abuse his authority and ask of Jesus anything unnecessary or purely selfish, let alone sinful. Here we see a richer understanding of obedience as St. Benedict also understood it. Obedience is not just carrying out commands, but more broadly it involves accepting reality. Obedience to the Father's will accepts rainy days along with droughts. In humble, silent obedience, we trust that God will give us whatever we need in order to do what He wants us to do (see 2 Cor 9:8).

In his monasteries, St. Benedict prescribed the need for an "abbot" (derived from the Hebrew *abba*, meaning "father"), who serves as the monks' father in Christ, and he insisted: "The abbot must always remember what his title signifies."[7] Furthermore, he described what the abbot must do in order to be truly fatherly:

> Anyone who receives the name of abbot is to lead his disciples by a twofold teaching: he must point out to them all that is good and holy more by example than by words, proposing the commandments of the Lord to receptive disciples with words, but demonstrating God's instructions to the stubborn and the dull by a living example.[8]

This means that the abbot must strive to live the very same virtues he is teaching the monks to live out. And so we see that in the monastery, as in Nazareth, the teacher and the pupils are all striving to live out the same virtues.

---

[7] RB 2:1.
[8] RB 2:11–12.

When we think about Nazareth as a school where the teachers and pupils are all living out the virtues of obedience, silence, and humility, it gives us a picture of the kind of environment we can create if we take the Joseph Option. In such a place, there are superiors (e.g. abbots, mothers, fathers, business owners, managers, etc.) who must make decisions, but the decisions are made with care, forethought, and reverence for those who must carry them out. And for their part, the pupils carry out the master's instructions with trust and love. In this way, as St. Benedict described it, there are rules, carefully laid down to amend faults and safeguard love, but never anything harsh or burdensome.[9]

In a monastery, it is more obvious why we need an abbot and regulations, but one might question why the sinless Son of God and His sinless mother needed such structures in Nazareth. Therein we discover that human mediation is part of God's perfect plan, and so it is also part of the Joseph Option. St. Benedict was not only creating remedies for sin but was also implementing a divine pattern in his communities. It is a divine principle for God's love to be communicated through creaturely mediation. Although God could accomplish everything directly, He chooses to work through fragile human vessels (see 2 Cor 4:7). Thus, even if a monastery or a family were to be filled with saints, there would still be a role for order and authority under a leader. The hierarchy of mediation that reaches up to God Himself is part of the divine design and not merely a governance structure

---

[9] See RB Prol 46–47.

for sinful men. The divine pattern is always an inverted triangle, however, with the greatest being on the bottom in order to serve the least, as Jesus repeatedly insisted with His Apostles (see Matt 20:26, 23:11; Mark 9:35, 10:43).

Sometimes, in Christian practice, a devaluing of human relationships and human mediation can develop. Those who are struggling are sometimes dismissed by the strong to go and find God directly in prayer as if He would prefer to substitute a spiritual solution or even work a miracle rather than work through a human response to a human problem. Sometimes people even piously challenge the suffering not to need human support by claiming that God should be enough for them. The correction of St. James still applies, however: "If a brother or sister is poorly clothed and in lack of daily food, and one of you says to them, 'Go in peace, be warmed and filled,' without giving them the things needed for the body, what does it profit?" (Jas 2:15–16). As Jesus told the Apostles, "You give them something to eat" (Matt 14:16). Although God could have saved us in a different way, He chose to save us through the human flesh of His Son, born into the human marriage of Joseph and Mary. Jesus learned in childhood that His Father would provide bread, and so in the beginning of His public ministry, He could resist Satan's temptation to bypass human mediation by turning stones into bread. God continues to prefer human and angelic means to mediate His grace. It is the challenge for those in authority to learn a way of tenderness that most easily communicates divine tenderness to those in their care.

In the Joseph Option, the one who has authority also has the responsibility to provide for the others. St. Joseph has often been compared to the Old Testament patriarch Joseph because of the way he provided for the Holy Family as well as the way he continues to provide for us. In the Church's liturgy, the words of Jesus have been applied to Joseph in many of the prayers: "[This] is the faithful and wise servant, whom his master has set over his household," but the completion of the verse is also important: "to give them their food at the proper time" (Matt 24:45). Joseph received authority so that he could provide for the Holy Family. And when Bl. Pius IX declared St. Joseph the patron of the Church, he acknowledged that St. Joseph maintains that authority to care for the Church as he did for the Holy Family. Anyone who is in a position to care for the Church is thus summoned to choose the Joseph Option and care for her as St. Joseph does. When he was being ordained for diplomatic service, Pope St. John XXIII chose his ordination date as March 19, the Solemnity of St. Joseph, because he saw the excellence of St. Joseph as a model for his service to the Church. He explained that to Cardinal Gasparri:

> "This is the Saint We think would be the ideal teacher and patron for diplomats of the Holy See."

> "Oh! Is that so?" said the Cardinal. "I would never have guessed that."

> "Well, you see, your Eminence, it's this way.

Knowing how to obey; knowing how to keep quiet;
when need be, speaking with care and reserve.
That's the diplomat of the Holy See; and that's
St. Joseph. Just picture him setting out for Bethlehem at once out of obedience; carefully looking
for some place to stay; and then watching over
the cave; eight days after the birth of Jesus, pre-
siding over the Jewish rite that made a new-born
child one of the chosen people (cf. Gen. 9:12).
Just picture him receiving with honor the Magi,
those splendid ambassadors from the East. Just
see him on the roads of Egypt and then back at
Nazareth, always silent and obedient: showing
Jesus to people and hiding him: defending him
and taking care of him. And as for himself, just
following along quietly, remaining in the shadow
of the mysteries of Our Lord, and seeing a little
heavenly light thrown upon them every so often
by an angel."[10]

Lastly, we learn from St. Joseph a way of mercy that is
exemplary for leaders, as Pope Francis exhorted us:

Joseph's attitude encourages us to accept and
welcome others as they are, without exception,
and to show special concern for the weak, for God
chooses what is weak (cf. 1 Cor 1:27). He is the

[10] From an audience with devotees of St. Joseph on March 19, 1961,
published in *The Pope Speaks VII*, 133, quoted in Blaine Burkey,
O.F.M., "John XIII: Pope of Saint Joseph," *The American Ecclesiastical
Review* 149 (July 1963): 2–13.

"Father of orphans and protector of widows" (Ps 68:6), who commands us to love the stranger in our midst. I like to think that it was from Saint Joseph that Jesus drew inspiration for the parable of the prodigal son and the merciful father (cf. Lk 15:11-32).[11]

Living in the Mysteries

As we recognized earlier, Joseph was always living in the presence of God. A critical aspect of the Joseph Option therefore involves cultivating an environment that helps others become sensitive to God's abiding presence. This could be a description of St. Benedict's entire project in the Holy Rule. One can read the whole Rule through the lens of the verse "We believe that the divine presence is everywhere . . ."[12] Throughout the Rule, St. Benedict teaches the monk how to find God everywhere: in prayer, in reading, in work, in the sick, in the guest, in the young, in the old, in the abbot, in the brethren, in the refectory, in waking, in sleeping, in the ringing of the bells, and so on. The life of the monk is arranged by the Rule to cultivate contemplation: a constant, loving awareness of God's presence. The monk is summoned to practice this especially by paying close attention to God's presence in the Divine Office.[13]

---

[11] Pope Francis, *Patris Corde*, §4.
[12] RB 19:1.
[13] RB 19:2.

St. Benedict helps the monks tune in to God's presence by teaching them that the tools of the workshop are to be treated like the sacred vessels of the altar.[14] He teaches them to pay attention to God's presence in the voice of the young.[15] He teaches them to be obedient to the voice of God speaking through the abbot.[16] It is the responsibility of the monk, then, to practice this form of recollection. Remembering St. Benedict's words, along with the words of Holy Scripture, the monk can repeatedly stir up an awareness of God's presence throughout the day. We can think of how Joseph may have done that as he spent time in the presence of Jesus. While he watched his Son with a saw or a hammer, he was probably periodically caught up in wonder as he remembered the words of the angel he had heard in the dream: "He will save his people from their sins" (Matt 1:21).

The Benedictine life is also arranged around frequent restarts, which each allow a concrete opportunity for recollection. The repeated gatherings in the chapel provide one obvious way, but also the practice of beginning activities with prayer[17] or the arrangement of the refectory where the monks eat.[18] Although these are mundane tasks and can seem insignificant, our lives are made up primarily of such mundane things. The path for growth in the spiritual life follows from sanctifying such ordinary, daily activities. St. Thérèse exemplified this as she explicitly

---

[14] RB 31:10.
[15] RB 3:3.
[16] RB 2:3–5.
[17] RB Prol 4.
[18] RB 38:1–12.

reflected on her closeness to Jesus, Mary, and Joseph in the mundane task of eating:

> In the refectory we have but one thing to do: perform a lowly action with lofty thoughts. I confess that the sweetest aspirations of love often come to me in the refectory. Sometimes I am brought to a standstill by the thought that were Our Lord in my place He would certainly partake of those same dishes which are served to me. It is quite probable that during His lifetime He tasted of similar food—He must have eaten bread and fruit.

> Here are my little rubrics:

> I imagine myself at Nazareth, in the house of the Holy Family. If, for instance, I am served with salad, cold fish, wine, or anything pungent in taste, I offer it to St. Joseph. To our Blessed Lady I offer hot foods and ripe fruit, and to the Infant Jesus our feast-day fare, especially broth, rice, and preserves. Lastly, when I am served a wretched dinner I say cheerfully: "Today, my little one, it is all for you!"[19]

In order to stir this watchfulness in his monks, St. Benedict reminds them that God is also watching them: "Let [the monk] recall that he is always seen by God in

---

[19] Thérèse of Lisieux, *The Story of a Soul*, 238–39.

heaven, that his actions everywhere are in God's sight and are reported by angels at every hour."[20] While this could be a fear-inducing reminder, it reads better when we think about St. Joseph watching Jesus. Joseph could watch Him endlessly. He watched Him with a father's love, fascinated by His identity and His destiny. We wish he had reported more about those observations, but we can take consolation in knowing that at least the angels recorded everything, and one day we hope to hear the stories. Nazareth is a place where the Little One is always seen by His father and His father delights even in the little things He does.

St. Thérèse reflected on that quality of Nazareth in her autobiography:

> When I picture the Holy Family, the thought that does me most good is—the simplicity of their home-life. Our Lady and St. Joseph were well aware that Jesus was God, while at the same time great wonders were hidden from them, and—like us—they lived by faith. You have heard those words of the Gospel: "*They understood not the word that He spoke unto them*"; and those others no less mysterious: "*His Father and Mother were wondering at those things which were spoken concerning Him.*" They seemed to be learning something new, for this word "wondering" implies a certain amount of surprise.[21]

---

[20] RB 7:13

[21] Thérèse of Lisieux, *The Story of a Soul*, 249.

The Joseph Option cultivates environments in which the little ones are seen and cared for and delighted in. When one is in a place where everyone knows her name and celebrates her accomplishments, even when they seem small or insignificant, she can feel that God is very close to her at all times. Contrast that with environments that are governed by suspicion, criticism, negativity, and cynicism, where one must always be on guard against attack.

In the gentleness of St. Benedict's monastery, even negative responses were to be delivered with kindness. The procurator, who is the one chosen by the abbot to be responsible for the goods of the monastery, must be humble and kind even when he must sometimes deny a monk's request. St. Benedict wrote: "Above all, let him be humble. If goods are not available to meet a request, he will offer a kind word in reply, for it is written: A kind word is better than the best gift (Sir 18:17)."[22] Furthermore, St. Benedict is sensitive to those who have greater needs, while he calls those who are stronger to be grateful that they need less: "Whoever needs less should thank God and not be distressed, but whoever needs more should feel humble because of his weakness, not self-important because of the kindness shown him."[23] Once again, it is easy to imagine that St. Joseph could delight in his every opportunity to provide for Jesus. It was not a burden for him to offer Jesus his time, attention, kindness, patience, and every good at his disposal.

---

[22] RB 31:13–14.
[23] RB 34:3–4.

Ora et Labora

Modern man has an ambivalent relationship with work. From speaking to some people, one can get the idea that real life only happens on evenings and weekends after work is done. On the other hand, we seem to have lost our evenings and weekends. The reservation of these times for family and worship, times that once were protected by law, has all but disappeared in the Western world. The laws that used to protect menial labor from cash-thirsty businesses have dissolved in most places, resulting in shifts covering twenty-four hours of work each day and continuing seven days a week. While the forty-nine early Church Abitene martyrs refused to live without observing the Lord's Day (they professed: *"sine Dominico non possumus!"* meaning "without Sunday we cannot live!"),[24] it seems that modern man would be more likely to cry "without 24/7 Superstores we cannot live!"

Pope Benedict XVI observed the effect this is having on us:

> Technical progress, especially in the area of transport and communications, has made human life more comfortable but also more keyed up, at times even frenetic. Cities are almost always noisy, silence is rarely to be found in them because there is always background noise, in some areas even at

---

[24] Pope Benedict XVI, Homily for the Closing of the 24th Italian Eucharistic Congress in Bari, May 29, 2005, http://www.vatican. va/content/benedict-xvi/en/homilies/2005/documents/hf_ben-xvi_ hom_20050529_bari.html.

night. . . . It has reached a level such as to give rise
to talk about anthropological mutation.[25]

Some people seek the meaning of their lives in their
work, making their work an idol and making them work-
aholics. Others argue that if work were made optional,
as in the case of a basic guaranteed income, then many
people would devolve into helpless blobs of consumption.[26]
Christian doctrine has always provided a balanced
picture of work. On the one hand, Judaism and Christianity helped to establish the weekend for religious
and family purposes with an observance of the Satur-
day Sabbath for the Jews and the Sunday Lord's Day
for the Christians. When we put God first and rest well,
we work better. St. Teresa of Calcutta used to say to her
sisters, "Pray well, eat well, work well." St. Benedict and
St. Joseph communicate the same message to us, and a
healthy balance of worship, work, and recreation is a part
of the Joseph Option. Where communities are keeping
this balance, it is easier to encounter St. Joseph and his
healthy approach to work.
Pope St. Paul VI reminded us that work can be
a healthy source of joy. In a beautiful passage listing a
variety of joys that we can easily imagine were abundantly

---

[25] Pope Benedict XVI, Homily for Vespers at the Carthusian monastery of Serra San Bruno, October 9, 2011, http://www.vatican.va/
content/benedict-xvi/en/homilies/2011/documents/hf_ben-xvi_
hom_20111009_vespri-serra-san-bruno.html.

[26] The Pixar film *WALL-E* offers an image of this sad state of affairs,
while Neil Postman's strong critique *Amusing Ourselves to Death* or
Aldous Huxley's *Brave New World* provide similar descriptions.

present in Nazareth, he taught about the austere joy that comes with work and the way that Jesus would eventually proclaim such joys when He announced the kingdom:

> There is also needed a patient effort to teach people, or teach them once more, how to savor in a simple way the many human joys that the Creator places in our path: the elating joy of existence and of life; the joy of chaste and sanctified love; the peaceful joy of nature and silence; the sometimes austere joy of work well done; the joy and satisfaction of duty performed; the transparent joy of purity, service and sharing; the demanding joy of sacrifice. The Christian will be able to purify, complete and sublimate these joys; he will not be able to disdain them. Christian joy presupposes a person capable of natural joy. These natural joys were often used by Christ as a starting point when He proclaimed the kingdom of God.[27]

A balanced incorporation of work also provides dignity and meaning in our lives. As Pope Francis reminds us: "Saint Joseph was a carpenter who earned an honest living to provide for his family. From him, Jesus learned the value, the dignity and the joy of what it means to eat bread that is the fruit of one's own labour."[28]

Pope Francis, following in a strong tradition of papal

---

[27] Pope St. Paul VI, Apostolic Exhortation on Christian Joy *Gaudete in Domino* (May 9, 1975), §1.

[28] Pope Francis, *Patris Corde*, §6.

teaching going back to Pope Leo XIII's watershed encyclical *Rerum Novarum*, tirelessly proclaimed the importance of work with its natural benefits but also its transcendent meaning:

> Work is a means of participating in the work of salvation, an opportunity to hasten the coming of the Kingdom, to develop our talents and abilities, and to put them at the service of society and fraternal communion. It becomes an opportunity for the fulfilment not only of oneself, but also of that primary cell of society which is the family. A family without work is particularly vulnerable to difficulties, tensions, estrangement and even break-up. How can we speak of human dignity without working to ensure that everyone is able to earn a decent living?[29]

In following the Joseph Option, families and communities find ways to provide meaningful work for each person. St. Benedict did the same for his monks in such a way that a popular motto was applied to the Benedictine Order to summarize the whole regime of the Rule: *ora et labora*, meaning "pray and work." While the primary focus of the monk is the *Opus Dei* (meaning "Work of God" and referring to the Liturgy of the Hours), St. Benedict also prescribed hours of work each day for its own sake. He exhorted them not to grumble if they had to

---

[29] Pope Francis, *Patris Corde*, §6.

earn their own living[30] (rather than depend on benefactors who would support their work of prayer). He also required that they undersell any other local businesses because their focus was to be on the quality of the work and not on making a profit.[31] He encouraged them to work with the same kind of attention to God's presence that they gave to the sacred mysteries.[32] He warned them not to associate their identity with their work and become puffed up by it. He also helped them relativize their work every day by requiring them to drop whatever they were doing when the bell announced the time of prayer.[33]

When we keep our work in its proper balance, we place ourselves alongside St. Joseph and St. Benedict, who lived by the work of their hands. When we work in that way, we create an atmosphere of peace, recollection, intentionality, and excellence. Working alongside St. Joseph can help us give an eternal value to our work:

Entering the world as the eternal Son of God, He has taken up time into the divine eternity and by means of His humanity has founded, has given beginning to, and has become a measure of time itself. "According to this vision, time used purposefully is where time and eternity come together and this is time that has been completed and filled by God."[34]

---

[30] RB 48:7–9.

[31] RB 57:1–4.

[32] RB 31:10.

[33] RB 43:1.

[34] Donato Ogliari, Archabbot of Montecassino, *Saint Benedict and*

Our work can be part of our personal sanctification and part of the sanctification of the world, allowing eternity to break into time and time to be raised up into eternity. Working in this way, we can discover the virtues, love, and presence of St. Joseph in our daily labors and help others also to do so. As Pope Francis said:

> Working persons, whatever their job may be, are cooperating with God himself, and in some way become creators of the world around us. The crisis of our time, which is economic, social, cultural and spiritual, can serve as a summons for all of us to rediscover the value, the importance and necessity of work for bringing about a new "normal" from which no one is excluded.[35]

Promoters of the Joseph Option

Stepping back now, we can see some ways that the Joseph Option forms environments where people can come close to Jesus through the heart of St. Joseph. The Joseph Option forms a school for the virtues of silence, obedience, and humility where the pupils learn almost imperceptibly to imitate Christ. Authority under the Joseph Option is carried out as service, and God's grace and mercy flow through the tenderness of fatherly and motherly media-

---

*His Me*ssage (Abbazia di Montecassino, 2016), 58, quoting Anselm Gruen, *Nella Dimensione Del Tempo Dei Monaci. Come Vivere Il Tempo* (Brescia, 2006), 13.

[35] Pope Francis, *Patris Corde*, §6.

tion. In environments formed by the Joseph Option, there is a continual reminder of God's presence, and everyone is encouraged to practice continually the presence of God. Lastly, in places that cultivate the Joseph Option, everyone benefits from the dignity of work, but always in its proper place in relationship to love and prayer.

There are many saints throughout history who, like St. Benedict, were exemplary in choosing the Joseph Option and cultivating little Nazareths where others could share in the life of the Holy Family. Although it is not clear that St. Benedict had an explicit devotion to St. Joseph, it becomes clear in later centuries that an explicit love for St. Joseph leads saints to cultivate the Joseph Option and create places where others can live with Jesus, Mary, and Joseph like in Nazareth. Through forming religious orders, through teaching, through the establishment of shrines, and through personal witness, saints have helped others to know and to imitate the virtues of St. Joseph and so draw closer to Jesus through his heart. We consider a few of the more prominent lovers of St. Joseph in this section and highlight how they chose the Joseph Option to form places where others could encounter the love of God.

St. Teresa of Ávila

St. Teresa of Ávila was one of the greatest advocates of the Joseph Option, and her devotion to this spiritual father had a watershed effect on devotion to St. Joseph in her time and in the subsequent centuries. She promoted him in Carmel, and she promoted him in her writing.

In Carmel, she created an atmosphere analogous to St. Benedict's monasteries. The Carmel, meaning "Garden of God," is the name of the monastery where Carmelite nuns or friars live. In her reform, St. Teresa of Ávila renewed the spirit of Carmel to make her Carmels of the reform into schools where silence, obedience, and humility are cultivated, where authority is lived out in a tender way, where a spirit of recollection is fostered, and where work is properly balanced with prayer. All of this was carried out under the explicit patronage of St. Joseph.

Her unique contribution to living out the Joseph Option was in taking St. Joseph as her own spiritual father. That relationship developed after the loss of her earthly father and was an unprecedented relationship with St. Joseph in Christian spirituality.[36] With the confidence of a well-beloved daughter, St. Teresa of Ávila called on St. Joseph for her various needs in establishing a renewal in Carmel. As she wrote in her *Life*:

> I took for my advocate and lord the glorious St. Joseph and earnestly recommended myself to him. I saw clearly that as in this need so in other greater ones concerning honor and loss of soul this father and lord of mine came to my rescue in better ways than I knew how to ask for. I don't recall up to this day ever having petitioned him for anything that he failed to grant. . . . I have experience that he helps in all our needs and that the Lord wants us to understand that just as He was subject to

---

[36] Doze, *Saint Joseph*, 16.

St. Joseph on earth—for since bearing the title of
father, being the Lord's tutor, Joseph could give
the Child command—so in heaven God does
whatever he commands.[37]

She explained the reason for promoting him: "Because
of my impressive experience of the goods this glorious
saint obtains from God, I had the desire to persuade all to
be devoted to him. I have not known anyone truly devoted
to him and rendering him special services who has not
advanced more in virtue."[38] Furthermore, in her promo-
tion of St. Joseph, she cultivated environments in which
he could be more easily known and loved. She placed the
first monastery of her reform under his patronage and put
his image over the front door together with an image of
Our Lady. In the building of that and several other monasteries, she experienced his miraculous providence and
protection.[39] Furthermore, she helped her sisters to know
and love him as their spiritual father:

> As a result of her deep personal relationship
> over so many years with St. Joseph, Teresa found
> a model for realizing her dream of founding an
> enclosed monastery where the primitive Car-
> melite rule of poverty, prayer, and solitude would
> be observed and an apostolate of prayer for the

---

[37] Teresa of Ávila, *Teresa of Avila: The Book of Her Life*, trans. Kieran
Kavanaugh, O.C.D, and Otilio Rodriguez, O.C.D. (Indianapolis:
Hackett Publishing Company, Inc., 2008), 6.6.

[38] Teresa of Ávila, *Life*, 6.8.

[39] Teresa of Ávila, *Life*, chap. 32 and 33.

Church carried out. That model was the House of Nazareth, where St. Joseph's silent, humble service of and contemplative intimacy with Jesus and Mary became the prototype of the Teresian Carmel.[40]

St. Teresa is one of the founders of the Joseph Option, creating in Carmel another Nazareth where her sisters could come to know, love, and entrust themselves to the fatherly care of St. Joseph so as to grow in intimacy with Jesus and Mary.

St. Francis de Sales

St. Francis de Sales's devotion to St. Joseph was closely related to St. Teresa's. The two saints were contemporaries, and De Sales had assisted with the establishment of the first Carmel in France.[41] His great devotion to St. Joseph grew throughout his life and was articulated in his *Treatise on the Love of God* and his sermons, culminating in his famous sermon, delivered in 1622 to the Visitation Nuns, in which he expounded eloquently and at length on the virtues of St. Joseph. Like St. Teresa of Ávila, St. Francis de Sales entrusted his new foundation of Visi-

---

[40] Joseph F. Chorpenning, O.S.F.S., "St. Joseph in the Spirituality of Teresa of Ávila and of Francis de Sales: Convergences and Divergences," in *The Heirs of St. Teresa of Ávila: Defenders and Disseminators of the Founding Mother's Legacy*, ed. Christopher Wilson, (ICS Publications, 2011), Kindle.

[41] Chorpenning, "St. Joseph in the Spirituality of Teresa of Ávila and of Francis de Sales."

tation Nuns to the care of St. Joseph and also dedicated churches and chapels to St. Joseph. He knew the powerful patronage of this spiritual father.

As a great teacher, however, St. Francis de Sales's primary mode for promoting the Joseph Option was through expounding on the virtues of St. Joseph. He exhorted his listeners to imitate St. Joseph's example and to ask his intercession for growth in these virtues:

> For Francis, St. Joseph modeled the hidden ordinary, everyday virtues, what the bishop called the "little virtues," which are the very heart and essence of true devotion: purity of mind and body, poverty, humility before God, gentleness toward neighbor, constancy, courage, perseverance, obedience to the Word of God, charity of judgment (cf. Introduction to the Devout Life, Part 3, chs. 1-2).[42]

St. Francis promoted St. Joseph boldly, insisting on the great privileges of that man who was closest to God. He promoted the bodily assumption of St. Joseph and taught that St. Joseph's sanctification and sinlessness already began in his mother's womb. He believed that St. Joseph needed such graces to live out the high calling God had given him as the father of Jesus.

As a bishop, St. Francis de Sales chose the Joseph Option in the way he structured his diocese. Although

---

[42] Chorpenning, "St. Joseph in the Spirituality of Teresa of Ávila and of Francis de Sales."

he was exiled from the Diocesan See of Geneva, from his home in Annecy he cultivated a sort of Nazareth. He promoted the Josephite virtues of silence, obedience, and humility, among others. His *Introduction to the Devout Life* became a spiritual classic that has never gone out of print. In it he promoted the universal call to holiness, guiding everyone, especially the laity, to a contemplative way of living daily life. In living out his authority as a bishop, he modeled the gentleness of Joseph. His friend, St. Vincent de Paul, once testified that Francis was so gentle that it helped one believe in the gentleness of God. He believed as he taught: "Nothing is so strong as gentleness. Nothing is so gentle as real strength."[43] With his beloved Visitation Nuns, he developed a balance of work and prayer that was unique for women religious at his time. At a diocesan level, St. Francis de Sales cultivated the Joseph Option for his priests, seminarians, religious, and laity through his teaching, governance, and personal witness.

St. Bernadette

St. Bernadette's devotion to St. Joseph was more subtle but also led to the creation of an environment that promotes closeness to Mary and her husband. St. Bernadette lived as a peasant in a poor but devout family in France. One day while she was playing near the cave in Massabielle, a beautiful lady appeared to her. Over some months, that Lady introduced herself as "The Immac-

---

[43] St. Francis de Sales, *Sermons of St. Francis for Advent and Christmas*, vol. 4 (Charlotte, NC: TAN Books, 2015), no. 9.

ulate Conception" and asked St. Bernadette to tell the
parish priest she wanted a chapel to be built where the
cave was. She also directed St. Bernadette to dig in the
leaves and mud to unearth a spring that would be blessed
with healing powers. In her simplicity and humility, St.
Bernadette obediently carried out all these instructions,
and the result was the great shrine of Lourdes, where mil-
lions of pilgrims have traveled seeking healing and deeper
faith.

Meanwhile, St. Bernadette disappeared into a monastery, where she lived out the rest of her life. Her religious
community was particularly hard on her, especially since
she had been singled out by Our Lady and blessed with
such moving and transformative apparitions. In her more
difficult moments, she found refuge in a chapel of St.
Joseph located in the monastery garden, because it brought
her back to Lourdes. "Lourdes, in her heart, is the land of
Joseph . . ."[44] The cave at Massabielle that protected the
Virgin and overshadowed Mary like a veil was a symbol
of the protective presence of Joseph, who is never far from
his beloved wife. For this reason, St. Bernadette found a
safe refuge in the chapel of St. Joseph when she needed to
return spiritually to her mystical foundations.

St. Bernadette's personal devotion also became a gift
for us through her humility and obedience. Her perseverance through many trials and interrogations led to the
construction of a great shrine that continues to bring us
into a Nazareth of hope for healing, renewal of faith, and
deepening love. Countless pilgrims enter the shrine of

---

[44] Doze, *Saint Joseph*, 73.

Lourdes every year across a bridge dedicated to St. Joseph, where he stands holding the Christ child. At Lourdes, the strong serve the weak, and the pervasive theme is mercy and tenderness. The abundance of prayerful pilgrims cultivates an atmosphere that fosters a continual loving awareness of God's presence. There is a balance of work and prayer there, with countless legions of volunteers helping the sick into the baths each year, while endless processions and silent prayer take place throughout the day and night. In her humble, obedient love for Jesus and Mary, St. Bernadette promoted the Joseph Option, providing a gifted place of encounter for us, and a way for us to enter Nazareth.

St. Bernadette also gave witness to St. Joseph as the patron of a happy death as she entrusted the end of her life to him. In an amazing turn of events, the sisters decided not to bury her in the cemetery because of her privileged status as the visionary of the Immaculate and instead decided to lay out her body and bury her in the chapel of St. Joseph where she had found so much solace. Even more wondrously, after thirty years in the watchful care of St. Joseph, when everything in her casket had been destroyed by water, her body was exhumed for the canonization process and was discovered to be preserved perfectly incorrupt. She still looked like she had only been sleeping.

St. André Bessette

One cannot write about a Joseph Option without highlighting the example given by St. André Bessette. This holy man of limited education and diminished height called himself the little dog of St. Joseph and had one simple preoccupation. St. André looked to St. Joseph like a puppy to his master, and his simple guidance to everyone who came was to pray to St. Joseph.

Serving as the doorman at Collège Notre-Dame in Montreal, St. André was in a position to meet a lot of people. He greeted each one warmly with a smile. He lived in the loft above the nave of the college chapel dedicated to St. Joseph. The chapel was right at the streetcar stop, and St. André had the opportunity to invite many people to come in and say a prayer. He also readily anointed many people with oil that he took from the lamp burning by the statue of St. Joseph in the chapel. As more people reported wonderful and even miraculous answers to their prayers, St. André became more widely known. He never took credit for any miracle or answered prayer, however. He always redirected their attention to St. Joseph.

St. Teresa chose the Joseph Option by founding religious houses under the care of St. Joseph, while St. Francis de Sales chose the Joseph Option in the way he governed his diocese and in the moving sermons he gave on the virtues of St. Joseph. St. Bernadette's humility and obedience led to the construction of a great Marian shrine, where the bridge of St. Joseph draws pilgrims closer to Mary and Jesus within the overshadowing of the rock of St. Joseph. St. André, for his part, fostered the construction of the largest shrine in the world dedicated to St. Joseph. On Mount Royal in Montreal, the little saint promoted a great building project that persisted through the Great Depression and eventually led to a home for St.

Joseph that draws more than two million pilgrims from around the world every year.

At the Shrine of St. Joseph in Montreal, the atmosphere promotes silence and humility as pilgrims pray and the sick humbly seek healing. The shrine was constructed through the perseverance of a little saint who moved the hearts of his superiors to act more like humble servants. Despite the resistance and detraction he faced from the powerful, he eventually gained permission and steadily developed the needed funds. At one point, he put a statue of St. Joseph in the open air of the upper chapel and stated confidently, "If St. Joseph wants a roof over his head, he will get it." In the shrine, St. André led the example of a prayerful presence open to the presence of God. As Pope Benedict XVI said, "For him, everything spoke of God and of God's presence."[45] Lastly, we see in St. André a balance of prayer and work in the tireless hours of availability that he offered to the pilgrims who sought him out in larger and larger numbers. In his death, more than a million people passed by his casket to pay their last respects.

All these saints show us the way that we can live the Joseph Option, no matter what our position in life. Strong and weak, rich and poor, powerful and powerless, we are all invited to find a loving father in St. Joseph. With him, we can then cultivate environments of silence, humility, and obedience where others can meet him through

---

[45] Pope Benedict XVI, Homily for the Canonization of New Saints, October 17, 2010, http://www.vatican.va/content/benedict-xvi/en/homilies/2010/documents/hf_ben-xvi_hom_20101017_canonizations.html.

authority exercised in tender love, a constant loving awareness of God's presence, and the proper balance of prayer and work.

Litany of St. Joseph

The Joseph Option aims to create an environment in which others can encounter St. Joseph and come to know his fatherly care, strong protection, hidden solitude, silent love, and solace in suffering. One of the ways to bring all these qualities to mind is through a regular praying of the Litany of St. Joseph. Officially approved by the Church, this litany gives us a trustworthy and robust image of St. Joseph and helps us draw on his graced qualities for our own spiritual growth.

Lord, have mercy on us.   *Christ, have mercy on us.*
Lord, have mercy on us.
Christ, hear us.   *Christ, graciously hear us.*
God our Father in heaven,   *have mercy on us.*
God the Son, Redeemer of the world,   *have mercy on us.*
God the Holy Spirit,   *have mercy on us.*
Holy Trinity, one God,   *have mercy on us.*
Holy Mary,   *pray for us.*
Saint Joseph,   *pray for us.*
Noble son of the House of David,   *pray for us.*
Light of patriarchs,   *pray for us.*

Husband of the Mother of God,	*pray for us.*
Guardian of the Virgin,	*pray for us.*
Foster father of the Son of God,	*pray for us.*
Faithful guardian of Christ,	*pray for us.*
Head of the Holy Family,	*pray for us.*
Joseph, most chaste,	*pray for us.*
Joseph, most just,	*pray for us.*
Joseph, most prudent,	*pray for us.*
Joseph, most valiant,	*pray for us.*
Joseph, most obedient,	*pray for us.*
Joseph, most faithful,	*pray for us.*
Pattern of patience,	*pray for us.*
Lover of poverty,	*pray for us.*
Model of workers,	*pray for us.*
Example to parents,	*pray for us.*
Guardian of virgins,	*pray for us.*
Pillar of family life,	*pray for us.*
Comfort of the troubled,	*pray for us.*
Hope of the sick,	*pray for us.*
Patron of the dying,	*pray for us.*
Terror of evil spirits,	*pray for us.*
Protector of the Church,	*pray for us.*
Lamb of God, you take away the sins of the world,	*have mercy on us.*
Lamb of God, you take away the sins of the world,	*have mercy on us.*
Lamb of God, you take away the sins of the world,	*have mercy on us.*
God made him master of his household,	*And put him in charge of all his possessions.*

Let us pray.

O God, who in your inexpressible providence
were pleased to choose Saint Joseph
as spouse of the most holy Mother of your Son,
grant, we pray,
that we, who revere him as our protector on
earth,
may be worthy of his heavenly intercession.
Through Christ our Lord.
R/. Amen.

CONCLUSION

So much more could be said in order to cultivate the reader's relationship with St. Joseph. Many books have been written to expand on various aspects of his life and explore various dimensions of his heart. The *Consecration to St. Joseph* contains a compendium of quotes and prayers with beautiful explanations of the various aspects of St. Joseph.[1] The many works of Fr. Joseph Chorpenning, O.S.F.S., explore the theology, artwork, spirituality, traditional teaching about, and devotion to St. Joseph.[2] The great compendium of Fr. Francis Filas, S.J., is a treasure containing an extensive collection of trustworthy Catholic teaching, along with explanation and analysis of that teaching on St. Joseph.[3]

---

1 Calloway, *Consecration to St. Joseph*.

2 See Joseph F. Chorpenning, *Joseph of Nazareth through the Centuries* (Philadelphia: Saint Joseph's University Press, 2011); Joseph F. Chorpenning and Barbara Von Barghahn, eds., *The Holy Family in Art and Devotion* (Philadelphia: Saint Joseph's University Press, 1998); Joseph F. Chorpenning, ed., *Just Man, Husband of Mary, Guardian of Christ: An Anthology of Readings from Jerónimo Gracián's Summary of the Excellencies of St. Joseph (1579)*, with an introductory essay and commentary by Joseph F. Chorpenning, O.S.F.S., illustrations by Michael L. McGrath, O.S.F.S., 2nd ed. (Philadelphia: Saint Joseph's University Press, 1995); Joseph F Chorpenning, *Patron Saint of the New World: Spanish American Colonial Images of St. Joseph* (Philadelphia: Saint Joseph's University Press, 1995).

3 Filas, *Joseph*.

One can look to St. Joseph as an example for many different vocations and professions. For example, St. Joseph can serve as a model for priests, as the liturgy of the Maronite Rite sings: "Though angels fear to behold him, you will raise him like your own son. Since Mary is God's pure temple, you will serve him like a high priest."[4] On the other hand, if one views Christ as the High Priest, one could look to Joseph as a model for the diaconate because of the way he serves Him. Of course, St. Joseph models fatherhood and marriage in an exemplary way as well. In fact, one can practically reconstruct a complete theology through the lens of St. Joseph, which we call a Josephite theology or a Josephology. We can read and think endlessly and never discover all the gems about St. Joseph. Indeed, "the world itself could not contain the books that would be written" (John 21:25). The most important thing for us to do, however, is to pray. Let us ask St. Joseph to reveal himself to us and ask him to deepen his relationship with us and make it more explicit.

In most works on St. Joseph, the focus is the exploration of who this man is. We discover so many great qualities of St. Joseph, most especially a beautiful, chaste, strong, fatherly heart in which many hidden treasures are kept safe in silence. This book has focused on the pathways by which we can enter into that heart and draw close to the treasures whose names are Jesus and Mary. Through the dispositions of vulnerability and littleness, we enter into relationship with St. Joseph, who is pro-

---

[4] Hymn in the Maronite Liturgy for Sunday of the Revelation to Joseph.

tector and father. Through hiddenness and silence, we enter into the hidden, silent depths with St. Joseph. And when we are suffering, poor, fearful, and doubtful, we find a guardian and guide in St. Joseph, who eases our pain and lifts our spirits as he remains steadfast in suffering. Finally, we are moved to choose the Joseph Option and intentionally create Nazareths, like St. Benedict and some other saints did, where others can find a heavenly home and be part of a holy family by entering in through the heart of St. Joseph.

St. Joseph, protector of the vulnerable, father of little ones, hidden and silent, comforter of the afflicted, pray for us!

BIBLIOGRAPHY

Aquilina, Mike. *St. Joseph and His World*. New York: Scepter Publishers, 2020.

Aquinas, Thomas. *The Summa Theologica of St. Thomas Aquinas*. Translated by the Fathers of the English Dominican Province. London: Burns, Oates & Washbourne, 1920.

Benedict XVI. Address on the Occasion of the International Conference Organized by the Pontifical Council for Promoting the New Evangelization, October 15, 2011. http://www.vatican.va/content/benedict-xvi/en/speeches/2011/october/documents/hf_ben-xvi_spe_20111015_nuova-evangelizzazione.html.

———. General Audience, December 28, 2011. http://w2.vatican.va/content/benedict-xvi/en/audiences/2011/documents/hf_ben-xvi_aud_20111228.html

———. Homily for Mass at Night for the Lord's Nativity, December 24, 2012. http://www.vatican.va/content/benedict-xvi/en/homilies/2012/documents/hf_ben-xvi_hom_20121224_christmas.html

———. Homily for the Canonization of New Saints, October 17, 2010. http://www.vatican.va/content/benedict-xvi/en/homilies/2010/documents/hf_ben-xvi_hom_20101017_canonizations.html.

————. Homily for the Closing of the 24th Italian Eucharistic Congress in Bari, May 29, 2005. http://www.vatican.va/content/benedict-xvi/en/homilies/2005/documents/hf_ben-xvi_hom_20050529_bari.html.

————. Homily for the Solemnity of the Epiphany, January 6, 2011. http://www.vatican.va/content/benedict-xvi/en/homilies/2011/documents/hf_ben-xvi_hom_20110106_epifania.html.

————. Homily for the Solemnity of the Immaculate Conception, December 8, 2005. http://www.vatican.va/content/benedict-xvi/en/homilies/2005/documents/hf_ben-xvi_hom_20051208_anniv-vat-council.html.

————. Homily for Vespers at the Carthusian monastery of Serra San Bruno, October 9, 2011. http://www.vatican.va/content/benedict-xvi/en/homilies/2011/documents/hf_ben-xvi_hom_20111009_vespri-serra-san-bruno.html.

————. *Jesus of Nazareth: The Infancy Narratives.* Translated by Philip Whitmore. New York: Image Books, 2012.

————. *Verbum Domini.* 2010.

Bernard of Clairvaux. *Homilies in Praise of the Blessed Virgin Mary.* Translated by Marie-Bernard Said. Cistercian Fathers Series, no. 18-A. Kalamazoo, MI: Cistercian Publications, 1993.

Bottaro, Dr. Gregory, and Jennifer Settle. *Consecration to Jesus through Saint Joseph: An Integrated Look at the Holy Family.* Self-published, 2019.

Brannan, Rick. *Greek Apocryphal Gospels, Fragments, and Agrapha: A New Translation.* Bellingham, WA: Lexham Press, 2017.

Burkey, O.F.M., Blaine. "John XIII: Pope of Saint Joseph." *The American Ecclesiastical Review* 149 (July 1963): 2–13.

Calloway, Donald H. *Consecration to St. Joseph: The Wonders of Our Spiritual Father*. Marian Press, 2020.

Chesterton, G. K. *Orthodoxy*. New York: John Lane Company, 1909.

Chorpenning, O.S.F.S., Joseph F., and Barbara Von Barghahn, eds. *The Holy Family in Art and Devotion*. Philadelphia: Saint Joseph's University Press, 1998.

———. *Joseph of Nazareth through the Centuries*. Philadelphia: Saint Joseph's University Press, 2011.

———. trans. and ed., *Just Man, Husband of Mary, Guardian of Christ: An Anthology of Readings from Jerónimo Gracián's Summary of the Excellencies of St. Joseph (1597)*. With an introductory essay and commentary by Joseph F. Chorpenning, O.S.F.S., and illustrations by Michael L. McGrath. 2nd ed. Philadelphia: Saint Joseph's University Press, 1993.

———. *Patron Saint of the New World: Spanish American Colonial Images of St. Joseph*. Philadelphia: Saint Joseph's University Press, 1995.

———. "St. Joseph in the Spirituality of Teresa of Ávila and of Francis de Sales: Convergences and Divergences." In *The Heirs of St. Teresa of Avila: Defenders and Disseminators of the Founding Mother's Legacy*. Edited by Christopher Wilson. ICS Publications, 2011.

Crosby, Dr. John. "On the Difference Between the Cosmological and Personalist Understanding of the Human Being." *Quaestiones Disputatae* 9 no. 2 (2019): 112–125.

Doze, Andrew. *Saint Joseph: Shadow of the Father*. Translated by Florestine Audett. Staten Island, NY: Alba House, 1992.

Dreher, Rod. *The Benedict Option: A Strategy for Christians in a Post-Christian Nation*. New York: Sentinel, 2017.

Dressler, Hermigild, and Roy J. Deferrari, eds. *Early Christian Biographies*. Translated by Marie Liguori Ewald. Vol. 15, The Fathers of the Church. Washington, D.C.: Catholic University of America Press, 1952.

Elizabeth of the Trinity. *The Complete Works of Elizabeth of the Trinity*. Vol. 1. Translated by Sr. Alethea Kane. Washington, D.C: ICS Publications, 1984.

Escrivá, Josemaría. Homily for the Solemnity of St. Joseph, March 19, 1963. https://stjosemaria.org/in-st-josephs-workshop/.

Filas, Francis L. *Joseph: The Man Closest to Jesus: The Complete Life, Theology and Devotional History of St. Joseph*. Boston: St. Paul Editions, 1962.

Francis. Address at a Meeting of Families in Manila, January 16, 2015. http://www.vatican.va/content/francesco/en/speeches/2015/january/documents/papa-francesco_20150116_srilanka-filippine-incontro-famiglie.html.

———. Address to the Homeless at the Charitable Center of St. Patrick in Washington, D.C., September 24, 2015. http://www.vatican.va/content/francesco/en/speeches/2015/september/documents/papa-francesco_20150924_usa-centro-caritativo.html.

———. Address to Young People in Manila, January

18, 2015. http://www.vatican.va/content/francesco/
en/speeches/2015/january/documents/papa-franc-
esco_20150118_srilanka-filippine-incontro-giovani.
html.

———. Angelus Address, December 22, 2013. http://
w2.vatican.va/content/francesco/en/angelus/2013/
documents/papa-francesco_angelus_20131222.html.

———. *Christus Vivit.* 2019.

———. *Evangelii Gaudium.* 2013.

———. First Meditation of a Spiritual Retreat Given for
Priests in the Year of Mercy, June 2, 2016. http://www.
vatican.va/content/francesco/en/speeches/2016/
june/documents/papa-francesco_20160602_giu-
bileo-sacerdoti-prima-meditazione.html.

———. Homily for the Feast of the Presentation, February 2, 2015. http://www.vatican.va/content/
francesco/en/homilies/2015/documents/papa-franc-
esco_20150202_omelia-vita-consacrata.html.

———. Homily for the Opening of the XV Ordinary General Assembly of the Synod of Bishops,
October 3, 2018. http://w2.vatican.va/content/
francesco/en/homilies/2018/documents/papa-franc-
esco_20181003_omelia-inizio-sinodo.html.

———. Homily for the Solemnity of the Epiphany,
January 6, 2016. http://www.vatican.va/content/
francesco/en/homilies/2016/documents/papa-franc-
esco_20160106_omelia-epifania.html.

———. Homily for the Solemnity of the Epiphany, January
6, 2019. http://w2.vatican.va/content/francesco/en/
homilies/2019/documents/papa-francesco_20190106_
omelia-epifania.html.

————. Homily on the Occasion of the Feast of St. Ignatius, July 31, 2013. http://www.vatican.va/content/
francesco/en/homilies/2013/documents/papa-franc-
esco_20130731_omelia-sant-ignazio.html.

————. Inaugural Homily on the Feast of St. Joseph,
March 19, 2013. http://w2.vatican.va/content/
francesco/en/homilies/2013/documents/papa-franc-
esco_20130319_omelia-inizio-pontificato.html.

————. *Patris Corde*. 2020.

Fry, O.S.B., Timothy, trans. *The Rule of St. Benedict in
English.* Collegeville, MN: Liturgical Press, 2018.

Garrigou-Lagrange, Reginald. *The Mother of the Saviour:
And Our Interior Life.* Translated by Bernard J. Kelly.
Charlotte: TAN Books, 2012.

Gaucher, Guy. *John and Thérèse: Flames of Love: The Influence of St. John of the Cross in the Life and Writings of St.
Thérèse of Lisieux.* Staten Island, NY: Alba House, 1999.

Glaser, Judith. *Conversational Intelligence: How Great
Leaders Build Trust and Get Extraordinary Results.*
New York: Routledge, 2016.

Gruen, Anselm. *Nella Dimensione Del Tempo Dei Monaci.
Come Vivere Il Tempo.* Brescia, 2006.

Guigo II. *Ladder of Monks and Twelve Meditations.*
Translated by Edmund Collegde and James Walsh.
Kalamazoo, MI: Cistercian Publications, 1981.

Ignatius of Loyola. *The Spiritual Exercises of St. Ignatius:
Or Manresa.* Charlotte, NC: TAN Books, 1999.

John of the Cross. *The Complete Works of Saint John of
the Cross of the Order of Our Lady of Mount Carmel.*
Translated by David Lewis. Vol. 2. Longman, Green,
Longman, Roberts, & Green, 1864.

John Paul II. *Redemptoris Custos.* 1989.

Leo XIII. *Quamquam Pluries.* 1889.

Lienhard, Joseph T., trans. *Origen: Homilies on Luke,* Fathers of the Church 94. Washington, D.C., Catholic University of America Press, 1996.

———. *St. Joseph in Early Christianity: Devotion and Theology: A Study and an Anthology of Patristic Texts.* Philadelphia: Saint Joseph's University Press, 1999.

Lombardo, O.P., Nicholas E. *The Logic of Desire: Aquinas on Emotion.* Washington, D.C.: Catholic University of America Press, 2011.

Marcel, Gabriel. *Homo Viator: Introduction to the Metaphysic of Hope.* Translated by Emma Craufurd and Paul Seaton. 1st ed. South Bend, IN: St. Augustine's Press, 2010.

Meinardus, Otto F. A. *The Holy Family in Egypt.* American University in Cairo Press, 1986.

Miller, Frederick L. *St. Joseph: Our Father in Faith.* New Haven, CT: Catholic Information Service, 2008.

Montfort, Louis de. *The Secret of Mary.* TAN Books, 2013.

Newman, John Henry. *Meditations and Devotions of the Late Cardinal Newman.* Edited by Rev. W. P. Neville. New York: Longmans, Green & Co., 1907.

Ogliari, Donato, Archabbot of Montecassino. *Saint Benedict and His Message.* Abbazia di Montecassino, 2016.

Paul VI. *Evangelii Nuntiandi.* 1975.

———. *Gaudete in Domino.* 1975.

Peters, Sr. M. Danielle. "Flight into Egypt." University of Dayton. Accessed May 16, 2019, https://udayton.edu/imri/mary/f/flight-into-egypt.php.

Pitre, Brant, and John Bergsma. *A Catholic Introduction*

to the Bible: The Old Testament. Vol. 1. San Francisco: Ignatius Press, 2018.

Pius IX. Quemadmodum Deus, December 8, 1870. https://osjusa.org/st-joseph/magisterium/quemadmodum-deus/.

Polanyi, Michael. *The Tacit Dimension*. Garden City, NY: Doubleday and Company, Inc., 1966.

———. Homily in the Basilica of the Annunciation in Nazareth during His Pilgrimage to the Holy Land, January 5, 1964. https://www.papalencyclicals.net/paul06/p6reflect.htm.

Potterie, Ignace de la. *Mary in the Mystery of the Covenant*. Translated by Bertrand Buby. New York: Alba House, 1992.

Rodrigues, José A. *St. Joseph: Son of David*. Victoria, BC: First Choice Books, 2014.

Rondet, Henri. *Saint Joseph*. Translated by Donald Attwater. New York: P. J. Kenedy & Sons, 1956.

Sales, Francis de. *Sermons of St. Francis for Advent and Christmas*. Vol. 4. Charlotte, NC: TAN Books, 2015.

———. *Sermon Texts on Saint Joseph*. Edited and translated by Joseph F. Chorpenning. Peregrina Translations Series. Toronto: Peregrina, 1999.

Sand, Faith Annette. *The Way of a Pilgrim and the Pilgrim Continues His Way*. Translated by R. M. French. 2nd ed. Pasadena, CA: Hope Publishing House, 1989.

Sarah, Cardinal Robert, and Nicolas Diat. *The Power of Silence: Against the Dictatorship of Noise*. 1st ed. San Francisco: Ignatius Press, 2017.

Servais, S.J., Jacques, ed. *Hans Urs von Balthasar on the Ignatian Spiritual Exercises: An Anthology*. San Francisco, CA: Ignatius Press, 2019.

Sheen, Archbishop Fulton J. *The World's First Love*. 2nd ed. San Francisco, CA: Ignatius Press, 2010.

Teresa of Avila. *Teresa of Avila: The Book of Her Life*. Translated by Kieran Kavanaugh, O.C.D, and Otilio Rodriguez, O.C.D. Indianapolis: Hackett Publishing Company, Inc., 2008.

————. *The Interior Castle*. Translated by Kieran Kavanaugh, O.C.D., and Otilio Rodriguez, O.C.D. The Classics of Western Spirituality. Mahwah, NJ: Paulist Press, 1979.

Teresa of Calcutta and Brian Kolodiejchuk. *Where There Is Love, There Is God: A Path to Closer Union with God and Greater Love for Others*. New York: Image, 2012.

Terruwe, Anna, and Conrad Baars. *Psychic Wholeness and Healing: Using All the Powers of the Human Psyche*. Edited by Suzanne M Baars and Bonnie N. Shayne. 2nd ed. Eugene, OR: Wipf and Stock Publishers, 2016.

Therese of Lisieux. *Letters of St. Therese*. Vol. 2, *1890–1897*. Translated by John Clarke, O.C.D. Washington, D.C.: ICS Publications, 1988.

————. *St. Therese of Lisieux: Her Last Conversations*. Translated by John Clarke. Washington, D.C.: ICS Publications, 1977.

————. *The Story of a Soul*. Translated by T. N. Taylor. London: Burns, Oates & Washbourne, 1912.

Tippett, Krista. "Xavier Le Pichon—The Fragility at the Heart of Humanity." The On Being Project. Accessed May 14, 2019. https://onbeing.org/programs/xavier-le-pichon-the-fragility-at-the-heart-of-humanity/.

SWITCHBLADE

Outlaw Fiction

Edited by Scotch Rutherford

Switchblade, Issue Seven, Volume One
First Printing, November 2018

ISBN-13: 978-0-9987650-7-5
ISBN-10: 0998765074

©2018 Caledonia Press

www.switchblademag.com

Stories by the authors: © Nick Kolakowski, © Stephen D. Rogers, © J.L. Boekestein, © David Rachels, © William R. Soldan, © Mathew X. Gomez © C.W. Blackwell, © Jack Bates, © Mark Slade, © R. Daniel Lester, © Arthur Evans, © Scott Hallam, © Michael R. Colangelo, © Jon Zelazny, © Bryce Wilson, © Bill Davidson

Front cover photo: ©2018 Scotch Rutherford
Back cover photo   ©2018 Scotch Rutherford

THE BASTARD GIRL OF TAMPA RAY

Nights I wonder why he brought them here,
and if here is where he did it,
in these thick and moaning groves,
each tree, each orange fruit a shimmering
witness to the end,
those soon-ghosts gutted in the warm breeze,
their lives spilled empty in the dirt,
brains bludgeoned in the bone hallows of their skulls,
a leaking nectar for thirsty birds.
I wonder if I ever would have known, who I am,
had Mama not let it slip
gin-soaked from a tongue dripping with loosed secrets
that had almost choked her.
That he was a carny baker, and she was the mark.
Where had the others been going when they fell inside
his shadow? I see them amble, oblivious, a stroll on
Bayshore Boulevard beneath the hissing palms,
wooed, rapt from a kiss they rent
and wrapped in a sheet. How many brothers and sisters
might he have raped into the world in that year,
years before his ride to meet the needle?
I wonder if Mama had been next
to lie along these quiet roads,
and what and where I would be then but an
undone sac of cells among the dead,
just another chained shade whispering at your backs,
telling you to run.
Don't let them lead you here...

CONTENTS

BRUCE
THOMAS

TOM
WISDOM

LEONA
PARAMINSKI

LOVIE
UNDERWOOD

CAYLEB
LONG

The Only Thing Necessary
for the Triumph of Evil
is for Good Men to Do Nothing

INTERFERENCE

IE RIGHTS PRESENTS A LDF PICTURES PRODUCTION IN ASSOCIATION WITH DARK PANDA BRUCE THOMAS TOM WISDOM "INTERFERENCE"

MATTHEW LESSAL MUSIC BY CHICO BENNETT COSTUME DESIGNER ELENA NAZAROFF EDITED BY LINDA DI FRANCO PRODUCTION DESIGNER MASS BEVERLY AND PETER CORDOVA

DIRECTOR OF PHOTOGRAPHY MASSIMILIANO TREVIS PRODUCED BY LINDA DI FRANCO SCREENPLAY BY LINDA DI FRANCO DIRECTED BY LINDA DI FRANCO

WWW.INTERFERENCE-THEMOVIE.NET

DOUBLE SHOT OF FLORIDA NOIR

S.W. LAUDEN

CROSSWISE

"Femme fatale, Florida heat,
and clues tougher to figure
out than a New York Times
Sunday Crossword Puzzle."
—Matt Coyle
*Anthony Award winning
Rick Cahill crime series*

"A zany, crazy, whirlwind
of a book that's easy to
devour in a single sitting.
Mystery and crime-capers
will love the fast-paced plot
and unforgettable
(ahem, Shayna....) characters."
—Steph Post
Author of the Judah Cannon series

S.W. LAUDEN

CROSSED
BONES

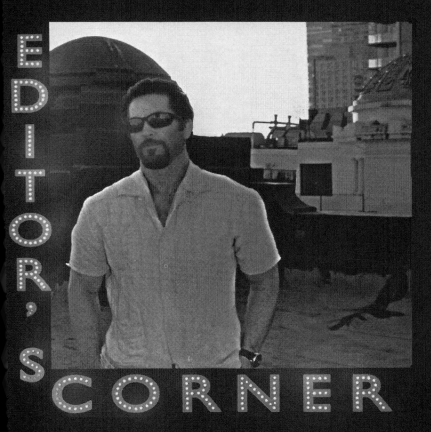

EDITOR'S CORNER

Pill mills, hurricanes, sink holes, alligators, mosquitoes, sharks, snakes, oh, and *Wally World*. Those are the things I think about, when I think of the sunshine state. This issue could easily be dubbed "The Florida Rejects" Why, you ask? Well, about half these stories take place in Florida, and about half of them are about rejects. That said, I didn't make it out to Bouchercon this year, and neither did any of these stories. Maybe it's the conspiracy theorist in me--thinking half of these stories were rejected submissions to the B-Con anthology. (if so, it's their loss) Whether they are or not, these stories you're about to read are a damn fine lot of tightly spun criminal tales, ripe for reading. New Florida noir and more, from veteran and first time offenders. Just take a look at the back cover, and you'll see why they're best freshly squeezed.

—**Scotch Rutherford**
  (Managing Editor)

LOST FARE

Inspired by true events.

SEVENTH RAY ENTERTAINMENT PRESENTS
A FILM BY BRUCE LOGAN "LOST FARE" AARON HENDRY ALEXIS ROSINSKY
CINEMATOGRAPHY AITOR URIBARRI CASTING CAMBRIA HANKIN MUSIC BY HAL LINDES
ORIGINAL SCREENSTORY RACHEL REAUGH SCREENPLAY BRUCE LOGAN & RACHEL REAUGH
PRODUCED BY ELLIOT LEWIS ROSENBLATT PRODUCED, EDITED AND DIRECTED BY BRUCE LOGAN

Alec Cizak
Preston Lang
Olin Wish
Robert Petyo
Victoria Dalpe
G.A. Miller
James Harper
Beatrix M.G. Nielsen
Brandon Alexander
Tom Miller
James Harper
Joshua Hill

ECONO
CLASH
review
✻Two

QUALITY
CHEAP
THRILLS

Edited By
J.D. Grave

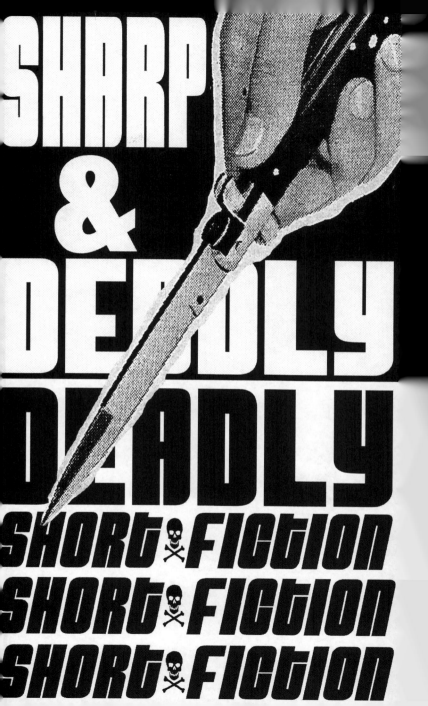

Dogfight

Bryce Wilson

There was a Bugs Bunny cartoon where Bugs
sawed through the border of Florida and sent the state
spiraling away from the union, into the Atlantic, where
it sunk beneath the waves.

In Michael's mind that let Florida off entirely too
easy.

Florida, home of face eating transients, black kids
gunned down in convenience store parking lots for
playing their music too loud and the hanging chad.
Florida had given Bush (and Trump) the presidency.
This meant that Florida had been directly responsible
for Michael getting his ass blown up in the desert for
three years. That had hurt. Then Florida had taken
Lebron James from him, and some shit you just
couldn't forgive.

But when you were in Michael's profession you
followed the circuit and sometimes, because the gods
were cruel, the circuit took you to Florida. He was not
pleased.

Michael was ready to go back home, even though
home was currently covered in three feet of snow.
Shit, he'd take Cleveland any day over The South. He
wasn't in the reconstructed, new South of Atlanta or
New Orleans, but the sticks. Real honest to God,
countin' down the days until they rose again, South.

Of course, his traveling companion didn't help
much. Didn't matter that they weren't lovers, a black
man traveling with a white woman in the rural South
still made for some uncomfortable situations; didn't
help that Petra seemed oblivious to the tensions that
her mere presence created. Actually, Michael
amended, given that it was Petra it wasn't so much
that she didn't notice as she just didn't give a shit.

Petra was a fire plug of a woman, pure Cleveland;
Polish Irish, auburn hair in a butch page cut, with a

7

spray of freckles across her face. In another generation she would have been a shop foreman, or run an industrial bakery with a firm authority that never gave way to tyranny but was never questioned. But not many of those jobs existed anymore, and people didn't much like firm authority, so she was his manager. She was worth the trouble, kept gigs lined up steady, and had more than once managed to turn a thousand dollar purse into ten through side bets and minor hustles. She took a fair cut, kept expenses down, and tucked a bit away for the both of them so he wouldn't have to get his face pounded for a living when he was sixty. He made more with her than he ever would without her.

Really wasn't that much trouble, considering just how many red hats they came across out here. They were such an odd couple. She only reached five two in heels and referring to her curvy was just barely not a polite euphemism. He was six and half feet tall, so black he was almost blue and lanky. Maybe even the most paranoid rednecks just couldn't imagine the two of them fucking.

They actually *had* slept together, the first night they'd met, mostly because both were just curious what it'd be like. What it had been like was fun, it just didn't take.

Also cutting down on the potential hate crimes was the fact that Michael obviously knew how to handle himself. It wasn't something people were conscious of. Michael wasn't aggressive, he didn't posture, he wasn't weighted down with show muscles. He just carried himself with confidence. You'd have to look real close at his hands to see the layers of scar tissue around his knuckles, to see the thick veins that traced up his forearms and over his biceps like earthworms burrowing in rich, dark soil. But people were animals, and their instincts were more active in their daily life than they liked to admit. People tended not to pick fights with Michael. No matter how deep in the deep South they got he and Petra drew nothing more than the occasional hard stare.

8

How he had got here was a bit of a winding path. He'd grown up in East Cleveland, and if you wanted to learn how to fight there were worse places to do it. He went from there directly to Iraq, which was another good place to brush up on one's technique.

He hadn't really ever wanted to be a fighter, his nature was actually pretty gentle, but when he got back the job market was crashing, and if prospects were bad for most people, then prospects for a black veteran from East Cleveland were fucking pathetic. He worked in a grocery store for a while but quit when he realized that the job made him want to kill people more than being in the army ever had. He had the GI Bill, but nothing in particular he wanted to study. He could keep a car running, but that was more for necessity and personal satisfaction. Getting covered in hot carcinogens all day for ten bucks an hour quickly lost its charms.

So he started working at a boxing gym where he'd trained as a kid. That led to his introduction to the world of underground bareknuckle boxing. Which led to contacts who started putting him in fights all over the state, which led to Petra expanding those contacts across the country, which led to him five years later, driving in North Florida, wishing he was back in his cozy Tremont row house and never mind the snow.

"We'll head back after this fight," said the grumpy voice next to him. Michael, turned surprised and regarded Petra who hadn't looked up from her John MacDonald paperback.

"I didn't say anything." Michael responded.

"I can always tell when you're getting homesick," Petra replied, deigning to glance over, "You get too fucking quiet." She shrugged, "It's OK, I'm sick of grits too. I've got a couple of prospects, but nothing that it'll break my heart to pass up. You fight tonight, and in two days we'll be back in The Land, and you can get some R&R while you try not to lose your mind because of cabin fever or die of hypothermia."

"Alright," Michael said, and he had to admit his voice sounded cheerful.

9

"But mark my words it's going to take you about five minutes before you're wishing you could be back on the beach. Don't say I didn't tell you."

Michael grinned, "Like you ever miss an opportunity to say you told me so."

Petra allowed a small smile and looked around to survey the landscape, "I can't say I blame you. I feel like I'm in *Stranger Than Paradise*." She looked at Michael expectantly and when he didn't respond she made a small disgusted noise in the back of her throat and turned back to her book, "This guy sure seems to think his cock is magic." She considered for a moment, "Then again I suppose most men do."

*

The site of the fight wasn't bad as far as these things went. The front was a small garage, the kind you didn't go to unless you knew the owner personally. The cracked concrete floor was covered in oil stains. About two hundred yards screened from the country road behind a clump of mangroves was a ring of red dirt and clay that was also covered in dark stains.

The owner of the garage came out to greet them, a white man in his late fifties whose face was obscured by an Osprey's ball cap pulled low and a tawny beard grown high that had gone half white. "You can park behind my house," he said, gesturing to a low wooden structure deep on the lot. Petra was behind the wheel now and obliged. She got out and scanned the road.

"You expecting any trouble with the law?" she asked. They both had clean records and aimed to keep it that way.

The old man shook his head, "Naw," my brother in law is an L T at the local department, and the county boys get a nice Christmas contribution. That's no reason to rub their noses in it though. It pays to be, whatchacall it, discreet." He grinned and held out his hand to Michael who shook it, "You're fighting second, any objections?"

Michael shook his head, "Who am I fighting?"

"Jim McNamara."

Michael nodded. He knew Big Jim, wouldn't call

10

him a friend, but they'd fought a couple of times before without doing permanent damage to one another or incurring any kind of animosity. Looked like a low pressure night.

"Need a beer?" The white man asked. Nodding to a plywood table that had a couple of long Styrofoam coolers tucked underneath.

"Not before the fight, but I'll have one after."

"I'll take one," Petra said, and they started walking for the table. The old man reached in and fished her out a Dixie. She drained a third of the bottle in one pull. She smacked her lips and asked, "How'd you get in this business anyway?"

He looked away, blushing on the bits of his face that were visible, "I started letting folk hold cockfights here about twenty years back, took my cut. About ten years ago, someone propositioned me about having some real fights here, and I stepped up my involvement. It's a little more risk," he opened a beer for himself and held it up in a small toast, "but you tend to attract a better class of people. "

"Ever traffic in Dog Fights?" Michael asked, he kept his question smooth on the surface but there was a dark and powerful current underneath it. Michael didn't have many demands, but he wouldn't fight on the same card as a dog fight. Wouldn't fight in a place that held a dog fight. Making sure he didn't was one of Petra's jobs; he felt her bristle beside him.

"Nah, that's a dirty business. Might sound odd coming from a former cockfighter, but way I see it, birds are just insects that happen to be covered in feathers. Sides, you run into too many low people trying to help yourself to that particular pie. Gangbangers from down South sure, but the Dixie mafia still has a piece of it too. No thank you, these days, I just deal with creatures who have enough wherewithal to choose to be in the ring." He gave a stained grin, "No offense."

"None taken." Michael said.

"There's a trailer out back of the house with an air conditioner if you want to rest up before the fight. I'm

11

sure you're sick of your car and the inside of the garage is no place to relax." ...

The trailer was nicer than expected, clean, with a TV in one corner, a mini fridge in the other, a small bathroom with a toilet and shower stall behind its own door, and couple of couches and cots lined against the wall. Michael was lying on one of the cots now, staring up at the ceiling. He was alone, Petra was out hustling and the other fighters had yet to arrive. He'd already performed his routine, shaving and then washing his face with Epsom salts to toughen the skin. Now he did what he always did before fights, let his mind go blank and float away. Tried to find that place in himself where he didn't have to think. Where he only had to react. Tried to get as close to that red core of instinct that would let him read his opponent and work on his weaknesses with a subtler, more complete knowledge than his conscious mind would.

In that place he would just know what to do.

*

It turned out that the old man's idea of discretion included two gas generator powered lights, and a PA system that played the Zac Brown Band. While parking in the field behind the old man's salt box house might be a nice gesture, Michael didn't think it was going to do much to disguise the fact that there were two hundred cars and five hundred people out here tonight.

He wasn't too worried; if the Old Man had ever been busted Petra wouldn't have let them fight here. Whatever deals he had in place would hold firm.

The atmosphere was nearly carnival like, the old man doing brisk business with his cooler, someone else was selling hotdogs and pulled pork. The weather was cold enough that the crowd's breath could be seen, but to Michael it felt downright balmy. Most of the five hundred were in a good mood. The split between men and women was surprisingly even, there were kids running around and no one found that strange. Michael wasn't the only black guy here, but

12

he had a feeling he wouldn't need much more than both hands to get an accurate count.

The opening fight was between two local boys, barely out of high school. One was so whippet thin that he made Michael look stocky, the other already had a generous slab of beer gut spilling over the front of his pants despite his youth. The niceties of weight regulations were not often observed in the underground.

The gut was overpowering the whippet with his mass, but really wasn't doing too much damage to the kid with his shoddy punches. It was just a generalized pummeling. Unbearably sloppy to Michael's yeoman eyes. Any half way competent fighter could have taken him apart, it just so happened that the whippet had more sinew than competence.

After five minutes and two rounds the gut landed an actual hit to the whippets chin and the kid went sprawling, flat on his back with a "Whodahr?" expression on his face. The old man lifted the big un's arm over his head and declared victory. Michael was sitting about ten yards away from his opponent on a long wooden bench and they exchanged a look of commiseration at the lack of professionalism.

This was actually pretty typical of fights at this level. For all its reputation of brutality bare knuckle fighting had its own set of rules of strictures, and since the fights usually didn't last near as long as legitimate boxing matches, the participants were usually in better shape afterwards.

Of course, you might get a young cowboy who thought it was real slick to open things up with a headbutt or a cheap shot to the groin. But word traveled quick in the circuit and such men either mended their ways or were quickly broken.

Michael had heard of places; places where eye gouging was not just allowed but encouraged. Places where boxing gloves were wrapped in barbed wire. Places where you could earn the money to live off of for a decade in a single night, or end up crippled, if you were lucky. Places where men in black rubber

13

aprons sat patiently in back rooms with hacksaws, bottles of bleach and bags of lime at the ready in case a loser had to suddenly disappear. Michael never wanted to see one of those places and he trusted Petra to keep him away from them.

They waited twenty minutes to allow people their second helping of pulled pork and fifth Dixie of the night and then with little fanfare he took off his shirt, went into the ring and went to work getting loose.

Big Jim stepped in after him. Also shirtless, swinging his arm getting the blood moving. Michael had fought him twice before, once when he was just getting started and Jim had soundly obliterated him, the second time a few years later where Michael had won on points. Michael wasn't sure which way tonight would go. Jim was a bit older than Michael, perhaps as much as five years, but he was still powerful and an experienced contender. Even if his frame looked more like a Dad bod than that of a gym rat's, only a fool would look at him and think he was anything but a dangerous force. In the legitimate ring Michael would be verging on over the hill and Jim would be down the other side. But out here in outlaw country they were both in their prime.

No bell, the old man just asked if they were ready and when the two nodded. He called out the start in a cracked voice that carried.

Jim came charging in, his style was aggressive and unforgiving, not quite boxing but not undisciplined enough to be called brawling. Michael came to meet him. His own style was more or less basic boxing, with a few principles from Karate and Kempo thrown in. For the most parts he didn't fuck around with the MMA shit. Arm bars were for white boys. His science still had sweetness in it.

He turned his shoulder and brought up his right to block Jim' first shot, then countered with his left jab. He connected but Jim twisted with it and the blow was glancing. They were still testing each other, they broke. It was Michael's turn to lunge with a straight right that Jim blocked. Jim swung big with the mean

14

hook that was his hurting bomb, and Michael connected with a solid blow to the face. Jim shook himself and smiled.

They were both fighters who liked to get in close, though Jim preferred to barrel over his opponent's defenses while Michael preferred to insinuate himself within them. They were both too good of fighters to get away with their chosen methods, so they sparred, got their hits where they could and waited for their opening.

Jim's opening came when Michael over committed himself to a combo. Michael knew the blow was coming just a moment before it landed. It caught him full in the face, he felt his nose crunch under Jim's knuckle. He didn't know if his nose was broken but it didn't matter, the effect was the same. His head swam and he staggered back, tucking in his elbows and his chin as he did. Distance was the only thing that could save him, if he let Jim get him while he was opened up like this he was over.

Jim opened up with a flurry of punches, catching Michael's ribs along with some glancing blows to the kidneys. They hurt. But that was OK; Michael was used to hurt. This was his advantage. His ability to manage pain. He put in more road work than any fighter he knew. It paid off at times like these, gave him something that steroids and show muscles never could. The ability to withstand, to endure, to be patient in pain, to protect himself as best he could and wait.

He sensed it, the hitch that saved him. Jim still had a lot of fight in him but he was getting older and the relentless pummeling he was delivering couldn't be sustained forever, his pace flagged, not a lot, but just enough to open up his rhythm.

Just enough for Michael to counter, hitting with some well timed jabs of his own, just when Jim was covering up, Michael crossed him with a hard left. It caught Jim on the brow, right above the eye and opened it up. A man's own blood in his eyes would always unnerve him, no matter how cool or

15

experienced of a customer he was. Jim lost concentration and Michael caught him again, this time in a solar plexus with a twisting punch that generated so much torque as it came forward that Michael winced to deliver it, Jim started to fall back. Michael decided he'd rather not have him get up again and hit him with an unsportsman like, but necessary, hook which twisted Jim's head around as he fell straight on his ass.

There was a tense moment of quiet as Jim lay in the red dirt. Then the old man entered the ring, bent like a hinge at the hip, peered down quizzically at Jim and declared the fight over.

The spectators cheered, maybe not quite as loud as they would have for Jim, but they'd come to see a good fight and that was what they had received. Jim groggily crossed the ring and after two or three attempts managed to place a magnanimous hand on Michael's shoulder.

Only one discordant note sounded. "Yah lost to a Jig?" A big man asked, "Guess it really is time to hang it up." His head was shaved, but dark bristles were already poking through the fishbelly white of his scalp. His grin split his bushy beard. If the man had said, "Nigger," there would have been a fight, but he was a true coward at heart, that was why he'd kept it at "Jig". So instead of beating his ass, Michael kept quiet, swallowed his pride and just dedicated himself to getting the hell out of Florida.

Jim looked like he wanted to fight anyway, but instead he stumbled and nearly fell. The bearded man laughed, "Fucking pathetic, at least the big 'un had heart." he didn't look at Michael as he said it. Michael felt someone tugging on him, it was Petra.

"Come on," she said, "Let's get out of here."

"Fraid I'll do something rash?" He asked.

"That's the next fighter, I've seen his record, rash wouldn't cover it." He could see the man a bit better now. He was massive; barrel-chested and already shirtless, like he couldn't wait for blood. The man had twin lightning bolts running up both ribs and a small

16

shamrock on his neck.

Michael had never been on the inside but you didn't have to be particularly street wise to know what those tats meant.

Michael allowed himself to be led away. Someone passed him a conciliatory open jar of moonshine. Michael took a sip, which hit harder than any of Big Jim's punches and tried to forget.

Petra led him back to the beer cooler, where the old man was waiting.

"I'll take that beer now," Michael said.

The old man handed him a Dixie.

"Something else," Michael coolly replied.

The old man looked confused but went back in and fished him out a Bud.

"Thanks," Michael said and walked away. Petra had already got his money, he was sure. "Let's get out of this fucking place," he said.

"Sure thing," Petra replied. "I have a few accounts to settle, but no reason we're not on the road in thirty minutes."

Michael grunted. He walked between the rows of cars. The sun had set and the sky was a crushed violet against which the mangroves swayed. Michael could smell the salt on the air. How could a place so beautiful contain so much ugliness? It seemed a question he had cause to ask himself far too many times in his relatively young life. It left a sorrow in his heart.

His reverie was interrupted by the sound of a creature that wanted to rip out his fucking bowels. Michael jumped, nearly dropped his shine but kept his grip. The animal in the back of the truck was locked in a putrid crate that smelled like it hadn't been emptied ever. Its left ear had been torn off leaving only a sickly nub and deep scars of pink mottled flesh showed through its thick black pelt, its eyes shone in the dark, its muzzle blasted foam off its bared teeth as it screamed its desire to end Michael's life, or the life of anyone.

17

Michael thought of his own Rot at home, a happy, affectionate, lazy, oil barrel of a dog. He thought about what had been done to this dog to make it this way and his heart was again seized with sorrow. This would not do, Michael decided.

He could let the dog go, but that would have mixed results at best. He couldn't have the dog run to the gathered crowd and maul some kid whose parent's reflexes had been slowed by too much pork, alcohol and violence to be of any good use as a protector. He could cut the bolt that was holding its crate shut. Give it a chance to get a jump on its master. But it could also force its way out and then he'd have the same problem as before.

He had learned long ago that you couldn't fight all the world's battles and injustices. He'd also learned long ago that there were some things you couldn't just turn a blind eye to and then look in the mirror and call yourself a good man. Both of those lessons had been hard won. And which one ruled in his life was a daily struggle.

He took a swig of his moonshine and considered. He noticed for the first time the side of the truck that held the poor animal. Two lightning bolts stenciled on either side. Michael didn't believe in coincidences. He looked back towards the ring. Zac Brown was still playing, the fight hadn't started yet.

*

Michael made his way to the trailer, he knocked on the door and Jim answered. "You wanted to get that bastard earlier; you still want to get him?"

Clarifying which bastard wasn't necessary, Big Jim just growled, "Yeah."

"How bad?"

Big Jim just smiled.

"That guy store his shit in here?"

Jim nodded to the corner, "It's still over there, that's how this mess got started. He came in early- we had some words."

"Anyone else in there?"

Big Jim shook his head.

18

"Come on," Michael said.

*

Five minutes later he and big Jim were carrying a forty pound crate containing one hundred and fifty pounds of confused Rottweiller between them. It didn't take long for the dog to start barking its head off and snapping at the mesh of its cage. But Michael wasn't worried about drawing attention. He figured that was what the dog had been doing since it'd arrived.

They made it to the trailer, Jim had the back of the crate and crab walked up the stairs. Michael followed, hoisting up the crate to keep it from tilting. Silently thanking himself for the extra reps in the gym. They brought the crate into the trailer's bathroom and set it on the yellowing linoleum. Jim stepped back right away. Michael picked up the bolt cutters, which he had retrieved from his own car and placed there earlier. With a snap he took off the cheap padlock that fastened the dog's crate, lifted the latch and took a quick step back past the threshold.

It only took the stunned dog a moment to leap forward, bursting the cage open. Luckily Jim was ready, and shut the door. The dog collided with it and cheap wood bulged and splintered. It took all of five seconds for the second hit to come. The dog would be through the flimsy door in half a minute. Michael picked up his bolt cutters and headed for the door.

"I'd hit the road Jim." Michael said. Jim picked up his duffle bag and nodded. "I'll see you at the next one."

"No," Jim replied, "I doubt you will." He held out his hand and Michael shook it. They closed the door behind them and headed in separate directions.

Michael called Petra, "You settle those accounts?"

"Yep."

"Get in the car and drive a quarter mile down the road, near those billboards, be ready to go."

"I will."

Michael found a couple of cars to hide behind. He had to make sure that asshole was the first through the door. Wouldn't do for the old man or one of his

19

lackeys to get mauled. He heard a cheer from the distant ring. Didn't sound like he'd have to wait long.

The dog barked for awhile and then went silent. People began heading towards the parking lot and leaving but not so many. The music started up again. Most were just looking to savor a night out with few responsibilities. It took ten minutes for the big Aryan Nation asshole to make it to the trailer, stepping with a swagger that told Michael that he'd won. You've got a tougher fight coming up Michael thought.

The man didn't have an entourage. He sauntered up the steps and opened the door, shut it behind him, and then screamed. Michael doubted that many heard over Zac Brown.

"Your day is over." Michael said to himself, he started running for where he'd knew Petra would be. The road work came in handy again.

The dog would die. He knew as much. Even if it somehow killed its master and got away, it wouldn't go feral. It would look for food in easy places and it'd be caught by animal control which would soon figure out its nature. Once you ingrained that kind of viciousness into a dog, there just wasn't much you could do to get it out. The dog would die, maybe even now by its master's own hand. But it wouldn't die with its throat torn out, bleeding into the sawdust, surrounded by cheering strangers and Michael needed to believe that was something.

He made it to the car. Traffic still wasn't pulling out in any meaningful way. "Drive," he said.

Petra didn't say anything, she just dry swallowed a pill, made sure the radar detector was on and made those four cylinders sing until they were three counties across the state line.

*

They drove through the night. Michael listened to the radio and kept an eye on the internet. He wasn't all that worried honestly; a cracker getting mauled by his own fighting dog wasn't going to cause a manhunt. Besides they'd already left Florida behind. They drove

20

twelve hours before they stopped for pancakes. Petra hadn't even yawned.

Michael took a sip of his coffee, "At times like this I wonder if we couldn't find a better use for our talents."

Petra was still stirring coffee into her sugar. "You talking retirement?" She asked.

Michael shook his head, "I'm talking diversifying, or who knows maybe diverging."

Petra nodded like she understood. Maybe she even did.

***

©2018 Bryce Wilson

Nowhere to Go but Dead

R. Daniel Lester

Inside the rusting Nissan Pathfinder, the woman breathes in deep. She breathes out. She does it again. She tries to *calm the fuck down.* She re-grips the steering wheel, resisting the urge to mash her palm into the horn. The highway is a winding river of brake lights as far as the eye can see. Everyone going nowhere fast, thanks to the blizzard in a place where it doesn't snow, not ever. What does Florida know about snow. Shit all and now it's bumper-to-bumper traffic on the only bridge out of town, and her in a stolen piece-of-shit SUV with a gut shot man in the back, bleeding all over the seat. But not just any man. No, it's Miami Frank, aka Ice Pick Frank, bad of the bad, King Asshole in a royal family of shitheads and scumbags.

An hour ago, his own people tried to execute him. See, Miami Frank's a snitch. Caught with his pants down, he drank the government Kool-Aid and turned rat for a new name, a new city and a fresh start. And today, the Fed transport, in transit from the safehouse in the Keys to the big city courthouse, gets ambushed. And she's watching from the SUV, slid down in the seat, freezing, window cracked so the glass doesn't fog up, hoping and praying for an opportunity to off the gangster herself. Before she gets her chance, a car pulls up out of nowhere and three bad guys jump out, opening fire on the Fed car. Real Hollywood shit. The Feds, trained in bad guy defense, return fire, guns blazing. The result: dead bad guys, dead Feds. What isn't like a movie at all is how quick the shootout ends, like a blink of the eye, no more than two.

When she's sure it's safe, she approaches the Fed car. And there, in the backseat, is Frank: shot, but alive--the lucky mutt. So she pulls the Pathfinder up to the Fed car and wrangles Frankie into the SUV, and they escape. Right, some escape. Trapped on the bridge, sitting ducks. She twists in her seat. "Hey, Frankie, you still with me?" She gets nothing back. Frankie's weak and delirious. He'll bleed out she doesn't get him to a hospital soon.

From outside, she hears voices. Discussion. In the rearview, in the split second that the back wiper clears a fraction of icy real estate, she catches a glance of a figure leaning into the window of the car behind her. Then, a knock on her driver side window.

"Police, ma'am."

She arranges the blanket in her lap. She rolls down the window. She smiles with her eyes. She says, "Yes, officer?"

The officer bends down and peers inside. "Everything okay? We're just making sure everyone has enough blankets and such. Big accident up ahead. Could take a while."

Slicked back hair. Designer suit. Wool overcoat. It doesn't feel right. He's no cop. She knows for sure when he sees Frankie in the backseat. His eyes light up. He shouts, "I got--"

She lifts the Lupara from under the blanket and pulls the trigger. Centre mass, 12-gauge shell, the spray of blood and bone as the man blows back onto the hood of the car in the next lane. She hears shouts. Bullets tear into the back of the SUV. The rear window explodes. She ducks low, wrenches the steering wheel left, and slams the 4-wheel drive transmission out of park, pounding down on the gas. The tires spin, spin, spin, then grab, rocketing the SUV through the gap between the cars and over the concrete divider

24

between bridge lanes. She nearly flips the Pathfinder, but miraculously, it stays upright and she mashes the pedal to the floor. The lane heading back into town is zombie movie empty. A snowy apocalypse. Only abandoned vehicles on the side of the road as witnesses.

"Frank, you don't get to die yet, motherfucker," she says, meaning it. Sure, she wants him dead. And yes, she was all ready to watch his light dim there in the Fed car, when his eyes focused on hers, alight with recognition, and he said the four words that changed everything.

He coughed blood.

He smiled blood.

He said, "Your son is alive."

*

Mob wife. Gangster moll. They don't tell you about that option in high school career counseling. Not a plan, it just happens. You meet a guy, go out on a few dates, you figure out pretty quick he doesn't live regular. Nine-to-five, punch the office clock, no, this is not his bag. But you look the other way because he's handsome, polite, well dressed and makes you laugh. And, truth be told, you like the attention and the sense of danger, plus the occasional fur coat or diamond ring that falls off the truck, as the story goes.

A movie plotline and you're starring in it.

And life goes on.

His mother, she sizes you up like a piece of beef the first time you meet, but she must know a prize cow with childbearing hips when she sees one and you get the cheek pinch of approval. Before you know it, you're married, until death do you part, and six months later, you're practically in the gang yourself. You wash blood out of clothes. You wrap raw knuckles. You look the other way so many times you get whiplash.

And life goes on.

Then, one of your husband's associates, a brutal man named Frank Zanatti, takes notice of you. Miami Frank, he misbehaved on his home turf, the land of sun and sand, so he's slumming it in the frigid Midwest until some heat blows over. But you wouldn't know it. Cocky son-a-bitch. Every other person in the world a mere toy to play with. And you're just his kind of doll, judging by the way he rubs up against you at wedding receptions and in the darkened hallways of restaurants where you never wait for a table and the maitre d' is trembling when he hands your husband the menu.

And life goes on.

One night, the doorbell rings while your husband is out of town. Standing there with a bottle of Barolo and the biggest shit-eating grin you've even seen is Frank. He feels terrible how he's been treating you, what with the inappropriate touching and the phone calls with no one on the other end but a heavy breather. So Good Wife, knowing that Frank is her husband's superior, says, "Fine, one glass, and then goodnight." And Stupid Wife wakes up in the morning, naked and groggy, face down in bed, feeling used hard and put away wet. The bullet sitting on the husband's pillow says yes, this happened. And to keep the mouth shut.

And life goes on.

One afternoon, you pee double lines on a pregnancy test. Nine months later, oops, you'll be damned if the kid doesn't take after your husband in the looks department all that much.

And life goes on.

Until it doesn't.

You're in the car with your husband, Frank and another guy who they must've got from the young mobster casting agency. He has shoulders like cement blocks and a face to match. And it feels wrong from the start, especially leaving the kid with a babysitter when all you want to do is sit beside his crib and watch him breathe, but no, you're Good Wife, so you dress up nice, pull a mink coat from the closet, and head out on the town. And it's unfortunate when Frank's car breaks down and they need a ride to the club, but they just don't make 'em like they used to anymore, do they?

Then, in the club parking lot, between two streetlights, the ice pick into your husband's brain from behind makes him gurgle. And the arm around your neck makes you fight, until you realize it's pointless. Cement Head is a strong son-of-a-bitch--but not incredibly skilled at his job yet or built for the task. His massive steroid limbs don't wrap that well around your delicate throat. And, yes, the life is running out of you, but not as fast as he may think. Then cop sirens pass by and Frank says, "You take care of her, I'll make sure they don't stop," and he gets out of the car and your eyeballs want to pop from their sockets but you've got an idea and you mimic dying and shake and gurgle and Cement Head thinks it's done— probably poppin' his kill cherry with you, lucky girl—so he doesn't check vitals before getting out of the car.

And it's such a good dead act you almost have yourself believing it. Heaven is the front seat of a Monte Carlo, who knew? Then, moments later, the door opens and someone says, "They left," and "Come with me," and "I'm sorry, but your house burned to the ground with your kid and the babysitter inside."

The words don't process. You and your husband weren't enough. Frank torched your house, your life. Because he could.

The man slaps you across your face—wake up and listen, or else. Your savior, he's about 5'10", sandy blonde hair, booze on his breath and an empty

27

gaze. Turns out, he's a Florida Fed on a self-funded, illegal vendetta against Frank Zanatti. Frank killed people close to him, once. Now, he's out for revenge and thinks you're just the ticket.

So your Fed squirrels you away, disappears you in a cabin on the outskirts of a small, nowhere place. Sticksville. A one-horse town but the horse is sickly and on its last legs. But there's a general store and a diner and enough regular, normal people so you can learn how to be one again.

Your saviour, he may wear a cape, but it's tattered and torn. He visits the cabin every couple of weeks. He gets drunk and punches the wall. He gets drunk and thinks that you ought to be grateful, pressing you up against the wall, next to the fist-sized holes. And you are but the knee to the balls lets him know you will pay him back in different ways. The fetal position and the tears in his eyes means he understands.

And life goes on.

You get new I.D. and a new life, but all under the table, hush hush. Don't fly with this passport, he tells you. You look at your face in the mirror, the one with the new name, and have no idea where this person would go anyway.

After a month, you get up off your ass and stop feeling so sorry for yourself. You start running again. You do wind sprints and calisthenics. You tire yourself out like an owner does a dog. Distraction helps ease the pain. Your husband, dead. Your son, dead. Everything you knew, burned to the ground.

And life goes on.

Until the day you get the call that Frank's back on his old Florida stomping grounds but about to turn snitch and even your Fed contact won't know where he goes after the trial. You listen. You know it's now or never. You promise no innocents get hurt by your

28

hand. You run more. You train harder. You start shooting, using the targets set up in the back yard. Your aim sucks so you start using a break-barrel Lupara shotgun that your saviour brought to the cabin in a leather sport bag. Try this, he says, grinning. Cast a wide net, you get more fish. You like the weapon, its heft, especially when you learn that the word "lupara" literally means "for the wolf."

You take the bus to Florida. It takes a gazillion hours. You stare out the window, preparing for a suicide mission. You wrap your conscience down tight with chain and remember the night Frank and his goon almost killed you, half wishing they did.

*

Doc Shaw is closing up shop for the day—hell, for the week, what with this weather—when a woman points a nasty-looking shotgun at his head through the window. The street is deserted. Not a car or another person in sight. Just the snow and the wind and the woman with the gun. Her eyes are a trapped animal behind zoo glass. The parka she's wearing has blood on it.

The woman taps the glass with the gun barrel and says, "Open up." He does and she sticks a foot inside, asking if he is alone, looking relieved when he nods. "To the back door," she says. "Now."

Doc Shaw does what he's told. The woman follows him through the veterinary office, past the front desk, past the surgery rooms, down the hallway to the alley exit door. She tells him to wait and keeps one hand tight around his wrist as she pops the back door, peering out. Satisfied, she nods for him to continue out into the alley, to a Nissan Pathfinder with bullet holes in the chassis and a shattered rear window. The man in the backseat has a bullet hole too, and they each take an arm and drag the man, dead weight, inside.

29

Like boating the marlin he caught last summer—
hoisting, pulling, cursing—they finally manage to get
the man up on an operating table. And though Doc
Shaw is in his early 70s, the woman has a harder time
than he does. She grimaces. Her forehead pops
sweat.

"Bad shoulder?" he asks.

She holds up the shotgun, wincing. "Looks easier
in the movies."

Doc Shaw grabs a pair of scissors and cuts the
shirt away from the man's wound, assessing the
damage. "He's lucky. No major organs or arteries hit.
But he's lost a lot of blood, miss. He needs a hospital."

"Exactly," she says.

"Not an animal hospital."

"No choice, doc."

"But—"

"You ever try and save a dog got run over by a car
and left for dead?"

Doc Shaw nods. "Last year. The Miller's golden
lab."

"It live?"

Doc Shaw shakes his head.

"Well," she says, "first time for everything."

*

Four blocks from the animal hospital, ten from the
police station, and they catch up with her. She's
moving slow--pulling Frankie on a stretcher that the
Doc helped rig up after he did his best to stabilize the
patient--when a blue van skids to a halt in the snow,
nearly fishtailing into a bus stop. The doors open. Two
men jump out with handguns. She dives to the ground
behind a parked car and drags the stretcher out of
harm's way. With one in the breech, she crouches,
turns, and fires blind. Panic mode. Desperation.

Her shoulder screams and so does she.

30

The snow, like a tomb, buries the sound.

Bullets slam into the car. Popcorn in a hot pan. She hits the ground, eating snow. A bullet ricochets into her left thigh. She bleeds. She muffles another scream, loading another shell into the Lupara. She makes herself sit up and lean out, catching one asshole close, on a reload. Boom—takes his knees. He topples.

She looks but doesn't see the other guy. Find the shell—where is the goddamned shell? Frankie moans.

She slaps him. "Wake up, fucker. Where is he? Where is my son? I just need to know."

Frank says, "Wha?" Dazed and confused. But his lizard brain is operating fine. Survival mode. He focuses, says, "Get me safe first," but it comes out more like, *Gemmesayphurst.*

The son-of-a-bitch is willing to take her son's whereabouts to his grave. If he even knows. Maybe it's all a big joke and she's the punch line. But she won't know until she gets him to the cops, or dies trying—because help won't come to her. She called an emergency burner from the vet's landline while the Doc was working on Frank and her saviour told her the system was overrun with 911 calls and blizzard-related mayhem, so not to expect any knights in shining armor. And why didn't she just kill the son-of-a-bitch like they planned?

"You know why," she said. "You knew all along."

His voice cracked, went low. "Knew what?"

"I saw it only I didn't know what it was. Every time you got drunk and made a move on me. Guilt for more than just the roving hands."

"I—the plan—"

"Spare me."

"I was going to tell you about your son…when it was done."

31

She'd heard enough. "Bullshit," she said and threw the phone against the wall.

Only now she was alone in a winter hell, a snowy wasteland, dead meat ready for the hook. Nothing left but to punch the ticket for purgatory. She can't move. Icicle hands and fucked nerves. Her shells, dropped. She hears the crunch of footsteps in the snow. Careful, controlled.

The Last Asshole Standing approaches, wanting a closer look. She is a curiousity, not something you see too often in his line of work. He gets closer, grinning a sick little smile when he sees her. He raises his gun. She prepares for it, welcoming death to the doorstep. But then a gunshot rings out and her executioner drops to his knees, pitches forward. She doesn't understand, until she does.

"Jesus, Doc," she says.

The vet approaches, confused, shaking, an ancient-looking revolver in his hand. "You looked like you could use some help."

"You shouldn't be here."

The vet, looking around, doesn't hear her. "What on Earth—?"

"Get out of here," she says. "Now."

But it's too late.

The gunman, only wounded, rolls over and shoots.

The doc clutches his stomach, walks a few steps, falls forward into a snow bank.

She kicks the gun out of the assasin's hand with her good leg.

He curses and begins to crawl for the weapon.

She feels for a shell.

A few blocks away, the sound of sirens.

So there is time.

Patience.

Haste makes waste.

32

She snaps open the breech of the Lupara and loads a shell. For the wolf.

The sirens get closer.

He turns, looks right at her.

She closes the breech, her eyes.

And pulls the trigger.

*

Sirens almost upon her and with the last of her strength, she crawls to Frank. Blood everywhere, spattered. Spent shells burned hot tunnels down into the snow. When she finally reaches him, she keys in the number from memory, on the cell belonging to the guy she just shot. He who has no face needs no phone. When the call is answered, she speaks before the Fed can spit out any more lies.

"Promise me. Promise you'll save my boy. Killing Frank won't bring my family back," she says. "Or yours."

"How did—?"

"I did some research of my own. Your wife and daughter were killed by stray bullets when Frank and his crew took down that diamond exchange in '86. He skated because no one was willing to place him at the scene after two eyewitnesses died in separate house fires."

The silence on the line says it all.

"Promise me, goddammit."

"I promise."

"Hey, asshole." She slaps Frank on the face to revive him. "Hear those sirens? I did my part, now do yours." She holds the phone up to his mouth. Frank nods, whispering into the phone. She hears "Boys' School" and "Palermo" and "Preside Guiseppe" and the Fed says, "Okay, got it," and she drops the phone.

The snow is cool against her hot cheek.

The sirens stop.

Footsteps crunch in the snow.

Holy shit.

Over here.

The snow is still falling.

Clipped femoral, massive blood loss.

We're losing her.

The snow lands on her cheek, her lips, her tongue.

She tastes the snow.

She remembers how her husband and son used to make snowballs in the backyard then throw them at each other while she watched from the kitchen window.

She smiles.

She lets go.

Nowhere else to go but dead.

***

Jackass Junction
Jon Zelazny

Peter Townshend, the twenty-three-year-old lead guitarist and songwriter for the burgeoning British rock band The Who, was dreaming what he called "the motor horror mystery." He never remembered how it started, but it always picked up at his gran's house where he'd lived as a small chap when his parents weren't getting on. In the dream, he was alone and couldn't find her. He checked the back garden and the kitchen and the front room and then upstairs, which was where things became specific and super-clear: he peers out the window and sees a strange auto parked outside along the front walk, an old pre-war Humber Super Snipe painted flat black. He can't see in the windows, but the car is bouncing up and down, like there are kids jumping around in the back. Something about it alarms him. He goes back downstairs, calling for Denise, but no luck. He unlatches the front door, goes down the front steps, and stops when he hears a noise like an animal mewling in torment. He looks around, but the lane is deserted. Then he hears the strangled cry again and he knows it's coming from inside the car. He starts toward it, and that's usually all he remembers, but today it's different: he vividly sees himself crossing the walk. Now a grown-up, he grasps the back door handle, presses in the thumb latch—

Pete came to with a start. Daylight, yes. Childhood, no. England, no.

Their motor coach was still running—the familiar diesel thrum and cold air blowing from the vent overhead—but they weren't moving. Blinking out the window, he saw flat land dotted by clumpy vegetation; trees and shrubbery in the American South grew into each other, creating impenetrable green walls and hillocks. Squinting out the other side, Pete saw they were idling outside a combination Texaco-Stuckey's. The five-and-dime was a longhouse with a broad, peaked roof, and her twin fuel pump islands shielded from the sun by a great batwing-style overhang. It was part of a now-familiar culture: service stations, truck stop diners and six dollar motels, billboards proclaiming "Jesus is Risen" or "Hank's Nudie Bar," and all the other lonely totems that dotted the asphalt veins of America's endless motorways.

Rubbing his eyes, Pete arose and quietly padded down the aisle. Everyone else was conked out: Entwistle and the promoter's secretary, Moonie and the buxom waitress from Hardee's. Head roadie Big Ed, his henchmen Danny, Kenny, Fitch, and… whoever those other three were. Pete longed for sleepy-bye as well, but his perverse brand of insomnia knocked him out within minutes of closing his eyes only to fully reawaken him three or four hours later; their manager Kit Lambert called it the curse of a creative mind.

Reaching the empty driver's seat of their GM Buffalo bus, Pete spied co-manager Chris Stamp having a smoke outside with their coachman, a stubby middle-aged cowboy who insisted they call him Wild Bill. Seizing the handgrip, Pete retracted the accordion doors and stepped down into a crushing liquid bear hug of humidity. "Fucking hell."
Stamp mopped his brow. "Makes you homesick for the cold and damp, eh?"
Pete surveyed the aluminum-plated length of the vehicle. Nothing appeared amiss. "We low on petrol?"

"Nossir." Wild Bill indicated the front wheel. "That left front tire done blew. Fella inside called around;

37

found us a replacement outside Fort Pierce. Gonna take 'em an hour to drive it here, maybe another to change it."

Pete looked to Stamp. "We've got that sort of time?"

"It's four hours to Miami. Curtain ain't 'til nine."

"I left 'er runnin'," the driver added. "So y'all won't roast to death."

Pete grunted and looked up and down the two-lane road. Aside from the access loop back to the turnpike, the outpost was an island in a sea of scrub. "No pub about?"

Wild Bill jerked a thumb northward. "Like I told your amigo, you got the most famous saloon in Yeehaw Junction settin' right up the road there."

"Yeehaw Junction?"

"Shoot, in my daddy's day, this was Jackass Junction. 'Til some Tallahassee fella didn't think that were appropriate for no state map."

Pete nodded. The air temperature was too beastly to support life, but once Keith Moon awoke, the bus would be havoc again, and he could use a spot of quiet. Nodding to Stamp and the driver, he crossed the parking lot and set off down the cracked asphalt road, punting at chunks of gravel and shreds of rubber.

For some reason, the absence of any houses made him think of his own. Two months married and weeks after moving into their new place in Twickenham, here he was across the pond again, living the horrible, wonderful fantasy of the English fucking rock star. He told Karen he lacked the patience and know-how for home repair, but their to-do list was a mile long and growing. The new custom-built windows had arrived a half inch too wide, the floor tile in the kitchen was full of cracks and loose bits, the parlor wall plagued with rot.

38

He'd been walking less than a minute, but every stitch of his khaki trousers and navy tennis shirt was already soaked in sweat. Bravo, Stamp; packing them off to south Florida in late July. Mopping his brow, Pete saw a lone structure shimmering in the heat ahead, but it was too far. Looking back though, so was the bus. What would Lawrence of Arabia do? Probably push on for a good pint. Pete hastened his pace.

The Desert Inn Restaurant and Bar was a two-story roadhouse of termite-chewed wood siding with peeling white paint set in the V of a crossroads. A front beer garden intruded on a gravel parking lot that currently held a pair of weather-beaten Ford pickup trucks and a lone Harley-Davidson. Passing the deserted outside tables and a Bell South phone box with a cracked window, Pete grinned at the warped wood sign above the front door: "Welcome to Jackass Junction." British history bored him—all those fucking kings and battles, back to Roman times—but the U.S.A. was still a frisky pup of a nation, and he could tick off all her milestones on one hand: Yorktown, Davy Crockett, Lincoln freeing the slaves, cowboys and Indians, the motor car, blues and jazz, Bogey, D-Day, the bomb, Elvis. A place called Yeehaw Junction could only be part of that great mosaic.

He opened the wheezing spring door into a barroom cluttered with frontier bric-a-brac, a flickering Pepsi-Cola sign, and a few actual natives. Three brawny, roughhewn young farm workers drinking at a side table went silent at the sight of him. There was a decrepit old man studying a newspaper behind the bar, while perched on the stool before him was a bloke in greasy dungarees and a denim vest emblazoned with a fiery phoenix insignia and the legend *Warlocks*. Ten stools away was a slight young man with a sculpted blonde 'do. Pete saw it was his band mate,

39

Roger Daltrey, and adjusted course.

"Must be the girlfriend," one of the drinkers cracked. The other two snorted.

Pete raised a self-conscious hand to his hair. It was Beatle-length, nothing more. Rog acknowledged him with a nod. He had his cig and a bottle of beer and was poring over what appeared to be a thick stack of legal papers in a black three-ring binder.

"May I?"

"Suit yourself."

Too many bridges had burned between them in the last five years, too many unforgivable words savagely thrust like dirks into each other's guts, but touring had become easier once they'd reached a sort of détente, an armored equilibrium. It wasn't perfect, and they'd never be chums, but by and large it kept their operation on the rails.

Taking the offered stool, Pete hailed the barkeep. "Cup of tea, then?"

His order produced a fresh round of guffaws from the far table. He shot them a glare, but Daltrey slapped his forearm. "Here, don't start nothin' I'll have to finish."

Chagrined, Pete faced forward. Verbally, he could flay any man alive, but actual brawling was out. Plucking a napkin from a metal dispenser, he wiped his face, and took stock of the décor: faded photos of cowpokes, doughboys, and alligator wrasslers. Iron farm implements and wagon wheels. Life-size mannequins of an Indian and his squaw awaited service at a corner table, while what looked to be a jackrabbit mounted above the bar sported an enormous set of antlers. His eyes settled on Rog's folder. "What're you reading, then?"

"My contract."

"What contract is that?"

"Our contract. With Track Records."

40

The counterman materialized with his cup and saucer. Pete smiled. "Got a splash of milk?"

"Huh?"

"Creamer," Daltrey translated.

The coot regarded them sourly. "Where do I splash it?" The boozers had a good laugh at that too as the man shuffled off again.

Rog exhaled smoke toward the ceiling. "You know how much they're making?"

"Who?"

"Lambert. And Stamp. They get 40% as managers, right? Which is already pretty fucking steep. On top of that, they're our record company. That's another cut off the top. Then Kit's our producer, right? More for him still."

"Jesus, mate. We live like pashas. What more do you want?"

"I work hard for my pay. I want everything what's comin' to me."

They heard footsteps and looked over. One of the dumbbells was approaching. A squat fellow with an unshaven baby face dressed in bib overalls and unlaced army boots. "I seen you two somewhere," he declared. He had the whole joint's attention now. Even the biker turned to watch. Overalls pointed knowingly. "Wasn't you singin' on T.V.?"

The rockers exchanged surprised looks. "Yeah, that's right," Daltrey allowed.
"I knew it," the clod whooped. "You them two Jewboys from New York City!"

Pete looked to his partner as the old man returning with his cream shook his head. "Red, you drunk as hell."

Red stood his ground. Grinning, he pointed to Pete. "You're Simon. And he's Carbuncle. Am I right?"

The travelers burst out laughing. "Close, mate,"

41

Rog shot back.

The dimwit's face clouded in confusion. Pete chimed in, "Actually, we're Peter, Paul, and Mary."

Daltrey took the cue. "He's Pete. I'm Mary."

"I thought I was Mary?"

Glowering at his mistake, the prat slunk back to his jeering mates. Rog waved for another beer. It was good to share a laugh, Pete thought. Daltrey usually walked around with such a stick up his ass, it was easy to forget he wasn't as thick as he pretended to be.

Or maybe he was, at that. Look at him; nose parked in that ledger. Pete sadly clicked his tongue. "Money, money, money. It's not what life's all about, son."

Rog didn't look up. "Yeah? What you want to be when you grow up, then?"

"What are you talking about?"

"I'm talkin' about the future. I plan on having one. What about you?"

Pete chuckled. Poor dumb Daltrey, always on about something. The singer jabbed a finger at him. "Suppose you *don't* die before you get old? You could live to be forty. You wanna be some old, bald geezer still smashin' his bloody guitar?"

Pete looked away. It was a low blow. Civilized people simply didn't talk that way. "Look... you want to hear what I got for the opera?"

"No. I don't."

Undeterred, Pete dug a notebook from his hip pocket. He scanned his notes, but just as he took a breath to begin, the front door wheezed open behind them again and then banged shut. Turning, they found they'd been joined by a police officer; a solid figure in a pressed tan uniform with black piping, belt sagging with gear, mirrored sunglasses, and the ubiquitous

42

Smokey-the-Bear hat.

The counter man cast aside his newspaper. "Afternoon, Sheriff."

"How are ya, Walt?" The copper removed his shades, hung them from a breast flap, and cast a piercing gaze at the three boozing locals, who immediately cut the chatter and even sat up a little straighter in their chairs. Shifting his piercing blue eyes right, to the two youths, the sheriff doffed his hat, revealing an abundant forehead exaggerated by receding blonde-white hair. Pete and Rog nodded, but he made no reply. Instead, he fixed on the motorcycle club patch dead ahead. "Warlocks, huh?" He came in for a closer look. The vest's owner didn't turn or flinch as the floorboards awakened under the patrolman's polished black boots, he just calmly took another pull of his beer. The Man halted a few steps behind him. "Seen more and more of these patches of late. Where you from, boy?"

"Kissimmee."

"Look at me when I talk to you."

He didn't have to ask anyone else. Every eye was riveted. Pete half expected the outlaw to whirl with six guns blazing. Instead, the biker set down his beer and slooowly revolved on his stool, keeping his palms low and open. He was well past thirty; clean shaven, dark hair trimmed military tight, but gaunt and battered-looking. His open left hand revealed a missing pinky and ring finger.

"Where ya headed?" the lawman pressed.

"Keys."

"What for?"

"Roofing job."

"Bullshit. You're too stupid to climb a ladder."

If the Law was hoping to bait his prey, he was disappointed. The Warlock wisely kept his eyes

43

lowered and his mouth shut. When The Man abruptly spun on his heels and drifted on toward the good ol' boys, the hoodlum silently resumed his libation.

Rog shook his head. "Fucking Gestapo."

Pete rechecked his notes. "So the story's about this kid who, like, lives completely in his own world. All he has is music, right? Doesn't see or hear what's going on around him and doesn't talk to anybody neither. Just grooves to this cool thing inside his head."

Rog lit a fresh cig. "Let me guess. His name's Pete?"

"Fuck you, Rog. It's just an idea." He started to tuck the book back in his pocket.

Daltrey waved in relent. "Alright. So this little fucker's deaf, dumb, and blind— "

"I never said that!"

"You said he don't see or hear or— "

"I know what I—y'know… that might work. Deaf, dumb, and blind."

"Anyway… ?"

"So this music, it goes round and round in his head… it's like patterns, right? It's mathematical. And he unlocks the patterns… and all the great mysteries are revealed!"

"What mysteries is that?"

"Why are we here? What's the purpose of life, and God, and the universe, eh?"

"Then what?"

"I dunno. Maybe he… becomes holy?" He let the thought hang there. Daltrey raised a hand but failed to cover his smirk. "What're you laughin' at? It's not a fucking comedy routine!"

"Nah, nah, nah. I was just thinking what Kit would say."

"What?"

44

Moon was forever parodying their erudite manager, but Rog did a mean impression as well. "Marvelous, Pete! Bloody brilliant! Could be a million-dollar idea!"

Pete snorted and the singer lightly punched his shoulder, a rare moment of *Hard Day's Night* comradery between them.

"You girlies telling jokes over here? I'd sure like to hear one."

The foreigners turned to find the unkind policeman planted a few meters back. Daltrey assumed the deference East End troublemakers used when addressing bobbies, headmasters, or magistrates. "No, sir."

"First visit to Yeehaw Junction?"

"Yes, sir," Rog answered. "Just passing through, like."

"Where from?"

"London."

"London?"

"London, England," Pete clarified.

"Whoop-de-fuckin'-do. Y'all run out of barbers in London, England?"

The rockers fell mute. As before, the whole room hung on every word.

"Any son of mine come home lookin' like that, I'd beat his ass red."

The rockers studied their shoes, though Pete's mouth was twitching. The cop saw it bubbling up in him and hooked two thumbs in his belt, eagerly awaiting any fool sass. When he again failed to draw any, he shook his head in derision and stepped away. Then Pete muttered, a bit too audibly, "Pig fucker."

The cop froze. And slooowly turned back with a big, shark grin. "Ladies, here in Osceola County, we got certain standards of decency. Drifters such as

45

yourselves—little sketchy-lookin'—win a night's room and board in our fine county jail, with a complimentary shave, buzz cut, and a good, long soak in a tub of ice water."

The travelers' faces fell. Daltrey slowly rose. "Sir, we ain't done nothin'. Our coach is just down the road. We'll be on our way, and you won't never see us again."

"That's a tempting offer, Blondie. Tell you what: why don't we just skip to the haircuts? We can take care of those right here, right now."

Horrified, Pete rose as well and they both instinctively eased back until their backsides touched the Indian table. Rog glanced about. They were penned in the corner.

Pete looked to him in panic. "He's havin' us on, right?"

"Shut up, you stupid git."

The cop grinned at the barkeep. "Got any prunin' sheers back there, Walt?"

"Aw, c'mon, now," the old-timer complained.

"Scissors, Walt. I'll do it with a goddamn steak knife if I have to." Pivoting again, he addressed the boozer table. "Chester, Red, Floyd, get your big, dumb asses over here. Y'all gonna be my deputies for the next ten minutes."

Hooting and hollering, the cretins pushed back their chairs and crowded forward, forming a footballer's defensive line between the unlucky patrons and the door.

"Look," Pete wailed. "We're rock stars, you know. What about our civil rights?"

The copper chortled. "Only right you got is to scream like a baby while I let these cracker peckerwoods take turns shovin' it up your skinny little punk keester!"

Clap! Clap! Clap! Clap!

Four sharp, staccato cracks came from behind the

46

enemy line. The sheriff looked back first, followed by his accomplices, and then a strangely haunted voice broke the air:

> *Don't you mind people grinnin' in your face*
> *Don't mind people grinnin' in your face*

Peering between their foes, Pete saw their mystery blues singer was the biker. The Warlock was on his feet, facing the four villains like a gunfighter, swinging and clapping a deliberate cadence, the words coming from some magnificent broken corner of his soul:

> *You know they'll jump you up and down*
> *They'll carry you round and round*
> *Just as soon as your back is turned*
> *They'll be tryin' to crush you down*

In spite of everything, Pete was enthralled. This was a voice of twisted metal, gin mills, and too many bad roads taken, a voice that shook the weak and made the mighty tremble.

> *So just bear this in mind*
> *A true friend is hard to find*
> *Don't you mind people grinnin' in your face*

The beat slackened. *Clap. Clap. Clap.* Then the biker again showed The Man his palms in supplication. Red and his friends seemed dumbstruck. They looked to each other, and to the cop, but the lawman seemed equally caught short.

"What do you say?" the biker drawled. "That enough entertainment for one day?"

All eyes were on the cop, who finally nodded, and then inclined his chin ever-so-slightly toward the rockers. "You boys go on. Me 'n this nigger-hollerin' sumbitch gonna have us a little set-to."

No further prodding was required. The rockers cut a path between two goons who let them pass

47

unmolested, and a heartbeat later they were out the door gasping for breath in the stabbing sunlight and crushing humidity. They dodged around the parked police car and the two pick-up trucks, but Rog came to a skidding stop as they reached the Harley.

Pete looked back to him, wild-eyed. "Come on, mate!"

Rog stood seething. "He didn't run out on us, did he?"

"Christ, Rog. That's a fucking copper!"

Daltrey stood rooted, fists balled. "Get back to the coach. Tell Stamp and Big Ed and the lads to get their arses up here."

"Aw, don't be daft, man."

"And no Moon, get me? Tie him to the fucking wheel if you have to."

Pete stood hopelessly. But even as his singer turned determinedly to the dreaded Desert Inn, the front door opened, and their savior strode out, apparently unharmed. Covering the distance between them, he nodded nonchalantly and straddled his machine.

Baffled, Rog looked between him and the villains' den. "You alright? How'd you get out of that, then?"

The Yank raised his hand missing fingers. "Two tours on a Medevac in Vietnam."

Fairly agog, Pete edged closer. "That was bloody amazing! You've got a fantastic voice, you know?" The biker shrugged like it weren't no thing. On impulse, Pete pulled his billfold and produced a cream-colored slip of paper. "Do you know Marine Stadium in Miami? We're playing there tonight."

The man took the ticket and squinted. "The Who. Y'all some new rock group?"

"Best in the world, mate."

"Yeah? Y'all keep covenant with the blues?"

The rockers exchanged surprised looks. "Yes,"

48

Pete assured him. "We do."

"Absolutely," Rog agreed.

The man studied the horizon. "Blues... and a good bike, man. That's about all you can count on in this world." He reached some decision and handed the ticket back. "Better give this to some chick you wanna ball."

The guitarist laughed. "I'm Pete. This is Rog. What's your name?"

"Ah, a name's just another label, boys. I'm the spirit of America." With a final nod, he kicked the big machine to life, gunned the throttle, and roared off down the road.

The rockers took one last look at the inn and all but sprinted back to the Texaco.

*

The venue sat on the shore of Virginia Key. It was built for fans of speedboat racing, but The Who weren't complaining. Five thousand screaming tossers had shown up to see them play against a scenic backdrop of Miami's barrier islands and the myriad lights of her downtown skyline. Midway through the first set, Pete told the crowd, "We'd like to do one of our favorites by the great Mose Allison. It's called "Young Man Blues." And we'd like to dedicate it tonight to all the Warlocks out there."

***

©2018 Jon Zelazny

Hollyw
Nipples &
PALM TREES
EVERY MAN DESERVES
A HAPPY ENDING

Kettle's Wake

Jack Bates

"I need your boat."

I recognized the woman on the dock looking down at me. She worked at one of Daytona's ubiquitous tiki bars. A five-dollar word for a two-bit guy like me. Doc says it's important I keep my brain revved. It was bugging me I knew the woman's face but not her name. It was Jodie…something.

I said I recognized her. I didn't say I knew her.

"My boat's not exactly passenger ready at the moment. I had a guy puke up a pint of cheap booze and some popcorn shrimp."

"Lightweights and waves, huh?"

"Yeah. I'm docked until I get it cleaned." I aimed the hose at the mess on the seats.

"You're Ray Kettle, right?"

So she knew my name. "You read that on the side of the boat."

She played to my ego. "I heard you were quite the powerboat racer."

My racing days were over. I still dug the feel of a boat on the open seas. The bounce off the water felt the way I always figured a stone skipping over the surface of a lake felt. A momentary break from reality where gravity abdicates its power over mass.

My addiction to speed wrecked me. I retired from racing in hydroplane boats a broken man. Figuratively and literally. I was also nearly out of cash. I tried suing the power drink company that sponsored the race circuit I competed for malfeasance. The company expected the six of us pilots to race in their boats maintained by their mechanics who didn't give two shits about us. The boats were constantly breaking down, or in my case, exploding. I should have known better than to hire a lawyer from a pop-up ad on a phone app. The settlement wasn't the windfall I expected. The goddamn lawyer took a third.

I missed the rush of racing, though, so I took my settlement cash and bought a used cigarette boat, which is another name for a powerboat. Yellow and black. Thirty-six feet long. Three outboards on the back. Sat six. I called her Kettle Won. Ironic, I know. I hadn't won anything except a mountain of debt. To get my fix, I took adrenaline junkies on full-throttle runs in a boat that cost me way too much money to own and maintain.

"My racing days are behind me. I'm sure you can find another boat."

"I know I can get a boat. I'm paying for you, Mr. Kettle." She reached into a large, canvas bag hanging from two large, wooden hoops on her shoulder. "Ten thousand now—"

"Ten thousand?"

"I can give you another ten when we get to Nassau."

She seriously offered me twenty thousand dollars to take her sixty miles. I had fees, expenses. I was two months behind on my boat payments. Twenty grand would provide some cushion. Hell, twenty grand would do a ton for me.

"When were you planning on going?"

Jodie Somebody looked at me like I was a moron. Then she smiled. "Now."

"Like right now?"

"Yeah."

Look. I'm not a moron. I may have suffered what they used to call a closed head injury after my boat exploded at a hundred and ten miles an hour but I could still put things together.

"You didn't make twenty large in tips at the tiki bar."

She scoffed, looked around the docks impatiently. "You don't know."

"I don't?" I opened a beer. Offered her one. She shook her head. "I know you want to give me twenty thousand dollars to get you out of Florida. That's not

53

something someone who's saved twenty thousand dollars in tips does."

"Who does?"

"Somebody who wants to get away fast. That's not what I do."

She folded her arms under her breasts. Her mouth was one long, flat line, her face tired and desperate. "If there's some other way I can convince you..."

Back in my racing days I jumped at opportunities like that. I had my pick of boat-bunnies around the gulf or up and down the Florida coast. Women used to line the docks before and after a race. So many of them popped their tops at me that after a while it was a bigger turn on when they didn't.

That was back in the day. Funny how fast three years can slip by a guy and things change around him but not in him.

Twenty grand and a little tail? Gentlemen, start your engines.

I held my hand out to her and brought her down into the boat. I showed her to a cushion that wasn't wet with soap and water and partially digested popcorn shrimp.

"You want that beer now?"

She took the bottle and twisted off the cap with a bar trained hand. "You mind if I smoke?"

"If you need to."

She went through her shoulder bag again. I could have sneaked a peak down her top when she leaned over. What really got my attention were the large, round bundles of cash in her bag.

And the gun.

She fished a cigarette out of a crumpled box. I held a lighter for her. She blew the smoke over my hand cupping the flame between us. She looked up at me with her big, brown eyes. Leaning back, she inhaled deep into her lungs, turned her face skyward, and blew out a long plume of smoke.

"You okay now?"

She shook her head on the inhale, spoke on the exhale. "No. I'm far from okay."

"You want to tell me what's going on?"

She looked around the marina. "I'd feel a lot better telling you this out on the water."

By then I had resigned myself to taking her. It was going to be dark soon. I wanted to get as much distance as I could with the sun still up. It took about twenty minutes to clear the Halifax River. A summer sun cast condo shadows over the waterway. It was like passing over an infinite stretch of finish lines. The entire way she watched the shores.

"Four weeks ago I found a backpack on the beach. It was under the pier, snagged on a piling. I don't know why I did what I did. I mean, it could've been a bomb, right?"

"But it wasn't."

"No. It was three kilos of coke."

"Three kilos of what?"

"Coke."

"Like that guy up in Ormond."

An old guy out with a metal detector found a kilo of coke and a couple of shell casings. He turned it into the police. They speculated a couple of traffickers capsized off the coast and the kilo found its way to the shore. That's the problem with amateurs and speed. Everyone thinks it's just as simple as opening the throttle and gunning it. No one knows the secret to speed is instinct. Knowing when to juke left or right or when to drop down. The bodies were never found so no one actually knew how the kilo or the bullet casings turned up on the shore.

She flicked her cigarette over the side of the boat. "Yeah. I'm thinking it was part of the same shipment."

"What did you do with yours?" I wondered how much went up her nose.

"Where do you think I got all the money?"

It was fairly clear why she wanted—she needed—to get out of Florida. You don't sell somebody else's coke.

"We were selling only to people we knew. Or thought we knew."

"We?"

55

"This girlfriend of mine. Janet. She works with me at Tiki Sid's."

Tiki Sid's! Of course. That was the where I'd seen Jodie Somebody. Sid's was a shithole of bar on the west side A1A. Tourists never crossed over to that side of the Atlantic Coast Highway. It was strictly for locals. Drifters. Losers. Guys like me. Who opens a tiki bar that's not on the beach? Someone desperate. Who works at tiki bar not on the beach? Someone even more desperate. Somebody who would sell someone else's coke and pocket the cash. Right then and there wasn't anyone more desperate than Jodie Somebody.

We reached Ponce Inlet where the Halifax River spills out into the Atlantic Ocean. I should have slowed. I should have told her I needed fuel and pulled in at New Smyrna. I should have taken us back. The twenty thousand dollars was just too juicy to ignore. I kept going and Jodie Somebody kept talking.

"Janet said she knew a guy who could show us how to cut it."

It was starting to get complicated as the cast of characters increased.

"And you trusted this guy?"

"Right? He was cool. Kept things light but serious. Took us to this guy who bought old storage units. He'd gotten a locker once that had belonged to a pharmaceutical supplier."

"You mean a drug dealer."

"The buyer doesn't know anything about who owned the storage unit. But he does know who to sell its contents to. The locker buyer had boxes of little glass vials just the right size for distribution. I just wish he'd had a machine that would fill them."

"You filled them by hand?"

"Every last one. We had to wear pollen masks and coveralls and rubber gloves. It took the four of us a couple of days to fill the vials."

"Four of you?"

"Yeah. We didn't have the cash to buy the vials so we cut the auction hunter in on the deal."

56

"All those people. Aren't you worried someone will talk?"

"Nobody is going to talk, Mr. Kettle."

"Then why are you in a hurry to get to Nassau?"

"We moved a lot of powder in a short time. Whoever owned that backpack with the three kilos in it is going to start looking for whoever is selling it."

We were far enough from shore I could open the throttle. Jodie Somebody dropped her shoulder bag to grab the seat in front of her.

"Why didn't you leave with your friend Janet?" I had to yell to be heard.

"Couldn't find my passport."

"You got it now?"

"It's in my bag."

"With your gun?"

Ever hear of crocodile tears? Jodie gave me a crocodile smile only there was nothing fake about it. "How did you know about the gun?"

"I saw it earlier when you were digging for your smokes."

"Most men look at my tits."

"Your girlfriend Janet. She's not in Nassau, is she?"

"Unfortunately for her, no."

"And Brian and the auction hunter. They're dead, too."

"You're pretty quick, Ray. From what I'd heard, you were a little thick in the head from the accident."

"My engine exploded. I was in a medically-induced coma for a couple of days to let the swelling in my brain subside."

"Is that all?"

"I came out of it."

"Not all the way." She picked up the bag. Found the gun.

"So that's your plan? Shoot me? Dump my body over the side? Go the rest of the way to Nassau on your own?"

"I said I needed your boat, Mr. Kettle. I never said anything about needing you."

I did a sudden, steep bank turn to the port side. The bullet meant for my head hit my left shoulder. Grazed it but it still hurt like hell.

I juked left, did an even quicker one to the right and then again to the left. It was enough to rock her off balance. Enough so that I could shove her over the side with a kick to her chest. Kick her in the gut, she doubles over. A kick to the chest knocked her backwards. She hit the water hard like a poorly thrown skipping stone. Gravity caught her and introduced her to the deceptive gentleness of an ocean's surface.

I slowed and circled back around to where I thought she might be. I waited for her cries for help but they never came. The bag with the money in it remained on the seat behind me. I grabbed it and disposed of anything that might possibly confirm she'd been on my boat. I put the canvas bag of money down inside the lower cabin.

There was still no call for help.

I could have done a variety of things. Called for assistance. Fired a flare. Turned on my spotlight. Like I said, I could have done a variety of things. Any of those actions would have led to a parade of questions from the police one of which undoubtedly would be, 'Why were you taking her to Nassau then if you suspected she'd already killed three people?'

I'm not a fool. I get confused sometimes but I still have my instincts and my instincts said, 'Go!'.

I started the boat and made my way back to Daytona. Behind me, Jodie Somebody, along with any thoughts of what I had just done, slowly churned in my wake.

***

©2018 Jack Bates

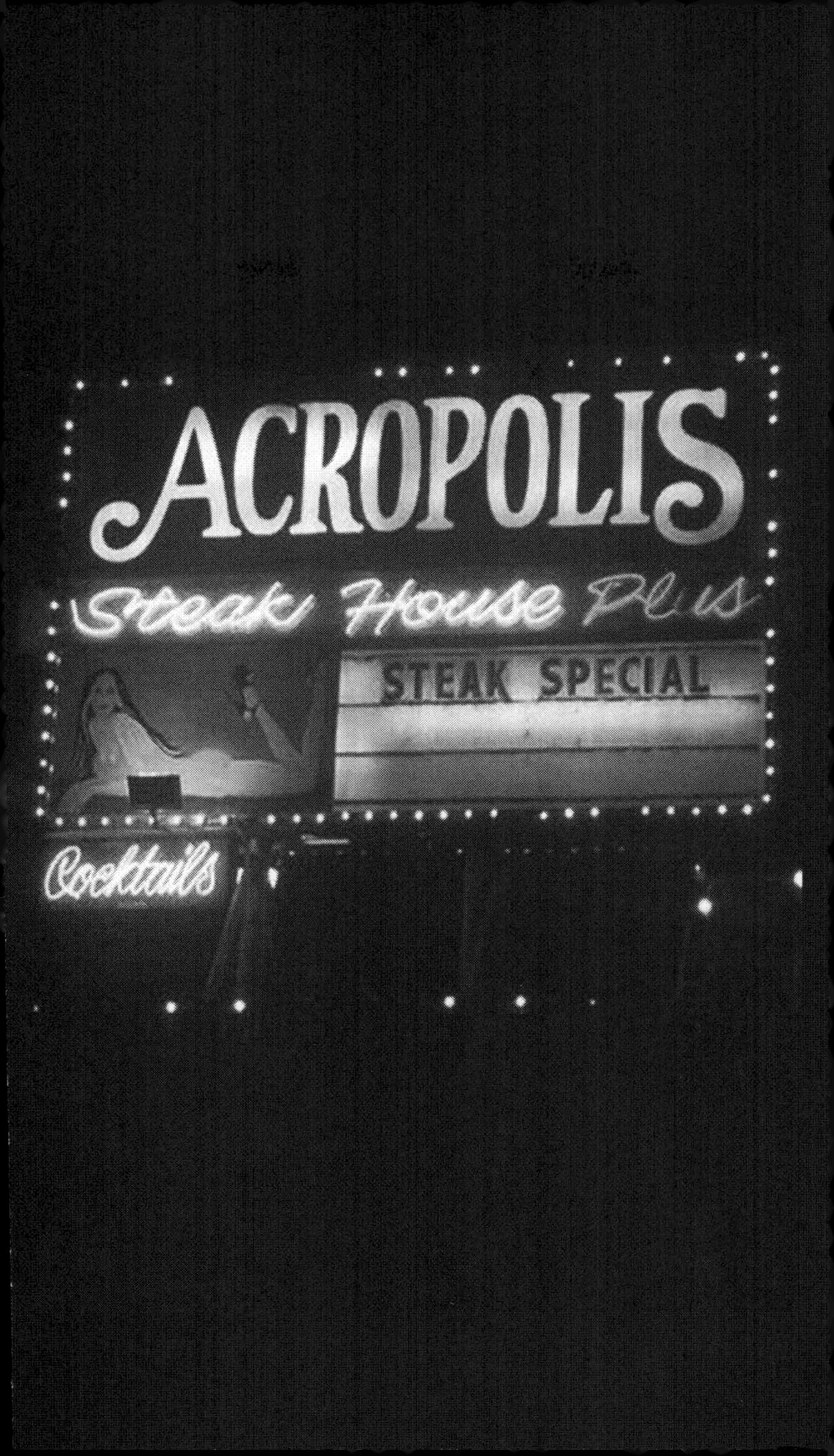
ACROPOLIS
Steak House Plus
STEAK SPECIAL
Cocktails

Tick Tock
Michael R. Colangelo

Jon was in the back room at *The Acropolis* again. He was pissing away the weekly paycheque in another one of Johnny Lambaros' crooked poker games. But he wasn't there to gamble anyway. Not really. Everybody knew that if you won at one of Lambaros' tables, Johnny would just dog you until you lost it all back to him anyway. And if you didn't; if you stood up for yourself; well; then Johnny would just hurt you in ways that weren't worth your winnings.

Lambaros thought this was hilarious, of course. And the owner of the Acropolis carried a strange affection for the losers that turned up for his poker games. One of the doormen tried to explain it to Jon once. He said that Johnny thought it was funny in the same way that slipping on a banana peel was funny. And if you made Johnny laugh, he might give you some work. And if you didn't fuck that up too bad, he might adopt you into the Lambaros organization. And that was where the real money could be had. And drugs. And girls.

There were three other guys at the table with him, plus the dealer; who was really just one of the girls normally from out in the front of the joint; moved to the back room. Of the other players, Jon recognized two of them; they were just regular losers addicted to the gambling and so far into the despair of it that they no longer cared about winning or losing.

And then there was a third guy. A new guy. Or, at least, a guy that Jon had never seen before. The dealer kept calling him Little Ray, so he must have been around. But Jon was clueless. Maybe he didn't know the scene at the Acropolis as well as he thought he did. But whatever, right? This 'Little Ray'; just another loser like the rest of them.

But this Little Ray; he was different. He was annoying. He wouldn't stop talking, nor would he leave anyone alone. For every hand dealt he had a snide comment or a sharp remark to make. And since Jon was the type of fellow who tended to wear his emotions on his sleeve, Ray seemed to pick up on whom he annoyed the most at the table, and he immediately honed in on Jon as the one to aggravate the most. It was like he'd done this before.

In fact, as the evening progressed and Jon began to gradually lose more and more money, thoughts of violence began to weave themselves together in his mind.

Jon had come to the Acropolis right after work, which meant that he still had his drywall knife in the pocket of his coveralls. It was a hooked, crooked thing with a taped handle and a strong gouging blade that was only a little on the dull side. He envisioned himself coming over the table with it; knocking cards and chips and drinks everywhere; to carve the expression off of Little Ray's face.

But Jon was still hesitant, because what would the consequences of such behavior be? Well, he could get hurt; although Jon was not a small man and Little Ray lived up to the 'little' part of his moniker. So this was an unlikely outcome, even if Ray had a blade of his own. He doubted

61

very much that the man carried a gun. None of them did. A handgun was an expensive and rare thing; more apt to get you arrested than serve a useful purpose; even among criminals.

There was, of course, the Acropolis staff to consider. Fighting on the premises wasn't looked too kindly upon, as it tended to attract the police. Cops weren't too welcomed at the establishment. They made it difficult to do business.

Little Ray might have friends in there too. Guys who might join in to batter Jon senseless. But, nah, Jon doubted it. Men like Little Ray didn't have friends. And if they did, they weren't the type of friends who had his back, unless it was to stab it.

But fuck it, Jon ultimately thought. Besides, that was the kind of thing that Lambaros found funny, if what the doorman had told Jon had any ring of truth to it. Maybe he'd give Ray a warning, he decided.

"If I gotta listen to any more trash spewing from that hole in your face," Jon said, abruptly. "Well, I'm just gonna have to peel it offa you, aren't I?"

It was as if Jon had frozen time with a sentence. The dealer stopped dealing in mid-deal. Ray stopped shit talking in mid-shit. The other players stopped playing in mid-play. Little Ray considered Jon's offer.

"I don't follow," Ray said. He squinted his eyes at Jon. "Do you mean you're going to peel my face? Or peel my mouth?"

Under the table, Jon's hand went into the pocket of his coveralls and found his drywall knife.

"Cause you can't really peel a mouth, you know. That's fucked up. Some real El Salvador Dali shit right there."

Little Ray snickered and glanced around the table, looking for approval for his smart mouth. But nobody was moving, and nobody was looking at him.

Everybody had enough of Little Ray. Jon too. He lunged. Little Ray didn't stand a chance. Jon's chair went flying backwards; and the bulk of his weight went crashing forwards towards its target and obliterated the table. Cards, poker chips, rum and Cokes, scraps of wood and green felt, everything -- It all scattered everywhere across the floor in a huge mess that somebody else was going to have to clean up.

Jon brought the beak of the drywall knife down in an overhanded cleave and the blade sliced into Little Ray's skull. This first swing tore a huge piece of scalp and hair away, like Jon was cutting kitchen linoleum. The second swing hacked off an ear. On the third swing, the knife got caught in Little Ray's face and Jon left it there. He released his grip on the handle and let Ray fall over. The man thrashed and bled among the scattered remnants of their poker table. Somebody was going to have to clean that up too.

Jon and Little Ray were swarmed by Lambaros' muscle; the doormen; and they were intent on separating the pair before Jon decided to go back to work on his bleeding victim; to finish the renovations, so to speak.

Someone sprayed Jon in the face with a can of pepper spray, then someone else clobbered him over the head with a steel-cased flashlight. The fight was over before it even really started.

63

They were really going to start laying into Jon with their boots, their fists, and their heavy flashlights, when a voice commanded them to stop. It was Johnny Lambaros himself, who had been sleeping on the couch in his office before all the commotion had started. He'd come out to investigate what all the noise was about.

Lambaros lit up a thin cigar and circled the carnage. Jon and Little Ray both lay on the floor side-by-side atop the shipwreck of the poker table amidst the sea of Little Ray's blood. Jon's eyes had cleared enough so that he could see Lambaros, and the owner of the Acropolis wore no expression on his face whatsoever. Here was a man surveying the violence with about as much attachment as an archeologist looking at rocks.

Finally, Lambaros stopped circling. He stopped and gestured towards the screeching Little Ray. "Get this bleeding fuck some first aid. Nobody dies here."

One of his goons shuffled away to retrieve a first aid kit. Maybe he could find a doctor too; drinking out front.

"Who started it?"

All fingers in the room pointed towards Jon. Lambaros tsked.

"Jonathan. I never would have thought that such a quiet guy like you could make such a big fucking mess."

Off the top of Jon's head, he could only think up two solutions to the problem as it was unfolding. The first solution involved making a break for the door; running out of the Acropolis never to return again. The second solution involved pulling the drywall knife out of Little Ray's face to replant it in Johnny Lambaros' face. Neither of these solutions particularly appealed to

64

Jon, and so he stood perfectly still and said absolutely nothing instead; a third solution.

Lambaros stared at Jon. He had an expression on his face like he was expecting some sort of explanation. But despite the intimidation involved in dealing with an irate Johnny Lambaros, Jon remained silent and still. And Lambaros broke his expression before Jon opened his mouth.

"Okay," Lambaros finally said. He gestured for Jon to move closer. "Let's go talk somewhere quiet."

When Jon got close, Lambaros wrapped an arm around his shoulder like they were old drinking buddies. The action was strangely comforting to him, even though he fully thought that Lambaros was moments away from shooting him with a concealed handgun.

But it didn't happen. Lambaros motioned to his office and herded Jon inside. He shut the door behind them and poured himself a drink; didn't offer one to Jon. Told him to sit down. John took a place on the couch. Lambaros sat down behind his desk. Put his feet up on its surface. Sipped at his drink.

"Look. Okay," Lambaros said. "Nothing bad's going to happen here. Nothing bad's going to happen to you."

Lambaros spoke quietly. It sounded more like he was trying to convince himself than he was addressing Jon.

Lambaros continued: "But you owe me, Jon. You owe me for damages. To my establishment and to my clientele; my guests. You did a bad thing, see?"

Jon didn't really see, no. But he wasn't going to argue with Lambaros. Especially not now when it seemed the owner of the Acropolis was about to let him off the hook.

"So I'm going to give you a package I need delivered. And you're going to deliver it. You understand?"

Jon nodded; animated again now that he realized that Lambaros wasn't going to murder him. Lambaros rose from his seat and went to a bench with a pile of suitcases balanced on top of it. He selected a brown faux-leather one from the collection and brought it back to his desk. He popped it open, and beckoned Jon to come and have a look.

Inside the briefcase was some sort of mechanical, clockwork contraption. An old alarm clock hooked up to a series of batteries with coiled electrical wire and duct tape. And clear plastic bags filled with some sort of cloudy liquid with the consistency of glue.

Lambaros began to wind the alarm clock.

"You know The N9ne 0ne? That club over on Stillwater?"

Jon knew it. One of those aspirational places where you could wear a cheap suit and shitty cologne to hang out with other guys dressed in cheap suits with shitty cologne. He nodded.

"Well, they run it as an after hours after two a.m. Problem is, guys that are supposed to be here in the backroom are over there thinking there might be drunk girls and cheap blow. There isn't. But it's still cutting into my business."

He was still winding the alarm clock.

"So. What you're going to do for me. Is you're going to go over there with this important package. And you're going to deliver it by launching it through the front doors of that place."

66

Lambaros finished winding the alarm clock. It ticked loudly and rapidly. He set the arms on the clock, then snapped the briefcase shut before handing it over to Jon.

"You got about an hour. Give or take."

Lambaros then reached into his pocket and snapped one link on a pair of handcuffs around Jon's wrist. The other end of the cuffs he snapped around the handle of the briefcase. He patted Jon on the back.

This was Lambaros' idea of a comedy routine. Now Jon was going to have to run across town with a loudly ticking briefcase cuffed to his wrist. And how was he supposed to toss it into the N9ne One if he got to the club in time? Lambaros had not provided him with a key.

Jon left Johnny's office and came out of the back room of the Acropolis. He stepped over the mess, and went out the front; he crossed its neon floor. It occurred to him then that Lambaros wasn't interested in whether he succeeded or failed in his mission to blow up the N9ne One. That wasn't the point of the exercise.

Jon got outside. It had started to rain. The suitcase ticked noisily tucked there under an arm. He headed down the sidewalk on foot towards Stillwater Road.

No, Jon understood that Lambaros didn't care about bombing his rivals. Not really. What he was interested in was killing Jon for fucking up Little Ray; for wrecking his table; for fucking with his business. Lambaros could have shot him but there was no sport in that. No, the briefcase bomb was funny. The briefcase bomb was hilarious. Maybe Lambaros had seen it in a movie. One of those old silent comedies that the guy was so fond of, or something.

As he approached Stillwater, he examined the cuff chained to his wrist. Nope; police-issue, spun-rivet, chain link construction with a black oxide finish. Jon wasn't just going to pull such a thing off his wrist.

The handle of the briefcase was another matter, though. A simple solution would be to pull the handle off and then Jon would be free of the bomb. It was well made and screwed into the case pretty tightly though. He would need a tool. It was too bad he'd left his knife back at the Acropolis.

Jon used the crosswalk and headed down Stillwater. He could hear the N9ne One before he could see it. They played their music just loud enough that you couldn't hear your conversations inside. Soon, he was standing across the street from the place.

There was no lineup in front of the N9ne One, just a couple of doormen standing about and an array of pillars with flame coming from the top of them. The club had always bothered Jon and he didn't know why, particularly. All that flash and glitz; like it might secretly be for homosexuals. He didn't know why.

Jon wandered into a nearby alleyway. He was looking for trash; a discarded piece of scrap metal; a good steel corner; anything hard and with enough leverage to pry the handle off the briefcase. He'd be only too happy to throw the bomb into the club if he could separate it from his person.

In the alleyway, he didn't find anything he might use as a makeshift tool. There was a vagrant though. An unwashed-looking fellow in a mesh back ball cap was rummaging the overflowed trash bin of the N9ne One. He stopped his activities when Jon stepped into the alley. He started to explain himself immediately; as if he'd gotten in trouble for doing this before. He stopped just as quickly once he saw Jon wasn't wearing the uniform of the club's doormen, and his excuses turned to complaints.

"They used to put the recycling out with the rest of it," the vagrant mumbled. "Locked it. But I used to pop it and take all the returnables they just throw away."

"Yeah?" said Jon.

"Well, yeah," replied the man. "But they caught me a few times so now they lock it up inside. Goddamn fuckers run this place. I hope you don't drink here."

Jon began to move towards the man. He said he used to pop the lock on N9ne One's recycling bin. That meant he had a tool. He probably had one on him at that very moment.

"Hey nice briefcase, man," the vagrant smiled as Jon closed in on him. "Are you some kind of secret agent? Say, buddy, you don't talk a whole lot. Is there something wrong with you?"

In hindsight, Jon supposed that he could have reasoned with the vagrant before he smashed his head like a melon against the steel of the garbage bin. Up close, he could smell that the guy had way too much to drink to defend himself properly. He felt a little bad about it, to be perfectly honest.

But the ticking briefcase that Lambaros had chained to Jon reminded him that time was not on his side. And that meant that he was forced to take this cruel shortcut rather than attempt negotiations with this chatty hobo. It likely would have ended in violence anyhow. He was having that kind of night.

Jon rifled the fallen man's prone body. He found what he was looking for somewhere in the multitudes of pockets of the man's unyielding layers of clothing. The guy was carrying a homemade pry bar. It was just a short length of pipe with one end crushed and flattened down. It was just thin enough that he could insert it between handle and briefcase, and then use his leverage to tear the handle away from the case.

Jon was free at last. There was the smaller issue of getting the dangling cuffs off of his wrist, but at least he was no longer under threat of being blown to pieces. He neatly returned the prybar to its place beneath his many folds and then apologized to the unconscious man. He tucked the handleless briefcase under his arm and returned to the street; to the front of the club.

Jon checked his watch. He doubted Lambaros' alarm clock was even remotely accurate in terms of when it might or might not go off. But Jon bet if he threw it hard enough, whatever unstable explosive chemical that was in those plastic bags would be agitated enough to go off by itself. He wasn't about to shake the briefcase to see if he was right either. There was only one way to find out.

Jon crossed the street and walked towards N9ne One until he was within throwing distance to launch Lambaros' bomb through its front doors, just like the man had asked. The doormen regarded him with disinterest. On a busy street like Stillwater, they'd seen all sorts of shit. A large sweaty man ambling towards them with a broken briefcase was no cause for suspicion or alarm. It was small potatoes.

They'd left the front doors of the club open, so Jon found it no trouble at all to launch the briefcase overhand with both arms right into the mouth of N9ne 0ne. One of the bouncers kind of flinched when he hurled the object. The second man immediately began crossing the front patio towards him.

Whether the bomb exploded or not was of little concern to Jon, because it was definitely time to go. He turned to speedwalk away from the scene, but he must have misjudged his distance. The doorman had caught up to him before he'd managed to take ten steps.

"Hey, man," the doorman started. But Jon cut him off with a square punch to the jaw. Sometimes if you caught a man off guard you could take him out with one good sucker punch. Not this time, though. The punch simply put the man on the offensive, and Jon soon found himself firmly caught up in a chokehold.

Jon wasn't a small man, but doormen were big too. And his neck; his throat; his windpipe; these were all frail parts that could be crushed no matter his size. He managed to loosen the hold just a little with a lucky headbutt. It was enough to keep breathing air, but not enough to escape.

The other doorman; the guy who had flinched; at some point he'd arrived at the place where Jon was struggling, and he immediately put his fists and feet to work on him while his coworker held his choke. He wasn't being gentle, either. He was laying into Jon with all the zeal of a man given free license to beat the shit out of someone else.

Jon did what he could, which wasn't much. Try to keep breathing and hope that the guy swinging on him didn't land a solid one. He got caught on the temple and the punch dropped him to one knee. The choke went tight around his throat again and he figured that was it for him. He was going to wake up in a jail cell or a hospital bed, if he woke up at all. These guys were scarily enthusiastic about their work.

Then the briefcase bomb went off, and the blast shattered all the glass across the front of N9ne One. Jon felt the heat bathe him like he was grilling hamburger on a barbeque in better times. A chunk of something; concrete rubble off the building; bounced off the skull of the man who was choking him as the trio was showered in rubble. The chokehold was gone; and he could breathe again.

Jon lunged at the man throwing punches. This guy was smaller; much smaller. And one-on-one he wasn't half as tough as before. Jon immediately overwhelmed him with his size; grappled him; and flung him headlong from the sidewalk into the street. It was a pity there was no oncoming traffic. Regardless, the fellow did not follow him as he made his escape.

Tired as Jon was; there was only one thing left to do now; and that was to go and settle his business with Johnny Lambaros.

*

"Look, yeah. So I forgot to give you the key. That's my bad. That's on me," Lambaros was saying. "I'm a busy guy. Look. I'll make sure you get compensated. I get the picture. I see your point."

Jon was back in Lambaros' office. This time the owner of the Acropolis was handcuffed to his own desk chair. In fact, Jon had attached so many handcuffs to Lambaros, the guy looked like a handcuff tree. Now that was comedy.

Even funnier though, were all the briefcase bombs. Lambaros had a whole collection of them. These were all stacked and piled high around him. Jon had handcuffed some of them to Lambaros' body, but he'd run out of room so he'd just piled them up all around him in compromise.

"Ha ha ha!" yelled Lambaros; it wasn't actual laughter. He spit in Jon's direction. "Ha ha ha! Fuck you! A comedian!"

The clocks. All the clocks. They ticked incessantly down.

***

Sleep Tight Hannibal
J. L. Boekestein

You get all kinds in the Red Rough Diamond.
Johns I mean. Yeah, yeah, you also get all kind of
strippers, but that's not what I'm talking about.
Anyway, you got single guys, groups, guys with
girlfriends, even guys who aren't guys but that is
another story. Johns aplenty, there is a whole range of
them: loners, losers, players, wannabee players,
saviors, sleaze balls… We working girls like to hang
around at the bar between shifts and categorize the
Johns. You got to talk about something and lifts and
tucks get boring after a while.

First time I met Leonardo, I thought he was sugar
daddy, or maybe a wannabee sugar daddy. You know,
the kind who thinks they are spending real big, but are
actually as tight as a virgin's ass around a but plug. He
had a goatee, a real old fashioned one, not the
hipster's kind, and he wore a three-piece suit, with tie
and all. And he was pretty old with grey whiskers and
horn-rimmed spectacles. He had a gold signet ring on
his finger.

"Gay," Victoria said after we spotted him. "Still in
the closet. Trying to prove to himself he isn't."

Yeah sure. Maybe. I looked at him. Gay or not, he
looked like money. Sweet Sugar. A guy who could
easily go five yards on the right girl. And a lot more if I
played my cards right.

Lula approached him first with the question what
he wanted to drink, or if he was interested in a private
show in a booth, or in a room upstairs. We got a cut on
the drinks we sold, the booths were our bread and the
rooms were the butter on our shiny butts.

Deidre whistled softly and made an explosive
sound when Lula turned away. She had been shot
down by Mr. Gray Gay. Like a bunch of hawks, we

watched her when she made her way to us. A professional smile on her face, but she wasn't happy. Lula didn't take rejection well.

"Sam, he's looking for Asian," Deidre said sourly.

Asian I am. Well, I was born and bred in Houston, but my ma and all my uncles and aunts plus grandpa—Jesus bless him, no doubt he was playing cắt tê in Heaven with his old cronies—and grandma were born in the old country, in Saigon where grandpa was something big in the Department of Agriculture. Sam is short for Samurai Girl, my stage name. Everyone calls me Sam.

So I walked up to Gray Gay John, smiled, stated that he had asked for an Asian girl and asked if he wanted something special. Easy as shooting dog in a barrel.

He looked me over, which I was used to. I moved a little, making sure my moneymakers followed. The trick is not to overdo it. Just enough to nudge the John over the edge.

"I would like to see you perform, Miss...?"

I eyed him. Did he know of my not-at-all-secret kinky lifestyle and was he addressing me as a wannabee slave?

Nope, his body language was all wrong. He was just being old fashioned polite.

"Sam," I replied. "We can take in a booth, which will cost you sixty for five minutes, or you can take a room, which gives us more privacy and time." *And will cost you a lot more.*

He nodded. "I guess a private room would be more convenient."

Gotcha! A room it was.

*

He paid up and I did my spiel, which was giving him a lap dance.

I think I made him a bit uncomfortable. Still he said thank you afterwards, and while I was putting on my top again: "You're a very alluring lady, Sam. Do you want to earn some extra money?"

76

I kept smiling. There are two types of guys who ask that question. The ones who mistake dancers for whores, and cops.

Mr. Gray Gay didn't look particularly aroused—which was a bit of an insult—which left the other kind.

"Are you a cop? We don't do that here," I lied. 'It' happened all of the time, no doubt about it. Other girls of course. Never me. Yeah, sure. Never done a hand job, or a blow job, or any orifice while performing, dear Mr. Judge. Never!

"No, I am not a cop, Sam. I am a collector."

Okay… That is a first one.

"I collect graphic novels and related art work Comics."

Uh…? If this guy was a cop he had the weirdest cover ever.

"And I want to know if you are interested in earning some money where you can use… your talents."

I decided to take the leap. "Hypothetically, what are we talking about and how much money?"

*

Men who dance well... It's true. If they got the moves on the floor, they know when to push and grind in bed, or on a parking lot behind a club. Which only happened once, twice, a few times. The last time it left me with a nasty cold which didn't do any wonders for my night job and day pleasures. "Crawl you... Achoo... Wait! Snort... On your knees you nasty piece of... Achoo... Shit. ("Gesundheit Mistress.") "Silence!"

Okay, men who dance well. The beat boomed, lights flashed, body against body, hips against hips. We weren't exactly dancing, that Roberto dude and I. Basically I was dry humping the guy and it was fun. Muscular, tanned white guy. Late twenties, bald, six feet two, obese gold bling everywhere. Sue me, that's the way I like them.

I myself wore a close-fitting mint green glitter dress, hard pink fishnet stockings, sexy Texas Longhorn heels and a black leather jacket. Not to mention extra-long eyelashes and my killer make-up.

It had been easy to get Roberto's attention and

hold them. He liked Asians and I am a professional performer. I can be any dream girl, from a hard-core whip wielding mistress to horny cheerleader virgin. Anything the John want, as long as he paid. Roberto wasn't paying, but Leonardo was. We were on first name basis now, the old comic geek and me. I knew his probably fake first name, he knew my artist name. He had actually grinned when I told I was Samurai Girl. "It fits you." Which was kinda sweet.

Back in the club. The remainder of the night went as planned: dancing, laughter, vodka, more sweat and foreplay—dancing—pills, giggling, warm, blissful glow, dancing. Roberto's muscular body and flowing movements were a blistering promise.

It was about five o'clock in the morning and he did not even ask if I was coming with him. That just was a given. I dived in the cab with him and as soon as we were riding Roberto pulled me towards him. Strong arms, demanding lips.

The cab driver could see everything, but if Roberto didn't care, I didn't care either. It was all part of the mission.

Yeah sure. Fuck, he was one horny bastard and I didn't mind at all.

His mouth on mine, tongue around tongue, his hands everywhere. A reconnaissance trip. Mr. Left Hand stroked me downstairs and upstairs: my neck, hair, titties; he was a real tramp. Mr. Right Hand was not such a world traveler, he went right to his goal. He dove right under my dress. The knuckles slid over my skin and the flimsy fabric of my stockings, his fingers found my panties.

He is not going to- I stopped thinking because he did exactly that. Roberto's hand disappeared into my panties and started rubbing the hot sweet spot between my legs.

Oohhhhhgggh. His mouth was tornado on speed, Mr. Left Hand supported my body and Mr. Right Hand... kneaded. The lower part of the palm of his hand rested against the cap of my clit, his fingers covered the rest my pussy. Without any shame—*Is the cabbie watching us? Fuck yes! Giggle*—Roberto opened my willing cunt. His index and ring fingers were on the inside of my hot flesh, but without really entering. They just rubbed and scratched while the rest of muscular hand kneaded my glowing pussy vigorously in the rhythm of his tongue, his breath and his body.

Uuuuuuuuhhhhhhwwwwjjjjjjjaaaaa.

It was damn exciting.

The cab drove through still sleepy Houston while I gasped and wriggled in the back seat.

I don't know how long it took.

Not long enough. I wanted still plenty more when we arrived at his crib.

The front door had three locks, and while they we were staggering across the threshold, Roberto released one hand to blindly enter the alarm code.

We didn't even make it to the living room, the first time. Nothing nice, nothing foreplay, we were done playing. Time to get nasty! We only took of the bare minimum of clothing before the first fuck.

Yesssssssss!

*

Someone had been watching us fuck.

Now I'm an open-minded girl and I have no qualms about fucking in front of friends, or acquaintances, camera crews or even random strangers. I've a damned nice body and I don't mind showing it off.

That's me, the world can deal with it, or just go finger or jerk itself.

Still, I was scared stiff for a moment when I looked up, pretty satisfied, after Roberto's final push. Although I wasn't a painting, he had done a good job of nailing me to the wall.

He was watching us. Those fierce, big brown eyes, that wicked smile and those teeth...

I froze. I like dogs well enough, but this was the type of dog that ate little Asian chicks for breakfast, as encore for a herd or bulls. The monster was sitting in the door opening, watching us.

Roberto followed my gaze and laughed. "Ah, that's

79

Hannibal. Don't go wandering around the house on your own. Hannibal doesn't like strangers. He is a fila brasileiro. In Brazil they were used to track runaway slaves."

Okay... So, this is the famous dog. I looked at the meat chewer on legs. *Hi Hannibal.*

Hannibal looked at me like he was calculating how much flesh was on my sweet little self, and how quickly he could gnaw my bones with those bear trap jaws.

I shivered. Smiles and charm would not work with this monster.

Roberto laughed again. "Come on."

*

After fuck numero two I was rolled up into a languid ball on the large, low leather couch. My panties were somewhere in the hallway, most of my other clothes were scattered through the living room. "No, keep those stockings on, I like that super sexy"

Roberto was sitting next to me, only covered in tattoos and the shine of perspiration. With a gilded razor blade he divided the coke on the black glass tabletop in three: two lines and a remaining mountain. A golden Y-shaped sniffing pipe was lying next to it.

"It's good stuff, directly from the source. Not that weak bunch that you can get anywhere else."

I only reacted by nodding lazily.

Chopchopchop. The coke was ready. Rob leaned forward and sniffed a line routinely.

"Aaaah." He leaned back, his arms wide, his head backward. After a few seconds he turned to me. "Go ahead."

It was good coke. Top notch. I let the energy flow through me and it blended nicely with the warm after-sex glow I already felt.

Roberto was meanwhile busy with the remaining cocaine. He licked his finger and pushed it into the white powder. "Have you ever tried this?"

He smeared the little crushed white crystals over the head of his cock which started to come back to life.

I looked at him. "Not yet."

80

Mr. Bad Boy grinned and leaned back, one hand stroking his stiffening dick. "Be my guest."

In the worst case, I will have numb lips and a tongue.

I wiped my long black hair back and looking dangerous as a wild, sexy tigress, I crawled over the couch to Roberto. I slowly licked my lips.

*

The third fuck—not counting the blow job on the couch—was finally in the bedroom. Robert had locked Hannibal out, but I knew the mutt was somewhere in the house. The whole time the thing had looked at me suspiciously, but I had tried to show no fear. "Never be afraid of dogs." Who would had ever said that? I couldn't remember. I just looked back and thought: *I am the boss, and besides, you will be sleeping soon. Just wait.*

As for sleeping, Roberto showed no signs of fatigue at all. Within ten seconds after closing the door we were rolling in the enormous bed over the black satin sheets. Thanks to the coke, Bad Boy as much energy as all the Houston Texans put together. From front to back, from left to right.

It sure was nice to be fucked with so much energy, but I was going to use the Rohypnol, otherwise the plan was never going to work.

I finally had the opportunity afterwards. "I'm thirsty. Going to get me some. You need some water?"

"Yes, do, honey. I'm as dry as a horse," Roberto croaked. He had lost some fluids the last few hours.

Horse. He sure is.

I opened the bedroom door, and immediately I heard dog feet approaching.

"Uh..." I looked back.

"Hannibal, sit!"

Hannibal sat and under his gaze I made it to the kitchen and the well-stocked fridge.

Bottles of glacéau vitamin water. I took a sip and dumped the crushed pills from my purse in the water. Shaking the bottle, I returned to the bedroom.

Stupid Hannibal watched. His tail didn't waggle.

81

Back in bed I offered Roberto the bottle.

"Ah, good, I needed that." Three, four big gulps and the water was gone.

Twenty minutes, then the Rohypnol should be working. Hm, I'll keep him busy for twenty minutes. A quick round four?

It was like my Bad Boy could read minds, because he pulled me towards him, his gun already cocked for a new round. "Okay, yeah. Get down."

There is something very satisfying with a big muscular body on top and in you. Screw all the porn movie positions, there is nothing wrong with some old fashioned missionary style fucking every now and then. Lay there and being pounded. Hey, it had been a long night! Just being on the receiving end without having to work for it, was nice.

The only thing was, I hadn't thought things through.

We hadn't been at it that long, when Roberto whispered: "I'm a little tired." He did not sound completely clear anymore. His head rested on my shoulder, I felt his big, muscular body on top of me relax. Suddenly he felt twice as heavy.

"Going to sleep now," was the last thing he managed before he blacked out.

Damn. It took me five minutes of careful pushing and maneuvering before I got free.

I grabbed my handbag. At first glance it was stuffed with the usual women's things, but in fact the bag it hid two important things. I riffled through the mess until I found the carefully sealed, bloody piece of meat. Raw steak, injected through the plastic with a nice cocktail of sleeping drugs.

With the nail scissors from my bag, I cut through the plastic. It smelled of blood and raw meat. *Bleh!* I made sure that I only touched the plastic of the packaged steak. The last thing I wanted was to come into contact with that dirty chunk of meat.

In stockings and with outstretched arm I walked to the bedroom door, encouraged by Roberto's snoring. I opened the door and within three seconds I heard the tip tap of approaching dog feet. My dear, big canine friend.

"Dig in, Hannibal," I whispered I threw the steak into the hall.

Within five minutes Hannibal slept and snored in almost the same way as his owner. By then I was fully dressed and had all my belongings, even my panties which were pretty torn up. I made as little noise as possible. If Roberto woke up I could talk my way out of it, but if that monster dog woke up... I didn't want to think about it. *Quickly do what I've come for and then get out!*

During my second fuck, the one on the couch, I had checked out the living room. It was furnished in the same way as the bedroom: expensive and modern, lots of leather and chrome, and lots of men's toys. A gigantic television screen dominated one wall, high tech boxes from an exclusive German brand were hanging on both sides. Along a different wall stood a lacquered rack with two Japanese swords, undoubtedly real. Framed posters, screen prints and blown up photos behind glass hung on the walls. Most of it was from movies or comics, with women in those metal bikinis or otherwise anxiously on the run as they were chased by a masked maniac who was waving an ax or chain saw.

I looked at all those things with my hands in my side and shook my head. *Boys will be boys. Some man- No, the most men never grow up. Anyway, I'm not here for that.*

I took my second hidden object from my purse. The black and white drawing was rolled up in a plastic cover and I flattened it out on the black glass coffee table. Even I knew who she was: Catwoman, from one of those superhero movies. Were those films about Batman or those films about that red-blue hero with those cobwebs, or was it that pretty guy with those knifes coming out of his hands? Leonardo had talked about the drawing extensively, but I had ignored most of the enthusiastic chatter. It was precious and the old collector wanted to have the original, plus he was

83

willing to pay for it. That was what counted. The drawing from my purse was a reproduction, but at first glance no one would notice.

The original hung framed on Roberto's wall, right under some weird movie poster of a flic called *Possession*. Snakes for hair? I didn't see it catch on.

Within three seconds I had pulled the drawing of Catwoman off the wall. Opening the frame took six seconds and replacing the original with the fake a further five seconds. I took me ten seconds to put the frame back and check everything.

No one would ever spot the difference. I grinned. Carefully I secured the original drawing in a plastic cover. Leonardo had at least told me ten times that I had to be very careful with the drawing. Do not crease, do not fold, do not even roll up.

I rolled up the drawing and stuck it in the inside pocket of my jacket. Once more I looked around. Did I have everything? My clothes? Yes. Bottle? Check! Roberto might wonder where I had gone, if he could remember me. Rohypnol often caused memory loss. Ha, at least I would have a few very good memories!

Satisfied in plenty of ways, I walked out the front door. I had a geek to meet.

*

Mr. Gray Gay, oh yeah, I could call him Leonardo, and I met in some coffee and bagels place near Westheimer Road. He was at his second cup of coffee when I showed up, only fifteen minutes late. Traffic was light, but I just left too late.

I sat down opposite him. An old suited up guy and a gorgeous hot, young Asian chick in hot pants and tank top. An elderly sugar daddy and his pet? I didn't care. It was a free country, people could think whatever they wanted. We were in a boot way in the back so nobody was disturbing us.

"You... You got it?" he asked. He couldn't keep the excitement from his voice.

"I got it." At home I had flattened the sealed drawing an put in the stiff brown envelope Leonardo had provided me. I pulled the sealed drawing from the

84

envelope, just enough to show it was Catwoman. "You got the money?"

He took his wallet from the inside pocket of his wallet and counted out twenty five hundred in crispy new banknotes. He put a napkin over them when the waitress, a small, fat Filipino woman, came to take my order. I shook my head. I was not going to stick around.

The waitress left and I handed Leonardo the cover with the drawing.

And froze when he reached once more under his jacket.

Leonardo didn't pull out a gun but a huge magnifying glass. "Excuse me."

Damn, he was real polite. The most polite fence I had ever met.

He studied the drawing while I watched the napkin with the twenty five hundred. I tapped with my heels, all nervous although I had no reason. This was the drawing I took from Roberto's crib. Sure, I could have switched it for another copy, but I didn't exactly have rich comic book collectors lined up. I would rather have the money instead of the hassle.

Leonardo nodded, there was a big smile on his face. "Yes, this is it." He pushed the napkin with the dough towards me.

I took it and counted it. The bread was all there. It disappeared in my purse and I rose. "It has been nice doing business."

Leonardo looked up. He hesitated. "I... Uh, Miss Sam. I... Would you like to earn another... say two hundred dollars?"

I should have walked away. I had what I wanted, safely in purse. But that is the damn thing with money: more was always better. Was Mr. Gray Gay less gay and more Mister then I had thought? Did he want another lap dance, or something else?

"What do you have in mind?" I purred.

*

I left the motel room two hundred fifty richer. I had haggled a bit. I was very satisfied with myself. I looked

85

at the pic on my phone. Leonardo had steady hand, it wasn't too bad. Maybe every comic collector was a wannabee cartoonist at heart.

He had drawn me, sitting on the motel bed, big eyes, hands in my sides, my boobs pointed forward like two battleship guns. It was cute!

No doubt the pic would be put away somewhere in his collection. Some folder named 'private drawings'. And every now and then he would look at it.

I grinned. A memorable series of fuck, a fistful of money and an unique piece of artwork. And I had also done Leonardo. I had seduced him, sitting on the bed. Not his hand over my skin, but a drawing pencil following my curves. No flesh on flesh, but his fingers sliding over the paper. Swift glances, a dry mouth of concentration, soft sounds, heavy breath. Oh, I had taken him in. I came, I saw, I conquered.

Fuck, life was good.

***

©2018 J.L. Boekestein

DEAD GUY IN THE BATHTUB

stories by

Paul Greenberg

The Last Savior

Mark Slade

"I killed him," Mya Stone said.

"I can see that," Barry London handed her a lit cigarette. "I see him in your bathtub…..facedown."

She was naked, sitting on the lid of her toilet, looking very morose. As a thirty-five year old woman, she still had a very nice body, even with a bit of a pouch from having two children. Her wet blond hair was cut shorter than the pictures in the magazine London was given. Mya Stone was mostly known for the terrible sitcom about a character that was a photojournalist and her Father who was also her editor. The sitcom lasted two seasons, was never a ratings success, but in syndication on cable channels, it was a blockbuster.

London was called in by Choaladi to find Haze Delegaura. Someone had kidnapped the famed gangster and Choaldi feared this getting out might cause a mob war. So he sent London to a former girlfriend's house to see what she knew. Turns out, Mya's father had business with Choaladi years ago when her parents ran a clothing store on 57th avenue. Haze was an old rival of just about everyone in the business. Choaladi didn't like Haze any more than anyone else. Choaladi was the type who wanted to keep the peace. His nature.

London worked for a lot of wise guys, but his main boss was Peter Choaladi. London did six years in state prison for the man. Choaladi had an interest in a jewelry robbery and it would have been his third strike. So London was picked as his stand in. He was given fifteen years, but Choaladi got it reduced to six with whatever deals he could make. They let him out in four for good behavior.

Mya was staring at the dead man, who was sitting on his heels, his head and arms in the bathtub. He too was naked. He had a long angular body that showed he worked out, but no muscle overstated anywhere; he was just toned. London slipped on a pair of plastic gloves, stepped to the tub and caught the dead man by his hair. He pulled the man's face out of the water. Huge dead eyes stared back, rested on a slim, slightly bearded face with a thin nose and wide fat lips that was smiling.

Mya said his name was Scarfe. A guru, or "humanities' last savior." Some kind of bullshit like that.

London wasn't sure, he thought he'd seen this fool on one of the cable news channels being interviewed. London did, however, remember reading an article about Scrafe in the newspaper. Talking about saving the world from humans, then saving humans from themselves by teaching them to look inward and how wrong it was for everyone to think he was preying on vulnerable, shallow people in Hollywood.

What else is new, London thought. But what the hell was he smiling about? Unless that was the sort of game the two of them played. Obviously they had sex. Semen was drying on Mya's small breasts. London was going to ask Mya about a lot of things, when she decided to come clean and she did so in such feverish way, she made London's head spin. He voice melded with the sobs. He didn't understand a word she spoke.

"Whoa," London held his hands up. "Slow down. Slow down. Smoke your cigarette, calm down." London sighed, wiped his face with a hand, which he did often when he became agitated. "This man is Wesley Scarfe. Correct?"

"Correct," Mya's voice shook.

"You two were…uh….having some fun, right?"

"We had sex, if that's what you mean."

"Yeah," London nodded. He started to say something else. Mya interrupted him.

"I had to," she said.

"Huh? You mean he forced you?"

"It was…my duty," Mya said.

89

London looked at her incredulously. "Okay. Did you want to or not?"

"Doesn't matter whether I want to have sex with Enigma. You just have to. If he picks you."

"Sex with…. what? What's an Enigma?"

"Enigma. That's his…real name," Mya said.

"Uh huh. I thought his name was Wesley," London said. He brushed his face with a hand again, caught himself and put the hand in his jean pocket.

"When he discovered the truths of the world, Wesley rechristened himself Enigma. You, as a person, are a mystery. In order to learn about yourself, you need Enigma to look into your mind and heart."

"I see," London had so much more to say, but couldn't think straight with Mya's brainwashed bullshit. London noticed she had a tattoo just above her vagina. "What's the tattoo of?"

"This?" She stood up so he could get a better view.

"This is not a tattoo."

London leaned in closer. It was not a tattoo, it was a branding of initials, two sets of initials as a matter of fact. He gently traced the branding with a finger. It was just the letter E. But there was the letters A and S, carved in her flesh in what looks like old English handwriting. "The E is for Enigma, right? Meaning Scarfe?"

"Yes," Mya shuddered at his touch, sighed deeply. She placed a hand on his shoulder, leaned down to kiss him. London pulled away. "What?"

"Not now," he said forcefully. "We have a problem to solve. I'm not here for…." London pointed at the dead man in her tub. "I'm looking for Haze, to be frank."

Mya sighed. "I-I-I don't know where Haze is. I haven't seen him in a year."

London knew Mya was lying. He checked things out before he came to Mya's place.

"And…after….?" The question lingered. "Us?"

London let it hang there without an answer. He stood, grabbed a towel and wrapped it around Mya. "Tell me about the branding."

"I…I….really don't like to talk about it," she said.

"I need to know everything. Tell me what's up with it? Some weird ritual?"

Mya nodded. "That's it exactly," she paused, continued. "Ten of us was chosen. We were asked to take photos of ourselves, naked……in compromising positions."

"As in what?"

"Masturbating. Different positions."

"That's what Enigma liked?"

"And his assistant. Second in command."

"Second in command. Is that his initials on the other side of Enigmas?"

"Not a *He*," Mya said. "A She. Anna Salvino."

"The news woman?"

"Former News anchor. She gave it all up for Enigma. She was the one who picked us for the branding."

"What's the purpose of that? Picked you for what?"

"To be their wives. To own us. Slaves," Mya said. "However you want to put it. They own us."

"What happened here, Mya? You seem fairly intelligent. Did he rape you—"

"No," there was a strange monotone in her voice. No emotion at all. "I wanted to give my body and soul to Enigma."

"And to Anna?" London said. Mya didn't want to answer at first. He could tell she was struggling with that. Was it a secret part of her sexuality she never knew existed? London reckoned it wasn't. He felt she was more of a rape victim.

"It's all a part of the education we receive to the higher self. So, yes."

"Why did you kill him if you care so much for him?" London felt something hard slam against the back of his head. He fell to his knees, eyes still on Mya. Blurred vision came first, then darkness.

*

When London awoke, Mya and Scarfe was gone.

91

Vision was still a little blurry, and the back of his head was still vibrating from the blow, London tried hard to collect his thoughts.

London slowly picked himself off the bathroom floor. He sat on the toilet, lid a cigarette. Pain invaded his thoughts. He closed his eyes and reopened them. He looked down at the floor. Water was all around the tub where they had taken Scarfe. Did Mya try to hide the body herself?

He noticed a trail of blood on the tiles that led to the kitchen and out the backdoor, which was left wide open. Someone made a mistake. They stepped in the blood, left a shoe print at the backdoor. London recognized the tread on the shoes. Excelsior tennis shoes. The shoes had an unusual tread, zig zags going one way and zig zags going across the other tread, three circles at the top and at the heel. London took his phone from his breast pocket. He immediately dialed Choaladi's number.

"Yeah?" The cracked voice on the other end said.

Got a problem," London said.

"Okay Barry. What happened?"

"Somebody ambushed me. The back of my head feels like mashed potatoes. Mya Stone and the body is gone."

"Shit," Choaladi said. "You know the guy?"

"No, I don't know him. But I've seen him on TV. His name is Scarfe. He runs a self-help cult."

"Son of a bitch!" choaladi went off line for a few seconds, coughed, then spat.

"What, Manny? What's wrong?"

"That jerk off gives thirty percent to Haze."

"Haze Deleguara?" London said.

"Yeah, Deleguara," Choaladi confirmed the news.

"She killed him?"

"That's what Mya said. She killed him. They were having some fun, decided to take it to the bathroom and she must've flipped out, drowned him. They had a weird slave-Master thing going on."

"Damn. What's wrong with people? Can't they just kiss and make love like in the old days?" Choaladi hacked something up and spit. "I never heard such shit in Cuba. Not until I came here to America. Okay, find the girl, Barry, before Haze finds out that jerk off is dead."

"What do you want done with Scarfe?"
"Make him disappear. Make it mysterious. Maybe they'll do books, even a movie about him and Haze can keep collecting from the jerk off's cult."

"Got it," London hung up, put his phone back in his breast pocket.

London happened to look up through the bathroom window and saw a man looking at him. The face was distorted some by reinforced glass, but London could see this guy was not all there. His little beady eyes sat on a bloated face and extended chin. The nose was flat and puffy with nostrils spread too far apart. What little hair he had was sticking up in the air.

The man noticed London. A frightened look creeped into those little black eyes and he backed away from the window.

London filled his hands with his Glock and sprinted toward the front door, knocking over trinkets on a shelf. He kicked the door open and ran full speed around the small cottage. The man was running across the lawn by now and through a wooded area. London remembered those woods led back to the cottage, so he switched directions to cut the man off, betting the fucker was so high, he thought he was floating. London put his Glock away and took off running.

London was right. The man had just circled around. He was back in the front yard. He was probably confused, because the man stopped for a second, did a three-sixty, twice, then kept going in the same direction.

London ran straight for the man and tackled him. London fell on top of the screaming, elbowed him once in the mouth. The man winced, coughed, spit the blood on his tee-shirt. The man struggled to get up. London held the man down with a knee on his chest.

93

The man realized he wasn't getting free and just gave up.

"Come on, man." He said in a tired voice. "Let me go."

"Who are you?" London growled.

"Come on…"

"Who are you?!" London shouted, retrieved his Glock and pointed it at the man's nose.

The man hyperventilated. "I'm-I'm Chester, man…I swear I just made a mistake…."

"Okay, crackhead, why are you looking through that window?"

"I'm no crackhead…never touch the stuff…" London pressed his knee harder into his chest. Chester screamed. "Give me break…please…..i'll…I'll tell you…"

"London eased up some. "Well?"

"I get a little high….Meth, man, makes me do things I shouldn't….okay. I…peep in houses sometimes. This lady who lives here….she has some nasty parties…."

"Did you see who else was here?"

"Man, I just saw you and another guy go in the house," Chester said. "I saw a jeep pull up, so I ran and hid in the woods. When I heard the jeep leave, I went to see what else was going on. Sometimes the lady has a lot people in there doing each other……Come on, man. Can you let me up?"

"You know this jeep?"

"Yeah, yeah. The people who own it has a farm a mile or two from here. Weird people. I don't fuck with 'em unless they have orgies in the ban. Then I might watch. Come on! Let me up!"

"Show me this farm and I might score you some Meth later," London removed his knee from Chester and stood.

Chester sat up, his eyes focused on London and a huge smile came across his face. "Really?"

Of course not, you freak, London thought.

"Yeah," London said. "You help me, I'll help you."

"Hell yeah," Chester found some spring in his shoes. 'I can show their spread.'"

"Hold on," London waved Chester back. Chester turned and saw the Glock was poking him in the ribs. He swallowed hard. "You fuck with me and I'll blow a hole in you the size of the Grand Canyon. You understand, freak?"

"I ain't gonna do that," Chester fumbled his words. "I'm a man of word....are you?"

London smiled, placed his Glock in his holster. "Yeah," he said. "Sure I am."

*

They jumped into London's '73 Cougar. Chester felt the interior, and London smacked his hand.

"I don't know where your hand has been," London said. Actually he did know, and he definitely didn't want that smell plastered all over his new seats.

"I was just admiring—" Chester tried to explain.

"I don't want you admiring anything I own, Freak," London started the Cougar and spun out of thin small driveway, leaving behind gravel and dirt.

They passed by woods on both sides of the highway. No city lights, no mountains, and no ocean waves could be heard. No other houses for miles at least ten miles. As a matter of fact, when London first tried to find the valley where Mya Stone lived, he drove by it several times. London and Chester found the dirt road that lead to the farm.

The cougar eased up to a barn where a flood lights lit up the scenery. Three jeeps and a Cadillac was parked near a series of six bungalows. London killed the lights on the Cougar as he pulled in behind a shrubbery. It didn't matter, he was sure the tires rolling across grass and gravel alerted someone.
He was right.

Three men in Gucci suits appeared, flashing shotguns and pistols. He knew instantly they were employed by Haze Deleguara. The man with the shaved head tapped on the window with the muzzle of his .38. London rolled the window down. In his other hand was a flashlight and the man kept shining it in

95

London's face, then Chester's. He repeated three more times until London said something.

"Keep shining that light in my face, baldy and you're going to eat that flashlight."

The man laughed. "Holy shit!" He nearly doubled over, laughed again. "I can't believe its Barry London!" He waved the other two guys to the Cougar. "Fellas!" He called out. "The one and only, Barry fucking London! This moron did six years for a robbery of a vault at a lumberyard. Guess what? There was no money but plenty of cops!"

London opened his door and smashed the man in ribs. The man dropped the .38 as he fell to his knees. London swung the door and then out, hitting the man square in the jaw. London quickly started the engine, placed the gear in drive and punched the gas pedal hard. The Cougar hit the man with sawed off shotgun. He fell on his back, discharged the gun, taking both blasts to the face.

Chester screeched, threw both hands on the dashboard.

London swerved the car to avoid an apple tree. The other man with the shotgun pulled the trigger and one shell shattered the back window.

"Mother fucker!" London screamed over top of Chester's screams. Now London was pissed. He'd just spent countless hours, days, and weeks, not to mention thousands of dollars to fix up the last vehicle he owned. He spun the car around and gunned it. The Cougar barreled toward the man who had now thrown the shotgun aside and fired a Walther. Two bullets struck the windshield. One barely missed London. The second struck Chester in the left arm.

Chester howled in pain.

The grill of the Cougar struck the man in the legs, jettisoned him in the air. The man landed on the hood of the car, slid into the windshield. His face was pushed close to the glass, disfiguring his visage. Chester screamed.

London took his Glock from the holster and jabbed the muzzle in the windshield where the man's face was glued to. He fired twice. Both bullet formed holes in the windshield as well as the man's.

Chester screamed.

"Shut up!" London ordered.

Chester was holding his arm, stifled his screams. He sobbed hard, watched the blood gush from the wound. London parked the Cougar, opened his door. He started to leave Chester, but had a change of heart. He removed a handkerchief from jacket pocket, and wrapped it tightly around Chester's arm.

"No crying," London said. "If you want to live through this, follow my every direction. Then you can crawl back under the rock you came from and smoke Meth until your head explodes for all care. But for now, you will not deviate from any instruction. If you get me killed, I will come back and haunt your ass! Got it?"

"Oh God," Chester whined. "I can't handle anymore ghosts....."

Suddenly the Cougar was surrounded by a mob dressed in white t-shirts and white cargo pants. Most of the mob were men, the others were women. They all flashed an array of gun, some with heavy artillery, some stepping back in the past with Colts. A tall woman with short blond hair appeared, illuminated in the Cougar's headlights. It was apparent she ran the show. She walked toward the car like a Lioness taking survey of all she owned. No one challenged this Lioness. She was dressed in white as well, but the clothing was a wrap of sorts, was made of silk and hugged her slim, athletic build snuggly.

London knew exactly who she was.

Anna Salvino.

Anna motioned for London to get out of the car. He shook his head no. Anna smiled. She gave her followers the sign to lower their weapons, then again urged London get out. London and Chester exchanged looks of concern. London opened the door and stepped out of the Cougar. Chester did the same, followed London until they met up with Anna.

"You have the money?" Her voice was choppy, direct, and could cut into a person like a hatchet.

97

London was thrown for a second. The money? That's what Haze's men were here for, London thought. They saw me and jumped to conclusions I was there to take the money from them. But what was the money for?

"Don't worry," Anny cooed. "You can have your boss back as soon as you hand over the two million." For Haze? This was a kidnapping? A mob boss? London had never heard a regular civilian committing such an act. How did they get away with it? He had bodyguards—"

London saw Tomassi walk out the barn. Lalo Tomassi was Haze's number two man. Tomassi is the reason you don't screw with Haze.

Pretty obvious Tomassi was working with Anna. They approached each other and locked lips, not sexy at all or any kind of passion most people would understand. They brushed lips, kissed hard, which was actually just bearing down had on each other's lower and top lip. London snckered. He didn't need Tomassi or Anna to explain further.

Tomasi and London only met once, and Tomassi never saw London's face. London was running with a crew robbing gamblers. They robbed Tomassi after a dice game one late night about fifteen years ago.

"Yeah," London said. "I have the money," London turned to Chester, jabbed a thumb pointing to the other side of the barn. "Go get the money out of the Cadillac."

Nervously, Chester nodded, shuffled off. One of Anna's men followed. Five minutes of staring at each other, Chester returned with a duffle bag. Anna's man did not walk him back. Chester acted like he had something to tell London. London brushed him off. Chester handed the bag to London. London unzipped the bag and saw stacks of fifties and hundreds on top. He handed the bag to Tomassi.

"Last payment," Tomassi rifled through the bag. He was pleased with what he found. "I bet you were surprised I was involved," Tomassi said.

98

"Oh yeah." London wanted to hit the man for patting himself on the back. "Very clever of you to pull this off."

Tomassi stopped grinning. He handed the bag to another member of the cult. "I don't like your smart ass tone."

"I don't like your conniving face," London told him.

"Have we met before?" Tomassi chuckled, looked surprised by London's statement.

"Yeah, it was a few years ago, and I knew you couldn't be trusted back then," London said. "I robbed you and it was easy-peezy, just like this con you've pulled on Haze."

"I don't think so, punk. Nobody has ever robbed me. That had to be another guy."

"No, it was you, wearing the same clown outfit as today."

"Funny," Tomassi took a step closer. "I get the feeling you aren't who we think you are."

"It doesn't matter," London said. "I want to take the old man. You got your money, Benedict Arnold."

"Traitor to what? A mob boss? A man who cared about no one or nothing but himself? He didn't give two shits about his family, even less about his employees. Haze ain't what he used to be," Tomassi laughed. "Anna here, she broke him. Just like all the other sheep that follow this dumbass Enigma, or whatever he calls himself. They don't have a brain. And what Anna did to Haze," Tomassi shook his head. "Proves he didn't have either. Then again, I already knew that. I used to bend that fucker any way I wanted. Go ahead. Take the old man."

London pushed past Tomassi. He looked behind him and saw Ann had her cult standing in single file, giving them a pep talk or a speech. They looked like a militia, the way they were holding their guns. Something struck London as odd. He referred to Scarfe in the present. So who the hell hit him over the head and took Mya?

London stepped inside the barn and saw Haze lying on the floor, dead from a bullet to the head.

There was a shadow by one of the stables. London sighed, unsheathed his Glock from his holster. Quiet footsteps came from the stables and out of the shadows came Mya. Still naked, her body covered in dirt and mud, blood stains on her face. She was pointing a .38 at London.

London noticed her arm was bleeding.

"What happened to your arm?"

Mya's eyes fluttered. She was racking her brain to remember.

"I brushed again the bathroom sink," Mya said. "Cut it."

"Mya," London spoke softly with an air of command. "Put the gun down."

"This isn't fun anymore," she said moving away from the stables. She knocked over some hay, which revealed some more weapons.

A few Barrett M 107's and a whole lot of Benelli M4 Super 90's. That one was a high powered shotgun. Fuckin-A, London thought. He shot a Super 90 last year. Talk about a weapon that could make a man cum in his pants. Or shit himself, if he wasn't prepared to fire it correctly.

"I know, Mya," London said. "The game is not fun anymore. Just…throw the gun away. I'll take you with me. Get you some help."

"I don't want any man helping me…they're all liars. They just use me."

"That man…that was in your tub. Who was he?"

"A computer programmer…I think," Mya was confused. She thought hard. "A friend of Enigma's. He paid Enigma a lot of money to fuck me. I didn't like it very much."

London nodded. "I could see that. Enigma did that a lot, huh? Sold you and the girls from his inner circle?"

"I had to supplement my income," Chester said as he entered the barn. He was carrying the duffle bag. Chester laughed, shook his head. His face suddenly changed. He was more serious. His eyebrows furrowed, sank downward to his nose. His voice

100

became deeper, no edge, calm as a gentle breeze. "Mya," he said, held a hand up. "Violence is not the way…not for you. You have too much love in your heart…..You are the mother of all that is pure….no evil exists inside your heart, no hate, no anger in your DNA….you were cured by me…..remember….?"

Mya listened to him. She lowered her gun. Dropped it to the ground. She fell to her knees, and wept.

A single bullet struck Scarfe in the back and exiting his chest cavity. He cried out once, fell forward. A loud voice coming from a bullhorn announced the ATF and FBI were there. London grabbed the duffle bag and ran to find a backdoor to the barn. There wasn't one, so he kicked out a lose board, making a hole in the wall just big enough to crawl through. He ran into the woods seconds before ATF and FBI agents stormed the farm. He stayed hidden in the hollow of a dead tree for hours until the helicopter above disappeared.

Ten AM the next day, London hitchhiked his way back into the city, leaving his '73 Cougar. He wasn't worried about it. What was in the duffle bag could afford him a new one.

***

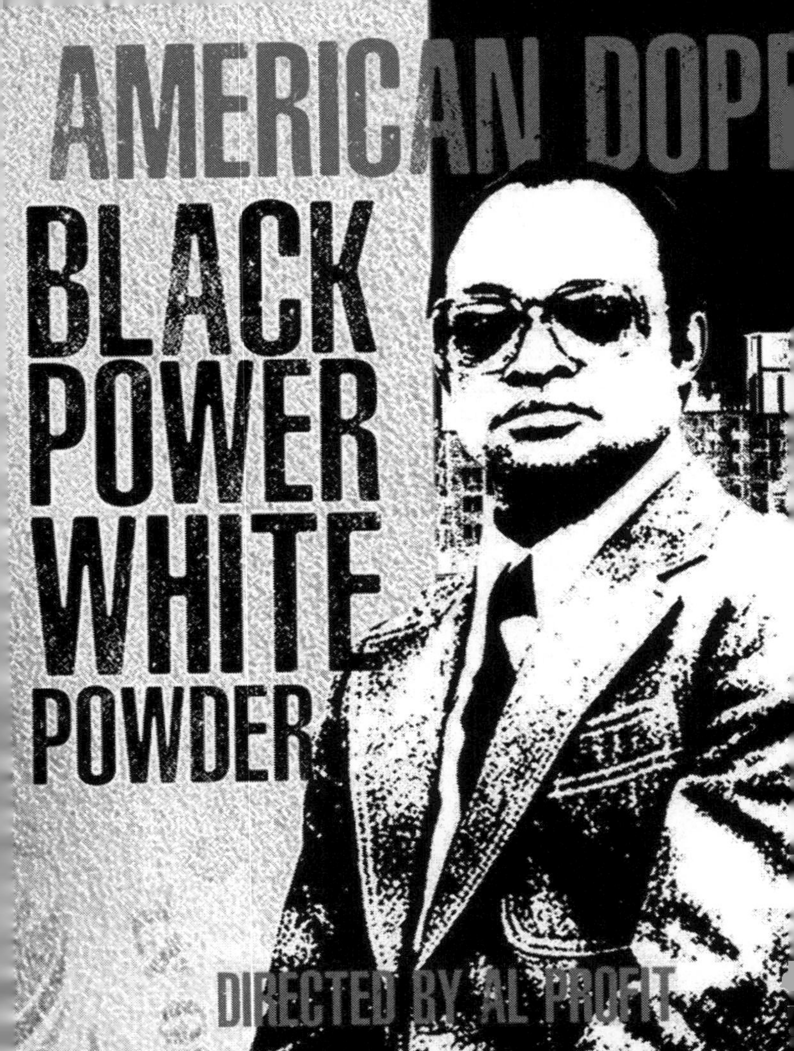
AMERICAN DOPE
BLACK
POWER
WHITE
POWDER
DIRECTED BY AL PROFIT

NOTICE

Alligators are common in this area. They can be dangerous and should not be approached, frightened or fed. Please give them the respect they deserve

KEEP YOUR DISTANCE

Kiss for Karma

C.W. Blackwell

The dead gator lay belly-up on the autopsy table, claws painted orange and white like candy corns. The guys from the Coroner unit had brought it in on a pallet jack that was usually reserved for the big Pensacolan stiffs, the ones whose insides looked like the grease trap from some Gulf Coast fish market.

The technician had just run a saw from throat to gonads.

Dana Parker looked at the carved gator, said, "Remind me not to die in this county when the doc is out of town."

The man laughed. Kind of a nervous chuckle.

"I'll be honest. I never done this before," said the tech. He was a gangly wisp of a man. Eyebrows twitching like his forehead wanted to shake them off. "Seen Doctor Havers do it once. They tell you she was in New York?"

"You the guy from Okaloosa County?" Parker said. She was looking him over with her arms crossed.

"Yep," he said. "I'm Gadsen. Came over when Havers called. Sounds like some case."

He was right about that.

The call came in from a drunk Northeast of the city. He was nearing the bottom of a pint of Early Times when the gator came strutting down Old Chemstrand Road. Dangling from its mouth was a silver crucifix and a wad of bloody hair extensions. No doubt he followed the thing a few hundred yards wondering how he'd get that necklace from its mouth and make it out with his drinking arm still attached. In the end he gave up, told the dispatcher: *Reckon that gator done et somebody.*

Gadsen was now working the gator's stomach loose from its spinal column.

"Think it's somebody's pet?" Gadsen said. His surgical mask was on now and it made him sound drunk.

Everyone sounded drunk in Pensacola.

"Not many gators paint their own nails," said Parker. She waved a business card in the air and set it on the tool tray. "Call me if you find out what it ate for breakfast."

Gadsen gave a nod. Saw blades catching the light just so.

He was probably right about the pet thing, too. It almost couldn't go any other way. Likely some old lady was painting the gator's claws when it caught a whiff of the shrimp po' boy she had for lunch. A decade of belly rubs, manicures and adorable crochet bonnets meant nothing to the gator for just one taste of shrimp on his master's greasy lips. Of course, with that first taste comes blood, then more tasting.

Parker was halfway across the lot with a still-dry pinch of tobacco in her lip when Gadsen shouted from the doorway.

"Detective," he shouted. He motioned with his blood-stained gloves. "I found a foot in there."

*

Gadsen held the severed foot in the cup of his hand. It was still a healthy shade of pink. Toenails artfully painted. There was a tattoo of a moon and shooting stars on the bridge of the foot, clear and dark as if the ink had not yet settled.

"Put on some gloves and hold it if you want," said Gadsen.

"There's not enough latex in the world," said Parker.

Gadsen set the foot on an exam tray. The toes were wrinkled like it had just gone swimming.

"There's something else," said Gadsen. He was now up to his elbow in gator guts, poised as if he were about to deliver the rest of the body in some dramatic reveal.

Instead, he just stared at his hand.

It sparkled.

105

"I think it's a necklace," said Gadsen. He held it up, mopped away the gore with his other hand. "Diamonds?"

"They're not diamonds," said Parker. "And we already found her necklace."

"A belt maybe? Eyepatch? I'm out of guesses."

"Rhinestones," said Parker. She was composing a photo of the severed foot with her phone. Cropping the shot with her fingers. "I take it you haven't seen a G-string in a while."

Gadsen stared at the thing in his hand.

"Who wears rhinestone G-strings?"

*

Tony's Lounge was a strip joint off HWY 98 with a dirt parking lot and steel-bar windows. Drivers always slowed when they passed as if somehow they'd catch a glimpse of what was going on inside.

As if it were some big fucking secret.

The owner was Tony Chicasso, a middle-aged transplant from Long Island. He had a reputation for paying his bills and keeping his nose clean. Still, he didn't like cops and never went anywhere without his bodyguard, who he always introduced as his *lawyer*.

There was only one space in the lot when Parker and the recruit rolled in. The other spots were jammed with a dozen crooked pickups and one Harley Davidson.

Even the Harley had mudflaps.

"Do we knock?" Deputy Tildson had sweat stains under both arms and was burying his hands in his pockets, taking them back out again. There were two kinds of recruits in the Escambia County Sheriff's Office: failed quarterbacks and tender church folk. Tildson was the latter, the kind that checked in with the almighty every time he got a little tight in the pants.

Parker pointed at the neon sign.

"When it says *open* you just go in," she said. "We aint selling bibles, here."

Tildson nodded, but he didn't open the door.

106

Parker crossed her arms, said, "I've seen you drag a two-hundred-pound decomp out of an airtight single-wide. Tellin me you can't handle a little *T and A*?"

"Just that it'll give me bad thoughts is all."

Parker looked him over like a bad deal.

"Give me your wallet," she said. Her eyes were stones.

"What?"

"Just give it to me."

Tildson offered his wallet and Parker took forty bucks from the billfold.

"What's that for," he said.

"For a lap dance and a ride home," she said. "Gas up the cruiser and get out of here, sweetie. Police work aint your thing."

*

On stage was a Cuban girl with a silver wig and six-inch stilettos. She was hanging upside down from the dance pole with her tits bound in Saran Wrap. No doubt she'd work that into her routine somehow, but the song was still near the start. There were half a dozen men at the drink rail with some variation of Budweiser in front of them.

A cocktail waitress shuffled across the room. Redhead, a little strung out. Empty beer bottles on a tray.

"Need a drink?" said the waitress.

"I'm looking for Chicasso." Parker thumbed her belt so the badge caught the stage lights. "He around?"

She looked at the badge, then the ceiling. There was a blinking security camera above the door. She gestured to it, said, "Wait here."

The girl on stage was slipping a straight razor down her cleavage now, working through the plastic. Some L.A. rock band on the house system.

In a few moments the waitress returned, trayless and agitated. She stood with her hands on her hips. Eyes heating up.

"He's in a real bad mood," she said.

107

"I'm sure I've seen worse," said Parker.

The Cuban girl freed her breasts from the plastic wrap to great celebration.

"I mean he's a real *fuck face*. You know? He's lucky I don't walk out."

"I get it. Still need to talk to him, though. *Fuck face* or not."

They went to a back room where the girls were setting up their costumes and dabbing makeup all over, covering up tattoos and needle tracks. They barely looked up, as if strangers barging in was part of the job. Parker grabbed the waitress by the wrist before she turned the corner.

"You can't just grab me," she hissed, pulling her hand away.

"Settle down," said Parker. "I might get what I need from the girls."

"Nobody gets what they need from the girls," she said. "That's why they keep coming back." She checked a video monitor on a wall shelf and clicked her tongue. "Jesus, the customers are wandering around."

"Take care of it," said Parker. "I'll let myself out."

*

Parker gave it to the girls easy. Nothing about the gator or the severed foot. Just that a girl was missing, probably left town in the middle of the night. Owed someone money. It happens *all the time*, she said.

None of the girls were concerned until Parker mentioned the moon tattoo. A tiny brunette in the corner had been staring at her smoky-eye makeup in the mirror, still as a statue. She was wearing a cop outfit with a plastic badge and fuzzy handcuffs on her hip. When she heard about the tattoo she buried her face in her hands and sobbed.

Parker went to the girl, asked what her name was.

The girl didn't answer. Instead she grabbed her purse and spun through the room, past Parker and out the back door, makeup streaking down her cheeks like war paint.

Parker followed.

It was sunset by now and the lights in the parking lot were just coming on. The lot was full, and men were standing around smoking and spitting in the dirt. The police cruiser was parked along the highway and leaning against the door was Tildson. The stripper cop tripped on the curb right in front of him and he rushed to help her up.

"You came back," said Parker. She had come out of the door at full sprint but was now sauntering across the lot.

"I gassed up the cruiser like you said, but I didn't want to get a bad eval," said Tildson. He jutted his lip and made an apologetic gesture with his hand. The girl was now embracing him and sniffling into his chest.

"You're never gonna get the glitter off your uniform," said Parker. Then to the girl, "You got a name?"

She coughed and wiped mascara over the back of her hand.

"Sierra Nevada," she said.

"Sierra Nevada," said Parker. "Like the mountain range?"

"Yes."

"That you're real name?"

"Nuh-uh."

"I didn't think so."

The back door opened again and two fat men waddled through the jamb. Sierra Nevada let go of Tildson and stood with her arms crossed, looking at the ground.

"I don't remember giving permission to talk to my employees." It was Chicasso. His hair was shiny, and he wore large eyeglasses that covered a third of his face. He motioned to the other fat man beside him. "This is my lawyer, Mr. Hinkleman."

Hinkleman crossed his arms and straightened when his name was spoken.

"A girl's missing, Tony," said Parker. "Might have been one of yours."

Chicasso rolled his head until there was a tiny pop in his vertebrae. He looked disappointed, like he couldn't believe he was interrupted by this small thing.

"Girls go missing all the time," he said. The lawyer touched Chicasso's shoulder and shook his head. "Still, my lawyer advises me against speaking freely on this topic."

"Just tell me if you've been short-staffed this week," Parker said.

Chicasso shrugged but didn't respond.

"Let us talk to the girl, then. Just for a minute."

"Sorry," said Chicasso. "She goes on in five minutes. Her face is a mess."

Hinkleman whispered into Chicasso's ear a long while, his mustache nearly touching his earlobe. When he was finished, Chicasso rolled his neck again but no pops could be heard.

"Tell you what. It's twenty bucks for a lap dance," said Chicasso. "If she's got something to say she can do it on your lap. And park the Crown Vic around back before the crowd starts to thin out."

*

"You don't have to dance," said Parker. They were in a shoulder-high stall with an open ceiling. Brown corduroy loveseat. Sierra Nevada straightened out the twenties on the coffee table and leaned in close, hand on Parker's thigh. She put a finger to her lips and pointed to an electrical outlet that on second glance didn't look like a real outlet at all.

"He's listening," she said. Her voice was just a breathy whisper. "I'll just talk in your ear, okay?"

"Fine," said Parker. She moved the girl's hand further down her leg. "But don't touch the Glock."

Sierra Nevada's real name was Julie Barton. She was a college drop-out from some Central California farm town, followed her boyfriend to Florida when he jumped bail for a string of auto burgs. When they finally hooked him, she ran out of cash and ended up on the Pensacola strip circuit.

110

"I needed a roommate," she said. "And that's when I met Karma."

"Karma?"

"Karma Sutra."

She couldn't remember Karma's last name, only that her real name was Connie and she was from outside of Atlanta. She danced at the 9th Street Gentlemen's Club and did a few nights a month at Tony's.

"Connie's a sweetheart. She was having a hard time though, trying to get clean y'know? She was into needles, the hard stuff. When she disappeared, I thought she was visiting home, but..."

Sierra Nevada was crying again, dabbing her eyes with a Kleenex she had found somewhere.

"But what?"

"She left her clothes. Toothbrush, makeup, hair dryer. And when you talked about the tattoo..."

"A moon and shooting stars."

"On top of her right foot. Oh God is she okay?"

"Pretty sure she's not okay," said Parker. A new song had started and Sierra Nevada was adjusting her top as if she had forgotten it was still on. "If you want to help Connie I'll need to know who she hangs out with. Who she uses with. Got any names, sugar?"

"Melvin," she said immediately, and when she said it her eyes iced over. "The owner's son. Real creep. He hangs two-dollar bills on the rail when he's holding. He doesn't even use, just likes getting the girls high so he can—"

The stall door swung open and the cocktail waitress stood in the doorway.

"Tony says time's up," she said.

"I'm not surprised," said Parker. She straightened her shirt, checked her badge and pistol. "It was just getting good."

Sierra Nevada hugged Parker and kissed her on the cheek, said: "Don't tell Connie I told you about the drugs. It would just tear her to pieces."

*

111

"You smell like tropical lotion," said Tildson. He was easing the Crown Vic off HWY 98, back toward HQ. "It smells nice, really."

"You say the creepiest shit," said Parker. "No wonder you live alone. Look, if you had a stripper on your lap for fifteen minutes you'd smell like goddamn tropical lotion too."

"I don't live alone," said Tildson. "I live with my—"

Parker held up her hand, silencing him.

"I'm going to fill the blank with something interesting so I don't lose all respect for you."

"Oh no, it's not that. I live with my grandma."

The radio clicked on. It was records.

"Sam Twenty-Three," said the voice. It sounded like Jane, the surly clerk with the red Polo shirts. "I have the address you requested. Last known for Melvin Chicasso is 998 New Haven Drive."

"New Haven? Is that in Myrtle Cove?"

"Nope," said the voice. She sounded irritated now. Jane didn't like follow-up questions. "It's off Old Chemstrand Road. By the refinery."

"Old Chemstrand?"

"That's what I said, Dana."

Parker slapped Tildson on the shoulder.

"The gator," she said. "It's where they found the gator."

Tildson was already getting back on the freeway.

*

It was full dark when they reached the end of New Haven Road. Heavy mist in the cedar groves. The refinery was just a mile away and you could see the orange lights melting through the night like molten steel. The house at 998 looked more like a small warehouse, the kind of place you'd store industrial supplies or farm equipment.

They circled the place once and stopped at a metal door by a rollup. Parker banged on the door with her fist. They waited. There were frogs croaking in the swamp beyond the treeline. Insects skittering against the porchlight.

"Not enough for a warrant is there," said Tildson. He stepped to the side and pounded on the rollup door.

Parker twitched her lips to one side. She was about to answer when there was a scream from the other side of the door.

"I think the judge just gave his blessing," said Parker. She rapped on the door again and announced herself. "Can you open the door?" Parker shouted.

The rollup jolted from the inside and there was another scream.

"It's locked from the outside," yelled a female voice.

Tildson was halfway to the cruiser by now. When he returned he was tossing a two-foot orange crowbar from one hand to the other. He jammed an end into the lock hasp and pulled hard. The lock didn't give easily, but after a few tries it clattered to the ground and Parker began working the door up the rails. When it opened waist-high, a woman scrabbled out on all fours wearing nothing but a silver crucifix around her neck. She collapsed at Tildson's feet and sobbed into his BDU pants.

"Why do they always go to you," said Parker.

"Grandma says I've got an approachable face," said Tildson.

The woman's name was Penny Nichols, and despite all the prodding, she swore it was her bonafide legal name since the ink dried on her birth certificate twenty-seven years ago. She was a waitress at Chubby's Diner on the westside of town, where Melvin Chicasso ate BLTs and strawberry milkshakes every Tuesday night.

"Did he promise you drugs?" Parker said. They were in the cruiser now with the heater on, waiting for the ambulance. Lynnyrd Skynnyrd on the radio. "You can say yes. We already know about it."

Penny nodded. She tightened the mylar blanket they had given her around her shoulders. "But then he went Pentecostal on me. Said he could heal my addiction with *the word*."

113

"What word?" Parker said.

"The *Good Word*," said Tildson. "Right?"

"Something like that," said Penny.

"Did it work?"

Penny shuddered and held herself tight, shaking her head. "He said I could score if I did something brave. Something that would prove my faith."

There were headlights coming down the road, and Parker looked to see if it was the ambulance.

"What did he want you to do?" Tildson said.

"He wanted me to kiss his alligator."

Parker and Tildson looked at each other.

"It wasn't very big," she continued. "But God it was ugly. He kept shakin' it and sayin' it was gonna bite me."

"Sounds like a bad metaphor," said Parker. "Was this an actual alligator with teeth and a tail?"

She nodded into her hands and wept. "What other kind of alligators are there?"

"Bigger ones," said Parker.

A big block El Camino passed on the road and made a slow U-turn at the dead end. Penny flattened herself on the back seat.

"Oh God that's his car," she whispered. "It's Melvin."

Parker squinted at the driver.

"Chubby guy in a Hawaiian shirt?" Parker said.

"Yes. Oh God it's him."

Melvin hit the gas, tires breaking loose and spitting gravel everywhere. The car fishtailed from one side of the road to the other, then launched down New Haven and disappeared.

Parker tightened her hands around the steering wheel.

"The ambulance is almost here," she said. Her voice had a dark tone. "Better get out."

Tildson helped Penny out of the cruiser. Their feet barely touched the asphalt when the Crown Vic peeled down the road with the passenger door swinging in the wind like some wild night creature.

114

She hit ninety-five before reaching the end of New Haven Road, just in time to see which way the El Camino was turning. It spun onto Old Chemstrand in a tumult of smoke, then sat with the headlights shining over the road, waiting to see if anyone followed.

Parker killed the headlights for surprise, but it was too late. Melvin hit the gas again when she came within a few hundred yards, engine screaming toward the refinery. On Old Chemstrand they broke 110. Every dip seemed it would launch the El Camino into a fireball of twisted metal out into the cedars, but Melvin was a better driver that she had guessed.

Just good enough to stay alive.

For now.

At the refinery gate, Melvin cut his speed enough to punch through the chain-link fence without wrecking. There was an empty checkpoint station with a plastic boom barrier that jackknifed into the air when he blasted through.

Parker followed.

The refinery was a maze of outbuildings and industrial stills. The roadways were narrow and lined with steel pipes of all sizes. Orange security lights on the chem towers. It wasn't the kind of place you'd pick for a vehicle pursuit.

Parker radioed dispatch and stayed on Melvin best she could. He weaved through the refinery grid like he'd been practicing his whole life for it, then disappeared around an array of gas stills.

Parker lowered the window, listening.

There was only the sound of electricity in the wires, crude oil in the pipes. The air smelled like grease and swamp grass.

There was a flicker in the rearview.

Melvin had circled back and flanked her. He was tapping his high beams. Parker spun the Crown Vic around so it faced him and flicked on the loudspeaker.

"Don't be an asshole, Melvin," she bleated from the speaker. "It's only me and you for a couple of minutes, then the entire Sheriff's Office. Come out and lay down before somebody overreacts."

He revved the engine, exhaust billowing all around.

Parker curled her fingers around the steering wheel, dropped the Crown Vic into low gear. She checked her seatbelt.

"Fine," she said. "Come and get it."

They launched at each other in a cloud of white smoke. Headlights blaring. At twelve thousand RPMs the two cars swerved only slightly, sparks arcing as they passed. Door mirrors snapping and looping through the air. Parker spun the car down a roadway and circled back, but Melvin clipped a pipe array. The El Camino careened off the roadway and flipped twice before settling on its side.

Parker ran to the car, pistol drawn.

Melvin was climbing out the window. Broken glass and fluids all over the roadway.

"On the ground," yelled Parker.

Melvin didn't listen.

He fired two rounds at Parker.

The shots missed.

Parker fired back. The round clipped his shoulder and he tumbled to the ground, then scrambled to his feet again and staggered for the open swamp beyond the refinery.

"You know, Melvin," Parker called after him. "Best not to keep racking up the charges."

Melvin didn't stop, only shouldered through the swamp grass until his boots sloshed in the mud. He swung around, and Parker dropped into a crouch with the Glock at center mass.

"She was just some junky waitress," Melvin cried. He looked haggard and desperate. Blood dripping from his sleeve. "I was trying to save her."

Parker kept him in her sights.

"You can't save them all, can you Melvin?"

"Just needed more time with her. I'd have fixed her."

"I wasn't talking about the waitress."

Melvin had been swaying and stomping in the water, but now he was still.

116

"That's right, Melvin," said Parker. "We know about Connie too. Sounds like she flunked your little program."

"Connie?"

"Karma."

"Couldn't do nothin for that one. The almighty looked into her soul and didn't like what he saw is all."

"Not the way I see it."

He itched the side of his throat with the barrel of his gun.

"How do you see it, then?"

Parker moved closer.

"You made a desperate woman kiss a hungry gator is how I see it. A gator that was used to taste of human flesh. It's biology, not religion."

"Those are the same things," said Melvin.

"Like hell they are. How many girls?"

"How many did I save?"

"No. How many failed your gator test."

Melvin sighed and counted on his fingers.

"Five. None of them sufferin anymore. Not even the Lord could save em. We both tried."

There were lights and sirens coming into the refinery now. Melvin started to moan and bang his head with the pistol.

"Careful now, Melvin," said Parker. "You're gonna make everyone nervous swinging that gun around."

He took a few steps into the water, up to his knees. He was looking to the other side where a cedar grove jutted into the swamp.

Parker drew close.

"You can't make it across," she said. "Not with a blown shoulder."

The sky was now clear, and a full moon cast over the water. A shape was cutting the reflection in a tiny wake, long and dark like a root curling from the mud.

"Get out of there, Melvin."

Melvin watched it move.

He dropped the pistol in the water and fell to his knees, water up to his waist. His good arm reached to the sky like some revivalist preacher.

117

There was movement all around him.

"You're bleeding in the swamp," Parker yelled. "Use your damn head, Melvin."

"The almighty knows," he cried. "*I give unto you power to tread on serpents and scorpions*. That's what the book says."

Parker was close now.

"I bet it don't mention gators," she said.

She reached for him, but when she touched his shoulder the alligator launched from beneath the water. Melvin's head disappeared in its jaws and his whole body submerged and twisted beneath the surface.

He didn't even have time to scream.

Parker saw the animal's white belly when it spun, and thought it was Melvin's best chance. Not that he deserved a chance, but she still hadn't heard who the other girls were.

When the gator spun again, she fired twice.

There was shouting behind her now.

"Where's the shooter?" It was Tildson, out of breath. There were six other cops running through the swamp grass with their weapons drawn, some stopping to kneel with rifles at their shoulders.

"No shooter," said Parker, holstering her weapon. There was a light froth in the water, but the swamp was otherwise still. "Bad news is the damn gators ate our killer."

*

They found what was left of Melvin just before sunrise. All that remained was a bloody Hawaiian shirt and a wallet full of two-dollar bills. The first gator had died from the gunshots, but others must have come after for a free meal.

There was a team roping off parts of the refinery, and the Coroner was standing by, waiting for a few bits and pieces to take back to the morgue.

Tildson handed Parker a cup of coffee.

"Gotta love the overtime," said Parker. They were standing by the wrecked El Camino watching Animal Control wade through the swamp.

118

Tildson just shook his head.

"Not the way I thought this would end," he said.

Parker took a sip of coffee, then gasped and spat on the ground.

"God, is this hazelnut creamer?"

"I thought you liked it that way."

Parker shook her head and glowered at the cup in her hand.

"You'd better be careful."

"I'm sorry, Sarge," said Tildson. "Wait, careful about what?"

She pointed to the swamp where they were hauling out the dead gator. "The thing about karma is," she said, grinning. "It'll come back to bite you."

***

©2018 C.W. Blackwell

119

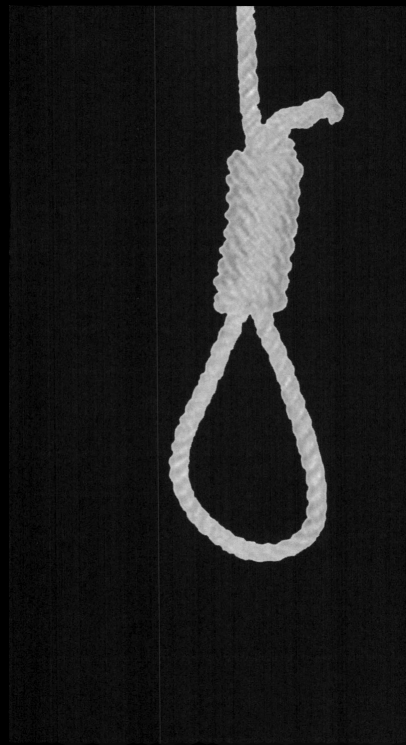

Dead Drop
Arthur Evans

She was filing out with the dawn arrivals at
Newark when the alert sounded. Sudden buzzers
like monster crickets. Every head swiveled. Behind
a clear partition the screening check was heaving
with TSA blue. There was a black smear on the
body imager's smoked glass, chest-high across
the jumping jack. Rubbernecks parked their roller
bags to watch. "Comin' by," she said. Then loudly:
"Comin' by."

A cab to the motor inn cost her twenty times four.
Getting out in the parking lot she spotted the Empire
State Building's lead-gray spire. Otherwise her view
was lost behind a toll plaza, eight lanes with blinking
signs feeding the Holland Tunnel. Holiday wreaths the
size of tractor tires hung above the tunnel entrance.
Ash-like snow was drifting around. There were
exhaust fumes on the cold air. Welcome to Jersey
City.

In the motel's office she found a lady elf grinning
behind a thick sheet of glass. She gave her name as
Esmerelda Chess, pushing her license and VISA
through the mousehole. Beside her a pot of coffee sat
on a credenza. She poured the last of it into a paper
cup. Tasted like solder, but it was a start.

The room was tolerable. Couple of burn holes in
the carpet if you looked. Traffic sighed through the
pulled beige curtain. She sat on the bed and watched
ten minutes of CNN. The airport came up on the
zipper, investigation, one dead. Slapheads. She shut
the TV off and took out her phone. Tapped, waited,
spoke a name. "At the water department," she said.

An hour later she sat in a waiting room at the City
Hall. The wooden bench was all hers. To one side a
whirring black fan slowly nodded no. She was studying
broken tiles in the linoleum floor when the water

121

manager opened his office door. A white button-down held back a mudslide around his waist. He beckoned her in, saying "Find us okay?"

"I only got lost in the building. By the big meeting room."

"The council chamber? It's a landmark. We're scraping for funds to restore it." Close in he smelled like new lard. She moved to an oak chair as he rolled around his desk. He lowered himself then said, "Emma, right? And you'd like to know about your brother. Ethan. About his job here."

"That's right. Can you tell me what all he was working on?"

"Ethan was a contractor helping with our accounts." Pause. "Lots of it was in sewerage." Pause. "Assloads, if you get me."

"Okay. But there has to be more."

He smiled. "More?"

"He left here one night and didn't go home. Never heard from after." The man's smile hung in there. "So I came to ask about it."

"Are you going to talk to the police?"

"I'm doing that, uh-huh. I'm set to see them today. That's to check on the missing person."

"Well then, *they'll* have more for you." His walrus eyes wandered to a dented file cabinet standing in one corner.

"Can I ask, what do *you* have?"

He let out a short wheeze. "I want to help, Emma. Your brother, we considered him one of ours. It's just that we don't have authority . . . if you get me."

She wasn't ready to kick up the anthill. There were better people to talk to. First off, that cop. The one who'd called the day after she reported Ethan missing. She wondered about that. *A police snake*, Ethan had said.

"Good of you to take time," she told the manager.

"Downstairs and either way gets you to the front exit."

"I won't get lost."

Strike one.

122

Once she was gone he picked up his desk phone and punched an extension. A moment later he said, "All done." There was a pause. "Right, Vi."

Emma checked the district cop shop on her phone map. Seven blocks, she'd walk it. Already skinned for a hundred and more in cab rides. She'd cartwheel it if she had to. She left the City Hall green with its Roman statue. The street turned residential. Waist-high chain link out front, houses a knife blade wouldn't slip between. The sidewalk was busted and cold wind cut through her suede jacket. She was getting the local feel. Nowhere to run to.

The station had a flat cement front and a glass door slapped with official decals. A sign said wait for the buzzer. She stood there till she heard a click, then went in. Just inside, railing made a hairpin track from the door to a wall-length desk. Behind it a female cop with one arm in a black sling sat staring at her. Emma followed the rails down and around to approach the cop. Under a stone gaze she related the who and why. "You might catch him on two," the cop said.

Up a flight of stairs she found an open room with vending machines. By the far windows a knot of men in jeans stood laughing. They ignored her, so she called out, "Alex Turnbull?" One glanced over, then stared. She marked a blue police sweatshirt, a shaven head, a starved-wolf face. "What?" he said, coming toward her.

"Emma Chess," she said. "Ethan's sister."

He nodded. "Sure. Let's do this." He stepped her over to some plastic waiting-room chairs and they sat down. "I knew Ethan," he said.

"Well then, maybe you know what happened to him?"

"We're getting on it. What we're here for." He studied her. His eye sockets were ringed dark red but he didn't seem tired.

"I went and saw his boss the water man," she said. "Ethan's not some accountant. He went straight from high school to basic."

123

"He always said he was ex-pert at diddlin' digits. Whatever fag farm they got him from." He stopped but she showed nothing. His look tightened. "Homes wasn't one to keep in touch, was he. But I'll tell you. He got in with some of the serious people up here."

"Maybe you could tell me where you think he went to?"

"I'm explaining. Homes had his little bee wick dipped all over Hudson County. My guess is there came a point he had to take off. No forwarding."

Emma said, "Serious people? What's that mean?"

"Just take the hint. Let us do our job."

"It's been a week."

He pointed at her. "You. And me." His thumb jabbed his sweatshirt. "Are going to take it slow. Do the slow grind. All righty? Miss Chest?" He sent a snicker to the group of men behind her. Spectators.

One corner of her mouth curled. "I have to say everyone's being a giant help today."

Now Turnbull looked bored. "You'll vouch for that? The dep chief's my dad. He'd be proud if he heard."

Strike two.

Outside she checked the phone map again. Again started off on foot. *That anger of yours, carry it light*, Ethan said, *a hollow-point slug never weighed much*. She still had one more of these fine folks to speak to, but after that — strike three. She made it back to the motor inn, used her key at the side door. In the badly lit stucco hall two backpackers smilingly blocked the way. "From where are you come?" one said.

"Texas," she told them.

"Ah!" A black beard parted to show perfect teeth. "Is it like so in Texas, the chain saw . . . mascara?"

"Massacre," she said. "Want to see?" She clocked from one to the other. The smiles vanished.

She went on to her room. She was sitting on the bed looking at her unopened travel bag when her phone sounded. "Emma here."

"I got your message," the caller said. "It's Violet DelGreco. From jungleland."

124

Unsure, Emma said, "I'm real glad to hear from you. Haven't had much luck here so far."

"We should get together. I'm city clerk, did Ethan mention? I dealt with him off and on. Some stuff I had knowledge of, some I didn't."

"Uh-huh."

"So. How about lunch? 12:30?"

"All right."

"We'll get 'za."

Emma paid a car to take her back downtown. When she got out, a short woman in business black was standing in front of Stanz Pizza. Emma went up and the woman extended a hand, saying "Vi DelGreco" as if that settled something. Her tan was dark as espresso. Curls brushed her shoulder pads. Emma followed her into a shotgun parlor where red vinyl booths lined one wall. They got a grin from the guy at the register. On Vi's advice, Emma ordered a sausage special.

They took the booth nearest the entrance, where a ballgame blared from an overhead screen. Tapping garlic from a shaker, Vi said, "Firstly, I have no idea where Ethan could be."

"Funny. I been hearing that one today."

"You spoke to him when?"

"Not spoke. He left me a voicemail last week. It sounded like strong trouble. He said to contact you if I had to. Then to use my judgment about the rest."

"And how's that going? The judgment part."

"It's going," Emma said. She lifted her pork-studded slice.

Vi bit off the tip of her plain cheese. "You're wondering, why her. Me."

Emma said, "Mostly not," then took a bite.

"To me Ethan was this Zorro man of mystery. At first. Then I realized he had no real existence here. So that was my in."

Emma had to finish chewing. Then she said, "Am I just hungry, or is this the best pizza I've ever tasted?"

Vi gave her black curls a shake. "He could be chirpy like that too. Had manners."

125

Emma shrugged. She really needed to eat.

"I would like to help find him," Vi said. Above them the sportscaster was yelling in what sounded like fear. "And so you know, we've been observed." Her eyes shifted sideward. Emma looked past her toward the pizzeria's rear. Two booths down a woman with a cloud of white hair sat staring at them through red cat-eye frames. Across from her was a set of broad shoulders and a bald spot. Vi said, "That's Estelle Quinn, acting mayor. She's taken charge since the old mayor's away. Lewisburg, a 30-month kick at Club Fed. You heard about this?"

Emma shook her head.

"Well, Estelle's had a so-called colorful past." Vi lifted her Sprite can, sipped through the straw. "Interested?"

Emma raised her slice and nodded.

"Going way back, she was a stripper called Vena Cava. She made good on the old fan-dance circuit. At 35 she quit to marry a developer and," Vi's voice dropped, "got involved. She was an earner. Got tapped for dep mayor and was in the right place for a vertical bump. As it were." Vi held up a finger, sipped more Sprite. "Her partner in crime sitting there's Coco C, a big boy on our city council. As reptiles go, he's Godzilla. Paid permits are Coco's private turf."

"Paid permits?"

"You heard right. He's got houses in San Juan, Miami. All the old-guard perks. Brother Ethan was one of Coco's guys. You knew that?"

Emma shook her head.

The mayor and councilman slid from their booth. They stood up, took a moment, then came over. "Shoowa," the mayor said. "Violet's here with a newfound friend. How ya doin', puss?"

"I'm Emma Chess."

"Shoowa. The yella rose of Texas." The mayor winked through her red frames. "Got time to check on a death certificate for me, Vi?"

The councilman, who wore a loose gray suit with no tie, said, "I wanted them files."

126

Vi wiped her lips with a paper napkin and said, "I can't help you, Coco."

"Big Al was in deep as Judas," he said. "Now everything'll move without us."

The mayor said, "Clam. It can wait." She pushed the door open and held it. The councilman puckered and made a kissy noise. Then they left.

Vi looked across the table. "So. Impressions?"

Emma was finishing off her pizza crust. "Can you drive us somewhere?" she said.

"I can. Where?"

"A mall. We need to bring a lock popper."

"Okaaay. What are we after?"

"I don't know. But Ethan told me there's a drop."

The mall was a ten minute drive. Emma said they wanted the parking garage, roof level. Vi took a ticket at the automatic gate and steered the car up. The roof lot was open to the sky, with bridges to the shopping. "No cameras up here," Vi said. "I don't think."

Emma said, "It's dark brown, the plates are B0Z." They did a drive-by crawl past the half-full spaces. "There." Vi pulled into a spot and they got out. Breath smoking in the cold air, they scoped the lot. Nobody around. Emma's boot taps scraped as they walked over to the drop car. A Maxima, backed in toward the perimeter wall. Vi went around and held one end of a steel tube over the trunk lock. She pumped the tube and the trunk cracked. She lifted it to reveal a manila envelope, which Emma reached in and took. Vi slammed the trunk and they quickstepped back to their car. She wheeled them down the garage ramps, her dark face moving in and out of the overhead lights. Beside her Emma unclipped the envelope and peeked, then slipped a hand in. "Only this," she said. She held up a flash drive. Vi glanced at it. "Something tells me Coco'd unleash the dogs of doom for that."

They joined traffic bound for the Holland. At the toll-plaza turn Vi spun the car into the lot behind the motor inn. A siren started to wail, growing nearer and nearer. Once it passed and faded they got out.

127

In the room Emma pushed the TV aside and booted her laptop on the dresser. A screen saver came up. Tanya Tucker: Outlaw. Vi slotted the flash in. It held two files, both labeled with strings of numbers. Vi clicked on the first one and a blurred face jumped onscreen, ox-eyed behind thick glasses, caught speaking in midsentence. ". . . kicking some major butt, Coco's up in it, he's the man to meet. Got these big wheels taking a number, I tell you that, your deal's nothing — I mean no offense my friend. Even those baller clowns down Jackson Ave won't go for a whiz less Coco says it's hundred percent okay. Man thinks of all kinds of angles, got a brain like a protractor."

Into the frame rose a hand clamped around a schooner of beer. The head tilted back for a long swallow. A date-and-time stamp ran in a lower corner: the past March, 3 PM. Vi said, "That's the ex-mayor. The one in Lewisburg." They watched him wipe his mouth with a wrist.

"I can tell 'em on Coco — heh! How 'bout this. He's the protection for this bar, the Rayos de Sol. Takes his cut in trade. Got a Honduran gal in there, sweeps the place up, he's waiting till she's fourteen — and he can barely stand it, see?" The face broke into a laugh, an angle of light turning the glasses into blank shields. "Just the price of doing business, all for the greater good."

The schooner came up again and tipped back till it was empty. The head turned and said "Hey!" The image scrambled and the window went black. Quietly Vi said, "Unbelievable."

"So why's Ethan doing this?" Emma said.

"I'm not sure." Vi said. "Wonder what the other one is." She moved the cursor to the second file. Ethan Chess appeared on the screen. He was leaning in, the cam picking up webs under his eyes and creases that made his chin look hinged. He pushed strands of pale hair from his forehead.

"The name is Ethan Lee Chess. This is my free and uncoerced statement." He leaned closer and spoke loudly. "On August 15 of this year I was ordered

128

by councilor Carlos Concepcion, my employer, to kill Sandro Annuzio, the political consultant. Concepcion explained to me that Annuzio had been working with the businessman Ken Lu against the interests of the city administration. On August 22 at 2 AM I entered the Crystal Cove condo where Sandro Annuzio lived. I was in the apartment for about twenty minutes. During this time he gave me surveillance video of mayor Isaiah Gross. The video had been excised from a recording in the US Attorney's possession. I'm including it here. I then applied pain to points in Annuzio's neck and temple until he fainted. I then used a glycerin tube in his throat to introduce a fatal dose of Klonopin and chloral hydrate." The eyes moved down from the camera and the image vanished. They waited but there was nothing more.

Vi spoke to the screen. "Not bad, Ethan." She pulled the flash out and closed it in her palm. Then she turned to Emma. "Don't you think?"

"You tell me what you want to do," Emma said.

"You don't seem surprised at the, uh, content. Family secrets?"

"You'll take this and use it."

"His intention, wouldn't you say?"

"Who was the man he talked about?"

"Big Al Annuzio. Our very own Seneca, once. Gave all kinds of aid and comfort to the local boys. They miss him, but not that much. At first the death was ruled suspicious, but later the ME cut a deal. Misadventure." Vi was toying with the flash. "If he was working for Ken Lu, that's treason. Ken Lu throws some major shade. He built up the Peking Palace joints and lately he went into some big-league land deals. Tax freebies. Percentages that would shame your corner crack dealer. Getting with him . . . obviously Al knew the consequences."

"They'd send somebody out after Ethan? He'd have to run?"

Vi nodded. "You heard. The price of doing business."

"You act like all of this is normal."

"Yep, pretty much." Vi smoothed her skirt as if their time was up. "And now I'm heading back to normal." She went across to the door and put a hand on the lever.

"The mall had a Sears," Emma said.

Vi stood still, back to the room, a silhouette in the dim light. Then she turned around. "A Sears?"

"I need gloves."

"Honey, listen. I have to hurry. But let me take this from here. How about it?"

"Good by me," Emma said. Chirpy.

Vi gave it a moment, then said, "And you should fly home now."

As soon as she was alone in the room Emma phoned the police and asked for officer Turnbull. He took the call. She wanted to know if she could see him that night. "Ethan left an actual confession," she said. "Plus he also gave me a drop location . . . his old office." Turnbull agreed to the meet. At 10 PM. City Hall.

At a quarter till she was waiting out in the shadows by the mayor's reserved parking. He showed up late. "I got real fine stuff for you," she said, fingering her shoulder bag's strap.

"Do you?" Turnbull said. "Know what, we'll go smoke first then T-Ball will have a look at your fine stuff."

One corner of her mouth curled. "The water office. Can we get in?"

"I go where I want," he said. They walked across the lot to the building's basement entrance. There was a barred gate with a keypad. Turnbull entered a code and the gate crept open. Just inside was an empty security booth. He went through first, saying, "I sent the guard off." They were in a freezing stone passage. "Better be worth all this. Better be extra fine."

"You won't be disappointed," she said.

"Huh. Nothing else to do tonight."

"No swingin' from the chandeliers, patrolman?"

"You're kind of mouthy. Know that? Like the big bro." He led the way past a service elevator and into a

130

narrow cement corridor. "New to the game and brought a big fat mouth. Both of you."

"Mind what I said."

He didn't seem to be listening. "That Ethan thought he was some hot shit," he muttered. "Some hick Dutch Schultz."

The corridor ended in stairs that they took up to the first floor. Shadows darkened the lacquered wood walls. The empty hallway reeked of cleaning fluid. They walked by a set of double-height oak doors. Emma stopped and said, "Let's do this," then opened one side and slipped through. Turnbull cried out, "*What* are you . . ." He closed his fists and followed her as lights blazed on.

It was the old council chamber. Worn carpeting the color of dried blood stretched beneath rows of hardwood benches. These faced a mahogany dais. Oblong windows and gold scrollwork rose toward the mighty ceiling. Bellying out in its center was a huge, filthy skylight dome. And suspended by chains above the benches were gold chandeliers set with round iron lanterns.

Turnbull came through the door to see Emma striding down an aisle toward the dais. She was reaching into her bag. "I said *what – the – fuck –* !" he shouted as she turned to face him. She'd put on work gloves and held a coil of white rope. He stepped forward. Emma pitched a fast backhand and a loop flew and dropped on his shoulders. She immediately yanked the rope taut and wrenched it back. Turnbull slammed to the floor and slid toward her, his hands at his throat. He twisted himself over as his tongue emerged and curled down his chin. Emma swung the loose coil upward. It sailed through a chandelier's thick gilded chains and she caught it coming down. She pulled off the slack, rope braids running like silk through the new gloves. She ground her bootheels into the carpet and leaned back at a diagonal, pulling harder. Turnbull scooted a few feet, then rose in the air flailing. His bald head went dark as a plum. The eyes were crimson knobs. She hauled till his toes

131

were off the ground, then backed to the wall and wound the rope onto a flag bracket.

Emma stood looking up at her work. Turnbull was twitchy for a minute, his body making noises, but he settled down. She kicked over the bench nearest his feet. Killer cop takes own life. Or however they'd put it.

She left the lights on. The way out led her back along the deserted hall, downstairs and through the open basement gate. She was remembering last week's voicemail from Ethan. Out of nowhere, since he wasn't one to keep in touch, was he. Ethan giving her Vi's name and the drop site with the license number. And some instructions. *First come out here and make that pickup. If I'm really not around anymore the responsible party is a police snake named Alex Turnbull. He needs to go. This could be goodbye, Em. They got me over a barrel.*

On the dawn cab ride to the airport she saw a band of dark gray all along the horizon, fading up into the blank sky. Huge construction cranes were visible like pencil sketches in the haze. She couldn't compare this place to anything she knew. On the flight to San Antonio she sat next to a piano player from Austin. He asked her about home. "It's outside Eden. We're ranchers," she said.

"Ridin', ropin', all that?"

She nodded. "All that. Learned the old way."

***

©2018 Arthur Evans

Sister

Bill Davidson

The big old car glides through country like a dusty ghost, its lumpy V8 sounding loose and lazy, throbbing unnoticed through our heads. It smells hot, of gasoline and leather, but I put my face to the side, so I can press it into Mari, my sister.

We leave the windows down, so dust and the chirp of critters floats in. This car has a radio and Mom sometimes snaps it on, searchin through the country stuff for Nat King singin his new song, Mona Lisa. She'll listen to Goodnight Irene or Chattanooga Shoe Shine Boy, but what she wants is Nat and Mona Lisa. She tries to hide it, but it makes her cheeks wet every time.

Mom takes back roads and I like to look behind us and imagine how the dust from our white walls might hang in the air forever. Like we leave our mark. It looks like that could happen.

Mom says, again, "We got to git us some gas, girls. Otherwise we'll be afoot."

It doesn't seem like there's goin to be any gas stations out here. Everything is hot and wet and scrubby and leaning and the whole place stinks like even the trees could rot and fall where they stand.

It doesn't seem like there's much of anything out here, cept maybe moss and creepers and snakes. I feel Mari shift in half sleep and suddenly I'm angry and I haul on our join. She cries out, cause it hurts, and looks at me with her big wet eyes.

She knows not to squeal, because if Mom hears and tears me up for hurtin her, I'll hurt her a whole other story. I bare my teeth and dig my thumb into the sore bit on her side of our join till I can feel the blood smear below my thumb. Her chin wobbles, and she scoots into me, putting her head on my chest till I put my arms round and shush her. Kiss her damp hair.

134

The first thing I know about the house is when the tone of the engine changes.

We sit up, as Mom brings the car to a stop, where it rocks on its springs, like an old boat.

"A house. You keep them firearms outa sight, but keep 'em ready, you hear me?"

I pull my Chief's Special out from under the seat and check the rounds, bein careful like we was taught. Not many eight-year-old's can be trusted with a sidearm and with good reason, Mom says. Mari gives a gentle tug, and I tug back. Her gun is pointed at the floor, just like mine.

The car eases forward and we get our first proper look at this house, way out in the boondocks. Clapboard, upstairs rooms and pointy roof bits. It was once fancy, I reckon, but it's not seen paint in a while. As we pull into the big dusty yard, setting chickens to flutter, a fat old woman is comin onto the porch, holding a cloth and rocking as she walks, like the car.

This lady must be a gramma, like gramma Nell, I think.

She's stepping down the steps, still moving funny. Not smilin, but that's ok. We're not smilin neither.

Mom is stepping out of the car, leaving the shotgun where she can reach it.

"Howdy, Ma'am"

The woman frowns, looking my Mum over. Then she says, "You got young 'uns in there?"

"Ay-yuh. Them's my daughters, Grace and Mari."

We are both of us up at the window, guns hid but ready, and the woman says, "They're like as two peas in the pod. Not like me and my sister, God rest her. She was skinny as I was fat."

"We don't want to inconvenience you none, Ma'am, but we was wonderin if you had any gas to spare. We're near out."

The woman seems to find this amusing, like it was some joke we was near afoot.

"I aint surprised, there's no gas station in fifty miles. None down this back road at all. What brings you here, if you don't mind me askin?"

135

"We're headed South."

The woman isn't laughing anymore.

"South?"

"We're headed that way, I reckon."

"Well, this is South, and this road goes Souther. That's the best that can be said of it."

"If you could sell us some gas, I'd be obliged. And maybe a bite to eat."

The woman looks at Mom, like she is coming to a big decision.

"I got some gas I could let you have. I also got my manners still. You been doin some hard travellin on bad roads and I'll not have you go past without a decent meal in them kids."

Even though Mom's back was turned, I could see she was thinking on that. This woman might be a trap.

"We don't want to put you to no trouble." Then, her voice careful. "Nor your family."

The woman, laughs, a short kind of bark. "I've lived here on my own this two-year past, if that's what you're askin'. Be glad of a bit of company, tell the truth."

Mom is a short woman, but stands straight. She's standin straight now, lookin up at the big gramma lady who has walked closer to her, and I see better than ever that one leg don't work like it should.

The gramma lady nods to us, Mari and me. We are just two fair haired heads to her, I guess. She don't see the guns yet, or where we join.

"Would you girls like to wash up some? Git yourselves a drink of my lemonade while I rustle up some chicken?"

We look at each other and ours eyes are wide. We would like that just fine. Then we look at Mom. She steps to the car, bringing out the shotgun.

We take our lead and tumble quick sharp out the door and onto our feet in the hot yard. The gramma lady is starin hard at Mom's gun, not happy about it. It seems she is about to say something choice when she glances our way and her head snaps round, surprised. We seen that look before.

136

I'm taller than Mari, but only just. We have to get a measure on us to show it. We're skinny and fair haired and wearing dresses Mom made special so we can get them on and off, joined up as we are. Nothing on our feet.

That's not what the lady is starin at and don't I know it. I'm on the left and the Chief's Special is hangin from my left hand. Mari is on the right, with her Colt. In the middle, we join.

The gramma lady stares and stares, till Mom says, "Now, you don't have nothin to fear from us, if'n you don't do nothin stupid. Do you have a telephone line in here?"

The woman doesn't even glance Mom's way. She is still starin.

"Sweet Jesus, woman." She says, "What in the world you thinkin? These are just babies!"

Mom gets that edge to her voice that we know, and it seems the gramma lady hears it just fine because her head comes round to attend.

"Ma'am you best mind your own beeswax, if you know what's good for you. I don't take kindly to bein judged regardin my parental duties."

"But..."

"Mind me now! Do you have a telephone line or not?"

"Out here? We don't have no telephone, nor 'lectric neither. They got one in town, maybe five miles back the way you came."

"Who else comes here? Don't be tricky, now."

The woman thinks about this, shiftin on her bad leg. "I can go one month t'other without anybody comin near. This aint exactly an on-the-way place."

I point. "What's wrong with your leg?"

That riles Mom up. "Haven't I taught you better than to point a loaded sidearm at someone, Grace?"

I drop my head, "Sorry Mom."

The gramma lady surprises me, answering my question. "I ruint my hip tryin to farm this Godforsaken bit of land. Now, come in and have some sweet lemonade, Miss Grace."

137

She turns and limps to the house, leavin us to follow if we're gonna. Mom looks surprised for a second, then hurries to catch her up.

The inside of the house is cool and smells of baking and soon we're sittin in the nicest room I ever saw. It's a kitchen, with a big stove and a bigger table and just as she said, the gramma lady is pourin cloudy water into glasses.

We sniff it and Mari takes a sip and smiles big and then we gulp it down, amazed.

The lady is lookin us over and she says, "Aint you never had lemonade afore?"

We shake ours heads and put out our glasses for more, but Mom says no. "It will gripe your stomachs, too much of that sweet stuff."

Mom would only take cold coffee and she steps to the side and sways suddenly, havin to put her hand on the table.

The gramma lady says, "When did you sleep last, girl?"

Mom shakes her said and says something about not needin no sleep, but then she sort of wilts.

She points at us. "Ok. I got to shut my eyes for a few minutes maybe. Don't you let this lady git too close. If she does, or tries to get away, you got to shoot her, hear?"

We raise our pistols and point them at the woman, serious in our business. "Yes, Mom."

The lady looks at us for a few seconds, but just seems sad. She turns to Mom. "I got a bed made up ready in the spare room."

"I don't need no…"

"For God's sake woman! Come!"

We are all surprised by the sharpness in the gramma lady's voice. She ignores all the guns pointed at her and stomps off and, after a second, Mom follows. Meek as a lamb.

It takes a while for the gramma lady to come back and we finish off the lemonade, gigglin at our own selves. When she comes in we point our guns, but she pays them no mind and walks right past, nearly

138

touchin the muzzle of Mari's Colt, and pulls some flat
breads from a cupboard.

We eat them, and they are delicious. She calls
them biscuits, but they're not like any biscuits we
know. All the while, she is standing at the back of the
room, watchin us, her eyes coming again and again to
our shiny join.

She says, "When was the last time you girls
washed?"

We look at one another, but neither of us know
and then she says she'll run us a bath.

Another amazement. This bath fills itself, the only
water we have to carry is a few jugs warmed on the
stove to take the chill off. She watches from way
across at the door as we get undressed and climb in.

"You can put them guns down, girls. I aint gonna
jump across there."

"Mom said…"

"Just put them down and have your bath! Gosh
sakes, you need it."

We look at each other and, just like Mom did, do
as we are told. The bath is lovely and cool and we sud
each other up with nice smellin soap and pour water
over our heads with a little pitcher. The water gets
darker, and we get slippy.

The gramma lady musta gone off at some point
and got herself a stool, because she is sittin now, still
at the door. She points to our join.

"You'll want to use that flannel to sooth that down
some. I got some ointment too."

We raise our hands and I tell her. "We was born
joined up. I came out first but left my arm behind.
When it come out, Mari was on it!"

We giggle at the story, but the gramma lady
doesn't like it. She looks so angry to hear it she can't
set still. She comes and kneels by the bath, takin a
time to get her bones down there. She is kneelin right
by our guns, but it seems ill mannered to speak of it.

She has a white flannel and she takes our join in
her knobby hands and we let her. It is a solemn
moment, because nobody has ever tended to the

139

cracks and cuts round our join 'cept for Mom. Not even Gramma Nell or Uncle Tobias, the only other people we really knew.

She still seems angry, but her hands are gentle and she washes away the crusty bits, tuttin and mutterin to herself like they were on her own skin. She gets us to come out and towel ourselves and she pats ours join clean and puts white cream on.

"There. That's the best I can do for now." She looks at me. "Is it only you who can talk?" Nell and Tobias made the same mistake and we could never fathom it. I look at her, mystified. "We both talk fine."

It turns out that our dresses are already in the wash and, when we tell her we don't have no others, she walks away. We have been forgettin our guns and pick them up now, pointin them at each other and giggling, makin pow noises cause we're on our own.

When she comes back, she's got cotton trousers and plaid shirts. "These were my boy's. They're old, but I guess they'll do a turn."

The trousers only want a fold at the bottom, but the shirts need cut along the side to fit our join. We look at each other and giggle, seein each other wearin boys' clothes. Then the old lady picks up our guns from the table and looks in them, checking they are loaded.

She puts them aside, telling how she could never abide a firearm on the kitchen table, and we run to pick them up, lest Mom finds out we been slacking.

It's dark by the time Mom gets up and finds us shuckin corn by the light of a paraffin lamp. The gramma lady is slicing up a chicken she just kilt.

When Mom comes into the light we go and hug her, holding our guns by our sides. Her voice is sharp. "Where you get them clothes?"

The gramma lady answers. "Their dresses will be dry by morning."

"You shouldn't a done that without askin."

"It's still my house, I guess. You can do with a wash yourself, girl. You're kinda rank."

140

Mom looks at her wild eyed and stiff, but the woman just ignores her and her shotgun. I don't guess she'd do that, if she'd been there when Mom shot the state trooper.

"We'll be eating in maybe an hour. Bath's in that room back there."

Mom bends over and sniffs us. "You smell like roses."

"It was in the soap, Mom. We can warm some water for you."

Mom don't take a bath. She sits lookin dazed and says nothing till the meal is on the table and then she says grace and we all of us bow our head over the chicken and corn and it's the best food there's been.

There's more rooms upstairs and the gramma lady takes us to one, showin us a bed with a feather mattress and a patchwork quilt. We sleep.

*

In the morning, we creep downstairs, wearing our boys' clothes and holding our guns, ready for trouble.

Mom and the gramma lady are in the kitchen, looking like they've been arguin although we never heard nothin. There's bread and eggs for breakfast, and coffee. Mom smokes a cigarette and stands to look out the window.

"We'll stay here for today, I reckon."

The gramma lady nods and looks righteous and we wonder if she's on the winning side of the argument. I ask if this was a farm.

The gramma lady laughs and pats ours heads. "That's too grand a name for this scrubby patch. Back along, in my great-granddaddy's day, it was a plantation. The war saw to that."

That made no sense. "What war?"

She looked at me and sighed. "The one with the North. After, the darkies got to be sharecroppers, and starved, cause the land was no damn use in the first place. Now, it's all gone back to wilderness."

"But you have chickens!"

That lit her up, like she'd heard a good joke. "You have that right, Miss Grace. I've got chickens and corn

141

and half dozen cattle. There's a few pigs round here someplace, but I wouldn't go so far as to claim ownership of a pig."

Then she says, "You girls can git out from under my feet, now. Don't go near the swamp and watch out for snakes."

We look at Mom but she's still staring outside, so we nod, "Yes'm."

As we run for the door, she shouts, "And stay away from the big house! It's a ruin and it aint safe."

We find that big house easy, and it was so big we wasn't sure it was even a house. For a while we just walk around it, skulkin through steamy trees all mossed and creepered up, with the insects near deafening us. We count sixty windows, twice the height of Uncle Tobias and he was bigger than most. It had been white once, but it isn't now. The roof had been sloped and peaked and fancy and some of it still is, but some is fallen in. We come back round to the front door and sneak up the path through high grass, comin up on statues and old tools and stuff we don't have a name for.

We step on the veranda, but our foot goes through the soft wood and after that we step careful, testing as we go. The house is full of creepers and stinks of damp and the plaster is comin off the walls and the ceilings are dropping. It's the best place we've ever been.

We creep from room to room and they're all huge. We can still tell the colors on the walls in some places, ducky blue and sea green mainly. And there's a piano sinking right into the floor that still makes a chimey noise when we whack it with a chunk of wood.

We really want to go up to the first floor, up the widest stairs there's ever been, but we don't. It's ghosty up there.

The best thing is the chandelier. It's filthy and spidery and wider across than we are and made out of big jewels. We call that room the jewel room.

I pick up a sharp bit of glass from beside one of the windows and pin Mari down, so I can stick her with

142

it, right behind her ear where it won't show. She squeals and squirms and cries and then puts her arms round me and I rock her till it's ok.

We are quiet coming back in case we are in trouble, so we get to hear some of what Mom and the gramma lady are saying.

The gramma lady says, "You think I don't know who you are?"

"You don't know me."

"I go into town every week or so. Read the papers. You're that woman on the run from somewhere's in Montana."

"I aint never been to Montana."

"Shot a state trooper right in his car and took off. Funny, the papers don't say nothin about those girls."

"Lady, your mouth is goin to get you shot, you aint careful."

"I'm not scared o'dyin. So, what else you got? Hah!"

They are quiet for a while, then the gramma lady says. "They say you 'scaped from one o' them prisons for kids, back in the 40's there. Been hidin out since with some crazy old woman in the badlands since."

No answer.

"You musta been what, fifteen?"

"I was thirteen."

"Thirteen! Mercy."

Words tumble outa Mom then, like she needs to tell it. "I wouldn't a run neither, if they hadn't put my sister somewhere else. They split us up deliberate. I hadn't been separated from my sister one day before that."

"You and your sister was twins, like your girls?"

"Yea, they separated us. I tried to find her, but couldn't do it before she died. Did it her own self. They oughtn't to have split us like that. They ought not to have done that to twins. I won't let anybody split my girls like that."

We look at each other. We knowed this stuff, but not from Mom. From gramma Nell, who wasn't our real gramma, but we loved her the same.

143

"Is that why you got them…"

"Don't be askin' me about that! I wouldn't a kilt that policeman, but they found us out. They would take us in and split us up. I won't allow it."

"But, this is no life for them girls…"

"We'll go South."

"This is a dead end, honey."

"We go back around then."

We hear the gramma lady take a big breath. "Can't you separate them girls? It's not right."

We look at each other and move quick, stomping our feet. Them two is sittin at the table and Mom is clean and wearin a dress too big for her, cinched in at the waist.

We tell her she's pretty and she smiles, and the gramma lady gets a tear that she wipes away.

Days pass, and we help with farm chores and eat good and even drink buttermilk. We go to the big house and find treasures and play but we don't go upstairs. One day a pick up truck comes, and we get scared and get our guns like we haven't done for a while, but the gramma lady, who is called Miss Matilda, shushes us and goes out to speak.

Mom hides behind the kitchen door and gets fretful and I'm scared she's going to go out there and shoot Miss Matilda and the truck driver man both.

But, after a while of wiping his face and bald head with a kerchief, the man is smiling and turning his truck and Miss Matilda is coming back and saying, everything's fine. Everything's ok.

"What you tell him about the car?"

"Told him I was lookin after it for a friend from Baton Rouge. Don't fret."

Mom does fret. She can't settle, and we put gas in the car and she says, we leave tomorrow, after breakfast.

Miss Matilda don't want us to go, we can see that. She says, "You can leave them girls with me. You got to know what you're doin to them aint normal. It's wicked. How can you do that to two young girls?"

144

Mom doesn't say a word. She just points us to our bedroom, but Miss Matilda aint done.

"Hear me!"

Mom has the shotgun in her hand.

"You shut up now, you busybody old woman!"

"It's a sin. You know it. What you're doin to them girls is a sin against God!"

Mom hisses at us and we take to our heels and run upstairs.

The worst day starts normal. We're drinking buttermilk and wearing our clean dresses. Mom is sipping coffee and looking out the window, and Miss Matilda is mending something with wool.

Mom stiffens and then I hear a car, comin fast. More than one car. We all jump to the window to see the Police cruisers boil into the yard. Mom is screaming at us to run out the back and Miss Matilda is on her feet, saying, calm down.

Mom points the shotgun at her, at Miss Matilda, and shouts, you told that man. Miss Matilda is shakin her head, hands up before her, but Mom shoots her anyway.

Then she screams at us to run, and we do. We hurry out the back and there are men already out there, but we know the land and run through the hole in the fence and into the trees. There's shooting from behind us, the bark of Mom's shotgun and other guns.

We can hear them shouting and crashing but we keep going fast, breathing frantic, even though ours join is hurtin and we want to stop. We run through the old fields and to the big house. We think we've lost them, but see them comin in a line.

We hide behind the piano, but they come in and find us and we shoot our guns and run with them at our heels, back to the big hall and up the stairs. The steps crumble as we climb, and the men are shouting, but we don't stop. We shoot our guns empty as we go but they are still coming, creeping up the stairs, complaining about it.

We run into a bedroom that still has a rotten bed in it and scoot under. They creep into the room, lots of

145

big men, steppin careful on the crumbly wood. We crawl out from under the bed, but there's no place to go. We're in a corner, holdin on to each other and cryin for Mom.

The men have stopped. They're looking at us and at each other and it's like they don't know what to do.

One of them says, "Well, shit. Don't that beat all."

Another man in a cowboy hat and a gold tooth is coming closer, bending right down, saying it's ok girls. Nobody's goin to hurt you no more.

Then they're all crowded round and they are huge over us and hands are on us and Mari puts her head in my shoulder and we are crying hard, clutching tight.

The man with the gold tooth takes a key from his belt, a tiny silver key that he takes a moment to show us. He's still sayin that it's goin to be ok. He's saying don't worry girls, you'll be free in just a second. Then he takes our join in his thick fingers and twists it round my wrist to show the little hole. He sticks that nasty key in and suddenly the join snaps clean off my arm, and off Mari's too, and he's holding it up by its silvery chain, smiling like he's done a good thing.

That's when we start to scream.

***

©2018 Bill Davidson

bowl

brisket

headcheese

eyeballs

blade

tongue

chuck

neck

sweet meats

shoulder

shoulder

ground

shank

release valve

stock

stew

ribs

soup

ribeye

fillet

BOISE LONGPIG HUNTING CLUB

NICK KOLAKOWSKI

My Worst Morning Ever
Nick Kolakowski

Before I became a cop, I was a grad student in the physics department at a major research university. If you're wondering why someone would leave behind writing equations on whiteboards for slamming freaks' heads through drywall, that answer comes later. Instead, it might be best to start with a discussion of probability, and how it led to my house exploding into a massive fireball one bright summer morning.

Probability rules our lives. When you purchase that lottery ticket along with your unfiltered cigarettes at the liquor store ("I swear I'll quit tomorrow. *Tomorrow.*"), you ask the universe to make you that one-in-fifty-million who takes the jackpot. Whenever you climb behind the wheel of your car and drive out into the bright and wonderful world, you face a one-in-twenty-thousand chance that another vehicle will run a red light and plow into yours head-on. Probability is sometimes a joker, and sometimes a savior: the best things rarely happen, but the absolute worst can sometimes take their sweet time finding you.

Sometimes.

On the morning in question, the chance of me in bed with a massive hangover was one hundred percent. Day Fifty after my wife Victoria had walked out the door, and I still had trouble dealing with her departure. By 'trouble' I mean that, unless I polished off half a bottle of scotch or a six-pack of beer every night, I inevitably found myself awake at 3 a.m., when the world of ordinary things turns black and merciless as roadway ice.

But when my alarm blared its cheery little tune that morning at 8:01, I broke my usual habit of hitting the snooze button five times, choosing instead to crawl out of bed and begin the day's useless routine. My head throbbed like a dying tooth. Aspirin, Lordy, please, stat. Shrugging on a threadbare white robe over my boxer shorts, I stuffed my feet into a pair of slippers and stumbled off zombie-style to shave and shower. Had I stayed under the sheets another eight minutes, the paramedics could have stuffed my mortal remains into a plastic lunch baggie.

In the bathroom I splashed boiling water on my face, lathered up, and readied my old-fashioned straight razor to hack away the bristles. Paused for a moment to stare at the photo tucked into the mirror's rim: Victoria from the waist up, nude, hands on cocked hips, wry grin, neck draped with long bead pendants of her own design.

My hand suddenly seemed possessed, the blade it held drifting from left cheek to throat, the cold edge notching against my windpipe. In the mirror my eyes gleaming like dull marbles.

The razor pressed down another millimeter, to the sting. Red bloomed on white cream. Watch me actually do it, this time.

Can we stop acting like a cliché now? Please?
Right. Onward. Sighing, I began to scrape the blade across my face in the recommended manner, losing myself in the ritual. The last stubborn hairs were mowed from the underside of my jaw when I heard that thin, high whistle.

Is that a kettle?

No. The sound kept rising, stabbing at my eardrums. I stepped away from the sink, thinking maybe air in the pipes, or else a piece of house in mid-breakdown. Except that was wrong, too.

The whistle came from overhead.

It sounded like a bomb.

Hangover or no, my reflexes hurled my body to the tile.

God sneezed.

Thunderclap, lightning, skull split, pain, hot air, gray dust, hurled against the side of the tub, howling, squeezed pummeled, ripped by a hundred claws, pain, air choking with dust, goose feathers, bits of paper, heat, burning, pain, blind, slick hands, head

Black.

149

My eye sockets stuffed with cold plaster. Digging them clear, trying to stand, knees quaking, pain, animal sounds like a trap-caught coyote in my throat.

No. Stop screaming. Stop.

Lordy be praised, my legs could move. That fantastic development in no way dampened my confusion. Coughing in the plaster snowstorm, I gripped the edge of the tub and pulled my aching body upright, almost slicing my head on the ragged curve of steel skewering the mirror. Plaster flecks sizzled on the 'NOT A STEP' stenciled on its edge.

I swiped at the hot wires sparking along its underside—a little 'fuck you' from me to probability—and limped to the bathroom doorway. Stared into the jagged hole where my bed had stood mere seconds ago, down to the disaster zone formerly known as my living room, where a charred and broken jetliner engine roared its last, hurling a tornado of pillow-feathers and insulation and wood-chunks upwards through the new gap in my ceiling. Craning my head upward, I spied through the hole a cloudless blue sky, sliced by a contrail of black smoke.

Try and calculate the chances of this happening. "Aw crap," I said, barely able to hear past the engine's dying howl, not to mention the ringing in my eardrums. At this point I should quote you the statistic, one I've used many a time when teaching undergrads the broader points of probability theory: The chance of dying in a plane crash is one in 11 million. This includes anyone on the ground, in the bull's eye of falling debris.
People like me.

The house emitted a deep and shuddery groan, my knees quaking along with it. The bedroom floorboards cracking and squealing as I toe-stepped for the hallway door. My entire second floor tilting worse than the deck of the Titanic, nearly throwing me off-balance as I retrieved my keys and cell phone and wallet from where they had been hurled along the baseboard. I paused long enough to stuff the three items in my robe pockets, cursing the jet engine for

150

pile-driving my bureau and real clothing into the basement.

Before making my exit I retrieved from the bedroom doorknob my shoulder holster, weighty with my department-issued Glock-40. Who knew what other weird and terrible shit awaited me this morning.

*

My house sat on the edge of a wide and untended field, stretching as far as the horizon's edge, where the distant spindles of high-tension towers glimmered in the sun. Above them, a gray cloud in the shape of a question mark stained the air.

The house's joints had graduated from crackling to moans of serious structural pain. Jogging into the yard, shoulder holster slapping against my bare ribs, I opened my phone and dialed headquarters, then each of my colleagues. An electronic voice put me on hold every time. Cursing, I tried 911 and received an earful of busy signal.

Well, as I once told my wife before punching her new celebrity boyfriend in the face: Some things in life are best handled by one's self.

Thirty seconds later my black Mustang boomed down Coalbiter Road toward the crash site. Let me tell you how difficult it can be, driving with one hand down a bumpy two-lane at seriously unsafe speeds, while fumbling through the glove compartment for aspirin. My hangover, the selfish little shit, continued to holler its needs over my fresh aches and pains.

Yet I felt no fear, despite that black pillar of smoke in the distance. The Job requires you lock away your emotions in a deeper place, lest the sight of yet another mass shooting (complete with the shooter's note: 'GUDBYE CRUL WERLD') send you on a one-way trip to the mental ward.

Looking back, the only thing protecting my already-teetering mind at that moment was a marvelous self-centeredness: my main concern was still whether my house would collapse, and if I could save my 54-inch flat-screen before that point.

In movies, the plane always crash-lands with a cracked fuselage, missing wings, almost certainly on fire, surrounded by screaming people—but mostly intact. A former physicist and current cop, I knew such things rarely happened in reality: the earth's forces do terrible things to objects that try to defy its laws. From a half-mile away, you could tell that physics had not been kind in any way, shape or form to that airliner, later identified as Trans-Globe Airways Flight 817.

The plane had hit the field at a shallow angle, carving a trail of fire through two hundred yards of dirt. At its end jutted a three-story chunk of fuselage, white paint crisping and bubbling as flames guzzled its length. Whole tonnages of plastic and steel and wiring and insulation scattered in hand-size pieces as far as the eye could see. It looked like a bomb had exploded on board. Maybe it had.

I skewed the Mustang to a stop on the shoulder of the road and barreled out, feeling that gassy heat baking my skin even from a football field away. The acrid stench of fuel and plastic burning my nostrils. Sprinting past flaming seats half-buried in dirt, broken luggage spurting entrails of clothing, crumpled beverage carts spurting soda in arterial bursts. My hangover burned away in the holy light of my new purpose: I would save lives, right wrongs, do my part to fix fate.

Then I saw the bodies. Every single one of them dead beyond dead, none of them whole, and dodging past I told myself not to look, that they were objects, nothing but more pieces of luggage. Sirens filled the air as the cavalry arrived, fire trucks swerving in epic dust-plumes onto the field, a helicopter chattering overhead.

None of it mattered. Survivors: zero.

I skidded to a stop, body shuddering with horror so pure it was almost ecstatic. The firemen and paramedics mistook me for a survivor, their hands patting my arms and chest until I yelled something about being a cop and pulled the robe open to show the pistol, and then they barreled away with their useless oxygen tanks and medical bags.

My cell phone rang. The screen flashed 'DON'T PICK UP.' My own private joke: it was my partner Harry, which meant that someone, somewhere, was having as bad a day as the passengers on that plane. I flipped open the phone.

"Buddy, we got a problem," I said as hello. My voice shook only slightly.

"Yeah, I know. You're on the news. Wave."

Spinning around, I saw the Channel Seven van nosed into the drainage ditch beside my Mustang. A cameraman rolled tape on the local newscaster in screaming negotiation with a firefighter, who looked ready to bury his fire-ax in the man's two-hundred-dollar hair. The camera angle meant I stood smack-dab in the background of their argument, ready for my close-up in plaster-coated bathrobe and boxer shorts.

I waved.

"You need to get your ass down to Glenmont Road right now," Harry said. "We have a situation down here."

"You mean compared to this?" I yelled over the crackling roar of the fuselage cooking off. A superhot inferno rocketed upwards, sending the emergency crew scrambling for cover. My heart sped to machine-gun pace, a Hiroshima-size panic attack coming due.

"John Doe cooked in car trunk. Our shift started fifteen minutes ago, and everyone else in the damn county is on crash duty." He paused, realizing how much that made him seem like the Jackass to End All Jackasses. "I'm sorry."

"It's okay," I said, even though the whole situation was pretty far from okay. My heart thrashed, primed to explode. The dozen cuts from bathroom shrapnel stinging and itching and burning. A nearby medic glared at me, probably convinced that my pale and shaking corpse would collapse any second.

"Oh, Jake?" Harry's abruptly gentle voice steeled me for the worst.

"What's up?"

153

"Your house is on fire."

Spinning around to see the pillar of white smoke rising from beyond the far trees. That Boeing engine with a little spark left in it, enough to set ablaze the two-story house where my wife once said we would live happily ever after, together.

Flames waved their red fingers at me from over the treetops, and even in my panic I felt no sadness, no regret. Absolutely nothing.

"Let it burn," I said.

***

©2018 Nick Kolakowski

WRITER TYPES
ⓅⓄⒹⒸⒶⓈⓉ

hosted by
Eric Beetner
S.W. Lauden

A crime and mystery fiction podcast
hosted by two Anthony Award
nominated authors

Interviews, book reviews, short fiction & more

Listen in for interviews with: Joe R. Lansdale, Megan Abbott,
Laura Lippman, Reed Farrel Coleman, Lou Berney,
Meg Gardiner, Ryan Gattis, Sara Paretsky Johnny Shaw
and many more!

New episode every month on iTunes, Stitcher & Soundcloud

HOME OF THE INCIDENT REPORT
SMALL PRESS CRIME FICTION

REVIEWS | NEWS | INTERVIEWS

UNLAWFUL ACTS

UNLAWFULACTS.NET

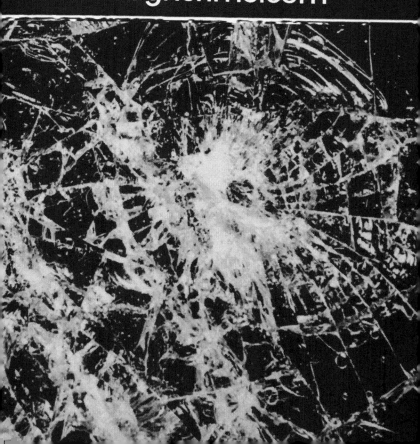

TOUGH
CRIME STORIES
www.toughcrime.com

TALL

PINES

LODGE

A
NOIR
PLAY

BY: J.D. GRAVES

INDIE RIGHTS

www.indierights.com

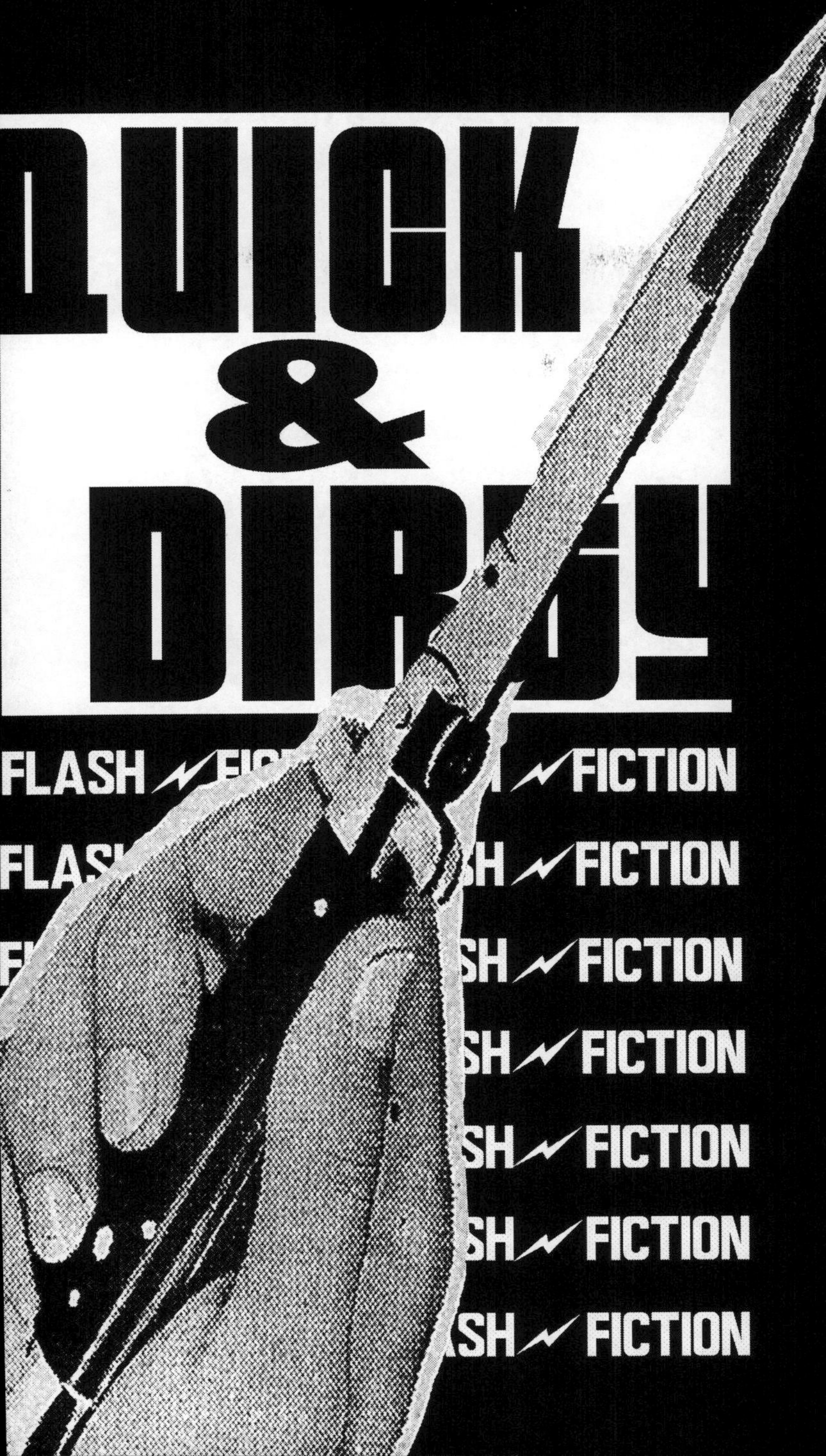

Last Day of Summer
Stephen D. Rogers

As I wrote in an assigned poem, "after the Columbus Day weekend, the tourists recede like a new-moon low." This year, the T-shirt monkeys left more than their trash on the beach. This time they left a woman behind.

A white and gray gull stood on her head, staring out into the bay. From where I stood, her long hair seemed to spread from her crumpled body like sea grass.

Her name was Jenny.

Or maybe Jerri.

Last night I'd come down here on my fifteen-minute break as I did most evenings, no matter the temperature. The summer season over, I wouldn't be disturbed as I walked along the line separating wet sand from dry.

She stepped from the shadows, examined my black pants and white shirt, and smiled. "You work at the restaurant."

"We don't deliver."

She laughed and moved closer. "That probably depends on what I'm buying. I want you to send Brian out here."

"Why?"

She dropped to her knees, flicked her hair back over her shoulder, and unzipped my pants.

My girlfriend was an on-again off-again relationship. At the moment we weren't talking, and hadn't for days. As if that was any justification.

I cleared my throat. "What's your name?"

She paused. "Jenny." Or maybe *Jerri*.

162

Even though she looked a few years older than me, I didn't think she was local. I would have remembered seeing her. Strange then that she knew Brian, or maybe she'd asked around.

Waiting tables was hard work, and I knew that some of the waitresses kept smiles on their faces over the long double-shifts thanks in part to Brian and the stuff I'd seen him sell. I managed to get by on coffee and soda but—

My legs buckled.

"Tell Brian to hurry."

I rushed back to the restaurant, repulsed and intrigued and enamored.

Brian seemed surprised by my question, his face reddened by the steam table. "I do. Didn't know you were interested."

"It's for ... a friend."

He laughed, flipped a colander of pasta.

"Seriously." I kept my voice low, as if anybody in the busy kitchen could have heard a word we said. "She's waiting outside, on the beach."

"How do you know she's not a cop?"

I remembered the sight of her kneeling in front of me, the hunger in her eyes when she stood. "I'm pretty sure."

Brian shrugged the pasta onto a plate, lifted it and three others onto the serving shelf. "Order up!"

"She seemed to be in a rush."

"They always are." Brian pantomimed a smoke to the other line cook and pressed past me out the back door.

My break over, I punched back in and went back to bussing tables.

Last night of the Columbus Day weekend, we were busier than we had been for months. Some of the highlights were a party of three who didn't speak

163

English, two speedboat types who were hammered before they walked through the door, and a family with six kids so unruly the hostess said the parents probably came to the Cape hoping for a series of tragic drowning accidents.

I noticed all this but thought only of her.

At some point, Brian was back on the line, and he acknowledged me with a wink.

She hadn't—no, Brian was running a business. There was no profit in bartering. What she'd done with me had been special.

After we closed and I finished my side work, collected my tips from the waitresses and another wink from Brian, I slipped out to the beach again.

With the restaurant lights out, I could barely see the surf breaking, but figured the flash of my white shirt would be enough to draw her back to me.

It wasn't. Or maybe she hadn't waited around. I would come back at first light to see if she'd traced her name and number in the sand above high tide.

I left the beach behind and walked up the street to our house where I tossed and turned before dreaming about her.

Woke early and ran back here, catching sight of her body as I crested the hill.

The gull took flight as I came closer. The bird landed on Manatee Rock, farther along the beach, and turned to watch me.

I looked down at her open eyes. They were a blue I'd never seen in the bay, a blue only hinted at by a sunset in late summer. They no longer looked hungry.

Dropping to my knees, I wondered how close I'd come to her last night, standing out here in the brisk wind.

I held two fingers against her wrist, her neck. Her breasts lay still.

There were no signs of violence. Maybe she'd overdosed or overtaxed her heart.

There was a slight smile on her lips, as if before she died she remembered me and our time together.

A woman screamed. Her dog barked, leaping back and forth, pulling at the leash that kept it from running towards us.

The woman produced a cell phone and spoke urgently. I'd seen her before at *The Village Mart*. Never at the restaurant.

I turned back to Jenny. Jerri.

The police would be able to tell me her name. Where she'd lived.

But not how to reach her.

I sat back on my heels.

There'd been no strange cars in the lot when I left last night, which meant she hadn't come here alone, not unless she'd swum, exchanging her tail for legs in order to approach me across the sand, drawn from the darkness by my white shirt.

Perhaps she'd been caught by low tide, been unable to get as far as the waterline, and so died of a thirst that would never be quenched.

Once again my throat was thick, and the rising sun made my eyes sting.

I leaned forward and kissed her forehead, tasting the salt.

As bitter a taste as I'd ever known.

***

©2018 Stephen D. Rogers

A Serial Killer Buys a Watermelon
David Rachels

On Thursday, September 24, 2015, serial killer
Samuel Grubb entered Taylor's *IGA* at 1717 Point
Road in Elderwood, South Carolina. As of this date,
Grubb had raped and killed four women in the area:
Michaela Tomlinson, 24, of Elderwood; Chastity
Moore, 33, of Friedel; Torrence Haney, 31, of
Elderwood County; and Noelle Williams, 19, of
Hugertown. At the time, local law enforcement
believed that these murders were connected, but they
had not yet made this belief public, as they did not
want to incite panic. Police hoped to solve the case
before local residents knew that a serial killer was
loose, and they were investigating six men whom they
believed to be viable suspects. Samuel Grubb was not
among them.

Surveillance footage shows that Grubb entered
Taylor's *IGA* at 6:41 p.m. and walked directly to the
rear right corner of the store, where the stand of
watermelons was located. Grubb tapped on several of
the melons and then hefted two of them before
selecting the melon that ultimately he would purchase.
There were three other shoppers in the produce area,
who are as yet unidentified, but Grubb did not interact
with any of them. Once he had chosen his melon,
Grubb carried it to the express check-out lane, which
was located at the opposite corner of the store.
When Grubb joined the line, there were two customers
in front of him. Phillip Starkey, 44, of Friedel, was
purchasing only milk. Hannah Burks, 66, of
Elderwood, was waiting to purchase a total of eleven
items, despite signage clearly indicating that this line

was reserved for customers who were purchasing a maximum of ten items. When Grubb got in line behind Burks, he appeared to count the items in her basket and shake his head.

While Grubb waited for Starkey and Burks to make their purchases, he held the watermelon using both hands. He spent time staring at candy bars, magazines, and Burks. He appeared to consider putting the watermelon on the floor so that he could pick up a magazine, but he did not. When Starkey and Burks had completed their purchases, Grubb stepped forward and handed the watermelon to the checkout clerk, Dayquelle Johnson, 17, of Elderwood. Johnson put the melon down on the scale next to the cash register.

The watermelon weighed 21 pounds and 1 ounce. At Taylor's *IGA*, however, watermelons are sold at a flat rate of $7.99 per melon, so the weight of Grubb's watermelon was not relevant to the transaction. Johnson entered the price of the melon into the cash register.

"Will that be all, sir?" Johnson asked.

"That's it," Grubb said.

Johnson told Grubb what he owed, and Grubb paid with a $20 bill. Johnson gave Grubb his change and receipt, which Grubb put in the front left pocket of his jeans. Grubb picked up the watermelon, and Johnson told him to have a nice day. Grubb told Johnson to do the same, and he left the store without further incident.

***

©2018 David Rachels

167

Choices

Scott Hallam

Joe

I bolt upright; the rattle of chains snaps me back to consciousness. My eyes dart around a dim cellar. I'm chained tight to a wooden chair, veins bulging from my forearms, and a man wearing a black latex outfit and mask is staring at me.

I feel like a ball of pain. Dozens of photographs are pinned to my clothes, my arms and hands. Blood caked on my skin. I can feel photos pinned to my cheeks. All of the same kid. Teenager or early twenties. Vaguely familiar. Damnit, where have I seen him before? And where the hell am I?

Man in Black

He's finally awake. This suit is sweltering, but it's having the desired effect. Let the horror sink in.

My legs are shaking so badly that I can barely stand. I hope I don't chicken out or vomit. But he deserves this. I hope he pisses himself.

"I see you're awake. Good. Before we begin, do you recognize the man in those photos? That BOY pinned to your body? No? You should. His name's Bobby. You killed him with that junk you peddle. So, now you get to choose. See the three syringes on the table next to the bottle of bleach and jug of water? Two water, one bleach. Take your pick."

Joe

This fucking creep has some voice changing thing going on. This is messed up. I have to get out of here; these damn chains are too tight. I hope he doesn't do any weird sexual shit to me. I still don't remember the kid, but I'm not gonna let on.

168

"Listen, I just sell the stuff. I don't want to hurt nobody. He was just a custom...wait, no, okay, okay, I don't want to drink the bleach. I pick the first one."

Man in Black

He chose wisely, the needle slid right into his vein. Fear dilated his pupils. I made sure to take my time. By the smell, he probably crapped himself. Good. My legs don't shake any longer. I can do this. Let's mix it up a bit.

Joe

Sicko. Just water. God, I smell. Can't believe I shit my pants. What does he want from me? Why does this nut job care? If I could find a straight-job that paid, I wouldn't be selling this shit. And I got a three-year-old to feed. It's all about the money. Period. Hell, what's he doing now?

Man in Black

"Five syringes this time. You choose correctly, I let you walk out of here, and we both forget about this little play date. Three bleach, two water. Choose now."

No more nerves. My voice strong, unwavering. I want to rip this asshole's eyes from their sockets. But this is better. Much better.

Hmm, he chose syringe number four. He can't see me smile behind this mask. I stacked the deck. He'll never leave this basement. But we knew that already.

Joe

Fuck, my veins burn like hell. Wrong one. I got to get out here, this hurts so bad. No, no, not another injection. I feel sick. I want to pass out. I want to die.

"Let me fucking die."

Woman in the Shadows

I breath shallowly to make sure the drug-pushing bastard doesn't know I'm here. This night was my brainchild. George just wanted to drink wine and weep

169

over his son's death. Sure, I cried as only a mother can. But my hot tears sparked this idea.

Clear liquid, liquid death. Slow, painful. But not as slow or as painful as how my Bobby died. Alone, cold, a needle sticking out of his bluing arm. It's an image I see when I brush my teeth, when I fall asleep, when I dream, and when I wake.

It was easy to find and capture the bastard, the one who sold Bobby that garbage. Two masks, a pointed gun, sodium thiopental, and a quick ride in the trunk of our Buick was all it took.

George is really taking to his role. I hope the pain doesn't knock the bastard out too soon. I'm enjoying this.

An eye for an eye, a vein for a vein.

***

©2018 Scott Hallam

Queen of Vice City

Matthew X. Gomez

I'm crouching down on the floor, the carpet worn thin from years of abuse, my hand in the proverbial cookie jar, when I feel something pressing hard against the back of my head. I freeze, my hand wrapped around a neat stack of hundreds, my eyes flicking to the revolver that's also stored in the safe. A bag is on the floor next to me, already stuffed fit to burst. Maybe not enough to retire on, but definitely enough to lay low and quiet for a time.

"Where are you going, Chase?" The voice, pitched low, asks. Ronnie. Veronica.

Fuck.

I try to turn, to face her, forcing a bullshit grin on my face, but she presses the object harder against the base of my skull. It feels a lot like the barrel of a gun and I hate myself a little for knowing exactly what that feels like.

"Stop," she says.

"I thought you weren't coming home until tomorrow."

"Guess you were wrong." But the pressure eases. I see one high-heeled shoe kick the bag. "Was it always just about the money?"

"Baby, you know that's not true." Even if it was. Even if I'd been planning this for a while.

Veronica Frederick, newly widowed. No kids. Her dead husband, Lars, had his fingers in more than a few pies and did a decent trade in local vice. If there was a drug you wanted or a kink you needed provided for, he was the guy you went to. After he died, everyone figured one of his lieutenants would roll up and take things over.

Veronica had other ideas and soon everyone was bending the proverbial knee to the new Queen of Vice. I was no exception.

Me? Yeah, I'd been one Lars' lieutenants, making collections and keeping things running smoothly. I liked the old man, and was as surprised as anyone when he got sick and died. Doctors couldn't do anything about it, despite the friendly persuasion we provided. I always figured Veronica was a bit of arm candy, not much going on upstairs as she could get away with her looks and a smile. So yeah, I was as surprised as anyone else when she called a meeting and told us who was calling the shots from now on.

Mostly we didn't complain, seeing as how she had control of the bank accounts, the ledgers, and the little black book of sins the local D.A. would have sold his soul to get his grubby hands on. Those that did either retired or disappeared. And I didn't complain when, six months after we put Lars in the ground I found myself in Ronnie's bed. I knew I wasn't the only one. She'd done the marriage thing and decided once was enough. I'd be lying if I said she wasn't sleeping with some of the other guys, using what she had to keep us in line. I tried to not let it bother me, but it bothered me, you know?

I'd been in this game for ten years and was getting tired. Tired of people looking scared around me all the time. Tired of the fake laughs from the other lieutenants. Tired of the plastic grins from the girls in the clubs as they fumbled for my wallet. Tired of putting bodies in the ground and wondering when my ticket would come out. Tired of being a side piece. Tired of cold winter nights out in the woods with a shovel and a tarp with nothing but a dead body for company.

So… my plan, if you could call it that. Wait until Veronica was out of town. I had the combination to the safe. Go in. Clean it out. Get gone before she got back. Yeah, she'd know it was me, but I figured I could put miles between us, go someplace where it never got below sixty degrees. Where the locals might smile at me and mean it.

Not a bad plan.

Except here I was, gun to the back of my head. Hand in the cookie jar.

"Let me explain—" but she cuts me off with a blow to the back of the head. I'm down, face pressing across the dirty carpet, can feel something warm trickling down the back of my head. She's angry and I won't be talking myself out of this one, will I?

Desperate I grab for the revolver in the safe, Lars' old piece. Rolling over, I see her standing in the middle of the room. She's in a shooter stance, gun held comfortably, finger on the trigger. My hand's not steady and I wonder how hard she hit me. I pull the trigger.

Clicks on an empty chamber.

Ronnie gives me a smile that's almost sad.

She pulls the trigger.

And my world disappears.

***

©2018 Mathew X. Gomez

173

JIM **JONES**   NICOLE "HOOPZ" **ALEXANDER**   ROYCE **REED**

WRITTEN AND DIRECTED BY DENNIS REED II

FIRST
Lady

DENNIS REED II PRODUCTIONS AND LOVE LOGAN PRODUCTIONS PRESENTS A FILM BY DENNIS REED II FIRST LADY CASTING BY LOVE LO
& DENNIS REED II MUSIC BY SUNNY SURFF, BIANCA MCCALL, AND KAZZIE STONER. STARRING JULIUS WASHINGTON, MIKE BONNER,
BLACK NOAH PRODUCERS SONIA RENEE MILLER AND CHEVAY HAMPTON COSTUME DESIGN BY DEAN HALL, ASSISTANT DIRECTOR TYLER RICH
BY DIRECTION OF PHOTOGRAPHY ERIC DE LA CRUZ "PRIME PRODIGY", PRINCIPLE DIRECTOR OF PHOTOGRAPHY BLAKE BRADY, AUDIO SUPERVISOR AND SOUND
TYLER RICH, EXECUTIVE PRODUCERS DENNIS REED II, AND LOVE LOGAN, MY LOCATION SCOUT & MANAGER AFRICA MCCLAIN MY PRODUCTION COORDIN
JACE R. YZAGUIRRE, MY PRODUCTION ASSISTANT SHANTE LEWIS, MY MAKE UP ARTIST SHANA SIMONE, MY PHOTOGRAPHER ERIC R. "BOOM" SALVA

            #FirstLadyTheMovie

AN ANTHOLOGY OF NOIR

SWITCHBLADE

Issue Sixx

SWITCHBLADE

NOW AVAILABLE AT

DESCONTROL PUNK SHOP

1725 E 7TH ST #C LOS ANGELES

OPEN EVERY DAY 12-8PM

SELL TRADE

BUY DESTROY

(IG) DESCONTROL_SHOP

CLOTHING • LEATHER • ACCESSORIES • RECORDS • TAPES

SWITCHBLADE

Outlaw Culture

switchblademerch.com

100 % ringspun cotton
preshrunk, with an
athletic fit

26 S Los Robles Ave, Pasadena, CA 91

ps://thebatterybooksmusic business sit

Author Bios & Acknowledgements

William R. Soldan lives in Youngstown, Ohio. He dropped out of high school in the 90s, traveled, and did some reckless things. Then he spent seven years in college, and now he has a couple degrees he doesn't use. His fiction has appeared in *Thuglit*, *Kentucky Review*, *Econoclash Review*, *Mystery Tribune*, *The* Best *American Mystery Stories*, and others. He's got poems here and there, too. You can find him on social media or at williamrsoldan.com if you'd like to get in touch.

Bryce Wilson's work has been featured in the anthologies, *Roadkill Texas Horror Vol. 2*, *Edge Of Darkness* and the upcoming *This Book Is Cursed*, among other places.

R. Daniel Lester's writing has appeared in multiple print and online publications, including *Shotgun Honey*, *Broken Pencil*, *The Flash Fiction Offensive*, *Bareknuckles Pulp* and *The Lascaux Prize* Anthology. Recently, his novella, *Dead Clown Blues*, was nominated for a 2018 *Arthur Ellis Award* for Best Crime Novella by the *Crime Writers of Canada*. The second book in the *Carnegie Fitch Mystery Fiasco* series is scheduled for release in May 2019 from *Shotgun Honey/Down & Out Books*.

Jon Zelazny is your typical stay-at-home writer-dad. A graduate of Syracuse University and the U.S. Army Airborne School, he began his Hollywood career with producer Joel Silver, then spent a decade in creative support of acclaimed director Uli Edel. His short stories have appeared in *Thuglit*, *Literary e-clectic*, and *The Binnacle*, and he's currently writing a novel about the British ballet.

Jack Bates is a three time finalist for a Derringer Award from the Short Mystery Fiction Society. This fall he will have a story included in the Bouchercon anthology.

Michael R. Colangelo is a writer from Toronto. Visit him at michaelrcolangelo.blogspot.com.

J. L. Boekestein (1968) is an award winning Dutch writer of science fiction, fantasy, horror, thrillers and whatever takes his fancy. He usually writes his stories in trains, coffeehouses and in the 16th century taverns of his native The Hague, the Netherlands. Over the years he has made his living as a bouncer, working for a detective agency and as an editor. Currently he works for the Dutch Ministry of Security and Justice. His English publications include stories in: *Cyäegha, Nonbianary Review, Strange Shifters, Lovecraft after Dark, Surreal Nightmares, Urban Temples of Cthulhu, Sirens Call, Mystery Weekly Magazine, Double Feature Magazine, After The Happily Ever After, Cliterature, No Safe Word* and *Switchblade*. http://jlboekestein.wixsite.com/jaap-boekestein

Mark Slade has appeared in *Weirdbook #32* and other publications.

C.W. Blackwell was born and raised in Santa Cruz, California where he still lives today with his wife and two children. His passion is to blend poetic narratives with pulp dialogue to create strange and rhythmic genre fiction. He writes mostly crime fiction and weird westerns. You can follow him on Facebook and Twitter.

Arthur Evans is an editor working in New York City. His stories have appeared in *Near to the Knuckle* and *Mysterical-E.* For his own sinister reasons, he uses a pen name.

Bill Davidson is a Scottish writer of mainly horror and fantasy. His recent work can be found in a number of publications from the UK and US, such as; *Flame Tree Publishing's Endless Apocalypse Anthology*, *Terrors Unimagined Anthology*, *Dark Lane Books*, *Storyteller*, *Under the Bed, Emerging Worlds*, *Metamorphose, Enchanted Conversation, Electric Spec, Tigershark publishing* and *Storgy Magazine*. Find him on billdavidsonwriting.com or twitter @bill_davidson57

Nick Kolakowski's work has appeared in *Shotgun Honey, ThugLit, Plots with Guns, Crime Syndicate Magazine, Mystery Tribune,* and various anthologies. He is also the author of "A Brutal Bunch of Heartbroken Saps" and "Slaughterhouse Blues," two short novels from *Shotgun Honey*, and the upcoming "Boise Longpig Hunting Club" from *Down & Out Books*.

Stephen D. Rogers is the author of "Shot to Death", and more than 800 shorter works. His website, www.StephenDRogers.com, includes a list of new and upcoming titles as well as other timely information.

David Rachels has published noir fiction in *Switchblade, Thuglit, Pulp Modern*, and other similar places. He is the editor of *Redheads Die Quickly and*

Other Stories by Gil Brewer, which was published by the *University Press of Florida* in 2012.

Scott Paul Hallam is a short fiction writer living in Pittsburgh, PA. His work has been published in venues such as *Cease, Cows*; *Ghost Parachute*; *Unnerving's* "Hardened Hearts" anthology; and *Night to Dawn magazine*. You can follow him on Twitter at @ScottHallam1313.

Matthew X. Gomez maintains his web presence at mxgomez.wordpress.com as well as on twitter @mxgomez78. As well as a writer, he is one of the two conspirators running *BROADSWORDS & BLASTERS*, a new pulp magazine that debuted in 2017. Other work of his has appeared in *Pulp* Modern, *Storyhack*, and in the anthologies *Midnight Abyss* and *Altered States II*.

Special Thanks to cover model **Lish Bliss**, **Battery Books**, **Eric Beetner** and **S.W. Lauden** of the *Writer Types* podcast, for their continued support of *Switchblade*.

Made in the USA
Columbia, SC
07 December 2018